9

09

DECEIVED

DECEIVED

A True Story

Sarah Smith

with Kate Snell

First published in hardback in Great Britain in 2007 by
Orion Books
an imprint of the Orion Publishing Group Ltd
Orion House, 5 Upper St Martin's Lane,
London WC2H 9EA
An Hachette Livre UK Company

1 3 5 7 9 10 8 6 4 2

A CIP catalogue record for this book is
available from the British Library.

Hardback edition: 978 0 7528 7622 1
Export trade paperback edition: 978 0 7528 8820 0

Printed in Great Britain by
Clays Ltd, St Ives plc

The Orion Publishing Group's policy is to use papers that
are natural, renewable and recyclable and made from wood
grown in sustainable forests. The logging and manufacturing
processes are expected to conform to the environmental
regulations of the country of origin.

Every effort has been made to fulfil requirements with
regard to reproducing copyright material. The author and publisher
will be glad to rectify any omissions at the earliest opportunity.

www.orionbooks.co.uk

Contents

Prologue   3

Part One: Entrapment   5

Chapter 1 − *Happy Days at Blue Door*   7
Chapter 2 − *Recruiting John*   18
Chapter 3 − *Entrapping Sarah*   28
Chapter 4 − *On the Run*   34

Part Two: Cat and Mouse   41

Chapter 5 − *Family Farewells*   43
Chapter 6 − *Safe Houses*   49
Chapter 7 − *On the Trail*   53

Part Three: Brainwashing   65

Chapter 8 − *Wage Slaves*   67
Chapter 9 − *Closing In*   83
Chapter 10 − *Phoning Home*   91
Chapter 11 − *New Recruit*   96
Chapter 12 − *Spreading Confusion*   100
Chapter 13 − *Spy on a Mission*   108
Chapter 14 − *Accessing the Joint Account*   113
Chapter 15 − *Showdown at the Pomona*   120
Chapter 16 − *The Last Friend*   126

Part Four: Birth of a Conman   131

Chapter 17 − *Mummy's Boy*   133

Part Five: Stealing a Fortune   145

Chapter 18 – *Targeting the Atkinsons*   147
Chapter 19 – *Cottage Life*   154
Chapter 20 – *The Prodigal Son*   159
Chapter 21 – *Rays of Hope*   169
Chapter 22 – *The Inheritance*   177
Chapter 23 – *To the Very Last Drop*   184

Part Six: The Net Widens   191

Chapter 24 – *The Night Porter and the Car Salesman*   193
Chapter 25 – *End of a Brief Idyll*   200
Chapter 26 – *Suspicious Behaviour*   207
Chapter 27 – *A Crucial Transaction*   217
Chapter 28 – *Living Rough*   225
Chapter 29 – *The Cottage Prison*   233
Chapter 30 – *Losing It*   243
Chapter 31 – *Lighthouse Spies*   252
Chapter 32 – *A Confirmed Sighting at Last*   258

Part Seven: Race Against Time   265

Chapter 33 – *Trains and Buses and Planes*   267
Chapter 34 – *The Photograph*   272
Chapter 35 – *French Holiday*   276
Chapter 36 – *The Sting*   279
Chapter 37 – *Seeking Sarah*   285
Chapter 38 – *The Pick-Up*   291
Chapter 39 – *Opening Up*   296

Part Eight: Legal History   299

Chapter 40 – *Building a Case*   301
Chapter 41 – *The Verdict*   306

Part Nine: Picking Up the Pieces   309

Chapter 42 – *New Horizons*   311

Acknowledgements

I owe a debt of thanks to my brother Guy that I can never repay, for being a tower of strength and putting up with me. Without him and my family and my friends things would have been very different for me. It would definitely have been a lot harder to come to terms with, and be able to mould a new life for myself.

I would like to thank all the people involved in making sure that I was found and that the case came to trial and found the correct verdict. Thank you especially to the police officers Bob Brandon, Mark Simpson and the Cathy Harrison for their personal contact with me.

I owe heartfelt gratitude to all those people who showed me generosity and unwarranted kindness over the years. It made an enormous difference to me and had a very positive impact on my life at the time. Those things that people may view as insignificant gestures can make the world of difference to a person when times are bad.

Finally a big thank you to Kate and her husband Mark, for their support and assistance over the past few years, it has been very much appreciated. Thank you Kate for putting up with my emotional outpourings and making sure that the book was written with sensitivity to all parties involved in such traumatic circumstances.

I am grateful to all those who have given me advice and help in rebuilding my life, if you are not mentioned it does mean not you are any less significant, I just have limited space so thank you all.

Sarah Smith

*   *   *

The events in this book are all true. They are drawn from the memories of people I have interviewed over the course of almost two years. Where speech belonging to those not interviewed has been included, it is a reconstruction of dialogue as remembered by those I have interviewed. In Chapter One, for the sake of brevity, I have collapsed various student conversations and background events into one day. However, the spirit captured by the scene, and with the exception of Freegard's lies, the facts relayed by the dialogue are true.

For all the victims and their families, immersing themselves in these events again has been very difficult and painful. Without their remarkable courage and resilience, the writing of this book would not have been possible.

I'm particularly indebted to Sarah Smith and her family for their unswerving support in my efforts to unravel this complex story. Peter and Jill have not only been extraordinarily patient with me, but their meticulous notes have greatly assisted my research. For Sarah this has been an emotional journey, but she has never once faltered in her desire to help me understand her ordeal. Thank you for your bravery.

So many others have been generous and kind in helping me unlock the various doors to this tale. Special thanks must go to John Atkinson for his remarkable candour and warmth. Thanks also to his parents, Russell and Margaret, who made me welcome at their Cumbrian home. Warmest thanks to Kimberly Adams, John Adams and Ann Hodgins – I promise to have tea with you in the desert one day! Wonderful Renata Kister found time in her busy schedule to recount her experiences and offer her insights. So too did Simon Young, Anna Jones, Mark Endersby, Simon Proctor, Rita Taylor, Michael Ingram, Jason Bennett, Darren and David Hancock, Richard Harbord, Hannah Bendon (née Wilson) and John Sims. I am grateful to you all.

Jill Mytton, Principal Lecturer in Psychology at the London Metropolitan University, and Colin Gill, chartered psychologist, have both given freely of their time over many months. Their insights have lent powerful understanding and credibility to the book. I also drew on two additional sources for the book: *Brainwashing: The Science of Thought Control* by Kathleen Taylor (Oxford University Press, 2004) and *Feet of Clay; A Study of Gurus* by Anthony Storr (HarperCollins Publishers, 1996). The ideas and research in both was interesting and compelling. DS Ivan Stallworthy, from Nottinghamshire police, and Cathy Harrison, from the Tooting Sapphire team of the Metropolitan Police Force must also be thanked for their unique contributions.

To my literary agent at Curtis Brown, Jonny Pegg, for his confidence in me, and his profound belief in the project; and to all at Orion publishing, thank you.

Finally I must extend my heartfelt thanks to the Crown Prosecution Service; to the Press Officer Russell Hayes, for facilitating my many and varied requests over the last couple of years, and above all to senior crown prosecution lawyer Andrew West. It is fair to say that without Andrew's unstinting efforts to assist me, this book would be much the poorer both in its comprehension of the case, and the forensic detail he has been able to provide. I extend my deepest, sincerest thanks to you.

Last but not least, no acknowledgement of my work would ever be complete without thanks to my husband Mark, whose incisive comments, reading of the various drafts, and patience and understanding never cease to amaze me. Thank you.

Kate Snell, March 2007

'The intent is to change a mind radically so that its owner becomes a living puppet – a human robot – without the atrocity being visible from the outside. The aim is to create a mechanism in flesh and blood, with new beliefs and new thought processes inserted into a captive body. What that amounts to is the search for a slave race that, unlike the slaves of olden times, can be trusted never to revolt, always to be amenable to orders, like an insect to its instincts.'

Edward Hunter, *Brainwashing*

DECEIVED

Prologue

A young woman steps out of a red single-decker bus by Dukes Meadows. Dressed in sweatshirt, jeans and trainers, with a misshapen leather handbag slung over her shoulder and carrying a supermarket bag, she cuts an unremarkable figure. Her dark, shoulder-length hair is streaked with purple, yet the effect is to make her blend in even more with the background. Her name is Carrie Rogers and she cleans houses.

Carefully crossing the A316, she walks briskly down Hartington Road. She has a tight cleaning schedule and it's important that she doesn't fall behind. This is the second call of the day; there are more to go.

It's a warm, fresh mid-June day in 2003, the sky's a bright blue and the trees a vibrant green as Carrie turns into Chiswick Quay. She makes for one of the modern town houses and, pulling a bunch of keys from her handbag, lets herself in. She strips off her sweatshirt in preparation for the work ahead and begins to hum as she grabs the bucket of cleaning things – cans of spray, bottles of creams and liquids, an assortment of cleaning cloths. She notices that there's plenty of ironing to do as well.

Before starting upstairs, she rummages in her bag for another set of keys, leaving them within easy reach on the dining room table. The keys are for Renata's new apartment. Her flatmate called earlier to say she'd locked herself out and could she borrow Carrie's set? Carrie just makes it to the top of two flights of stairs when her mobile rings.

'I'm at the front door,' says Renata.

'Give me a second,' replies Carrie. 'I'll be right there.' She hurries down the steps and opens the door.

'Hello, Sarah.'

The soundtrack to the everyday world disappears. Standing on the doorstep are two men and a woman she's never seen before. Her immediate instinct is to slam the door shut and run, but the sight of Renata standing behind them holds her back. Why is she here with these people? Carrie doesn't understand. Panic and confusion rope themselves together like a noose, tighter and tighter until she cannot breathe.

How do they know her name? With one exception, it's been years since anyone has called her Sarah; years since she has seen or heard from family and friends; years since she has been home; years since she has had a normal life.

One of the men is speaking to her about the government, about secret agents. Carrie hears the words, but they make no sense.

'We need to talk to you,' he says.

Carrie's centre of gravity collapses. Suddenly she's floating, detached from herself, body and mind disjointed. She feels the blood rush to her head. This cannot be happening.

'Let's go inside,' says the man gently. He leads her by the elbow into the front room and introduces himself as Detective Sergeant Bob Brandon.

What is going on? Someone needs to explain. What the hell is happening?

Brandon says, 'I'm very sorry, Sarah, but the last ten years have basically been one huge lie.'

part one

Entrapment

October 1992-March 1993

Chapter 1

Happy Days at Blue Door

Almost eleven years earlier
Sarah Smith, Shropshire

Radishes. That's the subject of my dissertation. I'm observing the difference that spacing and watering can make to their growth. I bend over my young seedlings planted in perfectly spaced rows, casting them a loving glance before jotting down their latest measurements in my notebook. Nothing in the world of farming is hurried; growing crops needs patience. But I'm not in a rush. I move through the dome-like greenhouse at the speed of a snail. The air is redolent with warm, sweet earth, in contrast to the brittle coldness outside this cocoon. I'm looking forward to finishing my degree next year and working as a farm manager somewhere in the English countryside. Perhaps I'll be able to get a job in Oxfordshire where I spent my sandwich year. First, I'm hoping this latest batch of radishes will give me some decent results to help me finish my dissertation.

Farming is in my blood. My parents have been growing wheat and cauliflowers on the Isle of Thanet in Kent all their lives. Their parents and grandparents did the same before them. In fact, my mother's family has been farming in east Kent for the last 400 years. My family's 600 acre farm stops just short of the North Sea, and in this south-eastern corner of the country the wind is so fierce that even conifers grow in a shield formation. This is where I spent my childhood, my hair whipped sideways and my nose constantly running with the cold. Nether Hale – my parents' farm – was the safe and loving world I grew up in.

It was only natural for me to follow in this well-established tradition, which is how, after some stops and starts, I come to be at Harper Adams Agricultural College in Shropshire. There's something about the solidity of the imposing red-brick building that chimes with my own traditional values and wholesome upbringing. I feel happier than I've ever been. I give my radishes a last watering before closing the door on the glasshouse and leave feeling utterly content.

It's the start of my final year and six of us – four girls and two guys – have decided to share student lodgings in a house we've nicknamed 'Blue Door' on account of the massive blue-painted wooden front door that lends the house an air of grandeur despite the peeling window frames.

The boys are John Atkinson and his friend Jim Cooper. My friend Hannah Wilson suggested they join us at Blue Door, and as they were looking to share a student house they agreed on the spot. John's family are cattle farmers in Cumbria, and he speaks with a broad northern twang. I can't help finding him attractive; his sense of humour, bonhomie and quick-fire repartee are infectious. I've known Hannah since I started my degree course. She is slender with short brown hair that's spiky on top. We're close friends and share confidences. The other girls are Maria Hendy and Marie Gilroy. We are serious about our careers; we're all studying to be either farm managers or take up food marketing once we've graduated.

We're also typical students, a boisterous group who like a drink and a good time. And at the moment there's a typical student problem vexing us: where to park our cars.

A couple of months ago my parents lent me a brown VW sports car, a Scirocco Storm. Sounds very grand, but it's a car with a history and I'm just the latest occupant of the well-worn driving seat. It once belonged to my aunt, before being passed on to my eldest brother, then it was used on my family's farm. But I love the car, it gives me a feeling of independence, and driving it soothes away any frustrations and anxieties. On the road I feel free.

But there's nowhere to park the Scirocco, or any of my housemates' cars. Blue Door sits right on a busy main road on the fringes of Newport, a couple of miles away from the college, and although we've explored various options, so far none of us has come up with a suitable parking place safe from traffic wardens and, we hope, thieves and vandals.

By chance, our local pub, The Swan, has a huge car park, twice as big as the pub itself, and it always seems to have free spaces. I wonder if we can come to some arrangement with the landlord and park there. John reckons it's worth asking.

The Swan is just two minutes' walk from Blue Door. The ceilings are low slung, and the two rooms that flank each side of the bar are cramped, but it makes for an intimate and cosy atmosphere as the six of us – John, Hannah, Maria, Marie, Jim and I – sit round a table socialising with our friends. The pub is filled with locals. Newport lies at the heart of a rural farming community, and many of the town's families have connections to the land that go back several generations.

John goes to the bar to order another round. The landlord, a cheerful oval-faced individual, pulls on the pumps.

'Any chance we could use your car park to park our cars?' John enquires.

The landlord looks up with a weariness that suggests he's been asked this question a thousand times before.

'We'll bring good business to the pub. We'll be regulars and bring our mates as well,' John enthuses. 'We're practically your neighbours,' he adds hopefully, pointing in the vague direction of Blue Door.

'How many cars?'

'Six.'

'Robert!' The landlord turns and shouts to his colleague, who's serving in the other half of the bar. 'What do you think of letting some students use our car park?'

Coming round from the other room, the barman swings into full view. He is slim, with dark hair and angular features.

'If they use the pub as their regular and encourage all their friends to join them I won't object,' he says looking over to where we're all sitting.

It seems the perfect solution to our problems. At last we have somewhere to park, somewhere to leave our cars without worrying if they'll be safe.

Manchester, 3 December 1992

Two IRA bombs explode in the centre of Manchester, one in the heart of the city's financial district, the second near the Anglican cathedral. Sixty-five people are injured.

Sarah, Blue Door

'Robert's coming round with some food. He says he's going to cook for us,' announces Hannah. Since we started parking our cars at The Swan two months ago, the barman, Robert Freegard, has become a familiar figure in our lives. We see him frequently, either at the pub or at Blue Door. In fact, he always seems to be around.

The news reaches me through the open door of my bedroom, where I'm pinning up another Athena poster. Our social gatherings tend to revolve around meal times.

'What time?'

'In about an hour.'

Good. That gives me time to finish what I'm doing. Bit by bit I've plastered over the ugly dirty wallpaper of my bedroom with posters. When I think of the rest of the house, the only word that comes to mind is 'brown': brown sofa, brown curtains, brown wallpaper and brown dining table. In protest, I've covered every inch of the walls in my own room with bright pictures; all available surfaces are alive with knick-knacks. I think I may have gone overboard, but everyone else seems to like the riot of colour. They call it 'the common room' because the door is always open and everyone piles in towards evening, usually to escape the drabness elsewhere.

I seem to have become the group's agony aunt, helping sort out everyone's problems. 'Sensible Sarah,' that's me. Maybe it's because I don't have the same boyfriend troubles as my other flatmates – for the simple reason that I don't have a boyfriend right now. I like having male friends but I've never been very confident around men, probably because I don't feel secure about my appearance and don't think they'll be interested in me. Make-up and high heels are not my style; give me a baggy sweater any day. John is different though. We come from similar backgrounds, loving families, solid farming stock. I feel relaxed with him and he makes me laugh.

This evening, we sit around our brown Formica-topped dining table, exchanging news about the day. As usual Rob is jovial, oozing energy and self-confidence. The other girls think he's charming, and good-looking with it. Our flatmate Maria Hendy has been going out with him for a month now. To be honest, I don't find him that attractive. He's known for having a string of women, aged anything from sixteen to forty-five, who are all apparently besotted with him. Something about him doesn't quite gel with me, but I'm not losing sleep over it. After all, he's just the local barman; it's not as if he's going to be in my life for ever.

'How's the car?' Rob asks, interrupting my thoughts.

In October, when The Swan car park had been full and I'd had to park elsewhere, my beloved Scirocco had been broken into twice. The first time, the roof was scratched and a window broken. Days later the windscreen was smashed and the stereo was stolen. I've now had an alarm fitted.

'It's OK, but you know it's weird, Maria's had problems too. Her car went missing and they found it twenty miles away, in Wolverhampton. And John's car has been broken into. There's definitely something strange going on around here.'

'Maybe it's the IRA?' volunteers John.

'Don't joke about it!' says Hannah.

'Well, it wouldn't be the first time,' says Jim.

They're referring to the bombs that went off in Shrewsbury — four of them, just before the start of term. The IRA claimed responsibility. Everybody thinks it's because of the city's links with the military.

'Scary,' Marie says. 'So close!'

'It's much closer than that,' says John. 'Don't forget the college link with the IRA.' There are a few raised eyebrows around the room. 'Remember that lad who was arrested for gun running for the IRA? What was his name? O'Donnell — Kevin Barry O'Donnell. He was a Harper student.'

'The one who was shot dead?'

'Yeah. Cleared of the gun running but then shot in an SAS ambush in Northern Ireland. Weren't you here when the police came round? I was. Heavy stuff. They told us not to make jokes about terrorism, or even wear balaclavas. Pity. I always wanted to turn up to lectures in a ski mask.'

'Would have been an improvement for sure,' jokes Jim.

The details come back to me. By all accounts Kevin Barry O'Donnell was a committed IRA activist. In 1989, just six months before we all started at Harper, the army barracks down the road at Ternhill was bombed. The bombs were aimed at the parachute regiment which is based there. Although the authorities never proved O'Donnell's connection, it was strongly suspected he was involved. Shropshire has made front page news more than once because of all the IRA activity around here.

These are troubled times, and we're all aware of the risk the IRA poses to mainland security. How could we not be? Britain is in the middle of the biggest IRA campaign on its soil since the 1970s. And then there was the Manchester bombing only four days ago. Even Manchester now feels too close for comfort.

'Where did you learn to cook, Rob?' asks Hannah, trying to lighten the mood.

'Worked as a chef in a London hotel for a while,' Rob replies, stabbing his fork into his food. 'Between studies, of course,' he adds.

'Up north we leave cooking to the women. It's what they were invented for,' John chimes in with a grin. 'Strikes me as a most sensible idea.'

'John, you're just a Luddite,' says Hannah.

'Unlike me,' says Rob. 'I'm a fine chef and one day I'll make a fine husband.' He turns to Maria and gives her a cheeky wink.

I get up to put on the CD that Rob has brought with him, *Liberty* by Duran Duran.

'Good taste,' says Rob. 'You know they've got another album coming out in February. My brother's given me a sneak preview of one of the tracks. "Ordinary World" it's called.' He looks pleased with himself, clearly expecting a reaction.

'How'd your brother get that then?' says Jim.

'Didn't I tell you? He's their bass player.'

'What? John Taylor?'

This is a surprise. Everyone's heard of Duran Duran, they were one of *the* pop bands in the Eighties. We're sceptical of Rob's claims, though.

'So why's your name not Taylor?'

'You don't think it's his real name, do you? Come on!'

'Can we meet him?'

'Well, he's away a lot; travelling, on the road, you know how it is. But yeah, I'll see what I can do.' My girlfriends exchange looks of disbelief. Can the brother of a pop star really be in our midst?

There's a raucous atmosphere round the table and the wine passes liberally between us. Rob asks who the television belongs to.

'That's Sarah's, of course,' says Jim Cooper.

'Sarah's got loads of gadgets and gizmos, high-tech electrical stuff,' explains Hannah. 'And she buys CDs like we drink water. Her room's full of them.'

That's a bit of an exaggeration. 'The TV is old and crappy, and I don't have that many CDs,' I say in my defence.

Led by John, the conversation degenerates into a happy

argument about age and Rob challenges us to guess his. John puts him at anywhere between twenty-two and forty-two.

'Forty-seven,' says Jim Cooper.

'I want to bid at forty-eight!' shouts Marie Gilroy. Bedlam erupts as we descend into silliness.

'Give the guy a break,' says Jim. 'He's not *that* old.'

We laugh until we're not sure if we're laughing or crying. 'I need a refill,' says Jim, thrusting his empty glass towards the middle of the table. The wine continues to flow. When things have quietened down, Rob looks at us all with great seriousness and announces, 'I'm twenty-nine, almost thirty.'

My mother nicknamed me the 'Chancellor of the Exchequer' because of my careful attention to money. While my brothers Ian and Guy seemed to spend all their pocket money the minute they got it, I preferred to save mine. Despite my parents' relative affluence, built on the solid foundation of the English countryside, I was thrifty from a very early age, putting aside money for my future.

Nether Hale has no immediate neighbours, and my nearest friend lived several miles away. The fields were my companions, haystacks and tractors my swings and roundabouts. Above all I was obsessed with riding. As a child it was all I thought about, and from the age of eight I owned a horse, Czarina, who was my constant companion; we grew up together and she was my passport to the outside world. I rode beyond Nether Hale, along the Kent beaches, a young free spirit.

If I wasn't riding I was helping out on the farm, so my childhood world was dominated by horses, tractors and trailers. Unlike other girls my age I wasn't interested in fashion; I was happiest in a pair of jodhpurs and riding boots; dresses were alien to me.

When I was nine, my parents sent me to boarding school. It was as if I'd been slammed into another world, one I couldn't relate to. I never felt I belonged and was truly miserable. The only salvation was that the upper school had stables and I was allowed to keep Czarina in a field in the school grounds.

When I turned sixteen I pleaded to go to St Lawrence College in

Ramsgate, a mixed school where my younger brother Guy was a pupil, and where I thought I'd be happier. There I encountered a new challenge: boys. I felt clumsy and shy. Growing up in an agricultural world and mucking in with everyone else on the farm meant I'd never felt the need to be particularly feminine – in any case it wasn't practical. This hadn't bothered me in the slightest. I was happy with my family and my horse. I didn't exactly avoid boys, I just never sought them out.

The biggest shock came when I was eighteen. My careers advisor persuaded me that I shouldn't waste time applying for degree courses in agriculture. Farming was a man's world, he insisted. This was a severe blow. I had always known that Nether Hale itself wasn't an option, since my elder brother Ian was already destined to run it when my parents retired. Now I was finding out that my gender meant I had little hope of succeeding in farming in the outside world.

With the occupation I'd always dreamed of pursuing apparently closed to me I embarked on a Computing in Business course in Huddersfield. I took this to mean business studies using computers, but I was wrong; it turned out to be a systems analysis course and involved writing computer programmes, which in turn required advanced maths. I was hopeless, and by the end of the first year I had failed so many modules I was told it wasn't worth carrying on.

Yet Huddersfield marked a social change for me. For the first time in my life I had a group of largely male friends. I felt part of a social circle, and in this North Yorkshire town I also met my first boyfriend, Hugh. We went to parties, took spins in the car and I got to know his family. Perhaps I was making up for lost time, but I had an absolute ball.

Despite the social life, my nine months in Huddersfield made me realise how much I missed the outdoors, so I vowed to make a life for myself in farming. I was determined to prove the cynics wrong. The course at Harper Adams Agricultural College at Edgmond in Shropshire sounded just perfect. I wasn't disappointed.

*

'Why did the hedgehog cross the road?' asks John Atkinson. I'm laughing before he's even told me the punch line. Today we're giving blood, and John is lying next to me in the mobile blood donation unit, his arm outstretched, eyes parked on the ceiling.

'Come on, Sarah.' John wiggles his feet at the end of the bed, impatient to deliver the one-liner. I've become very fond of this man. He has an impish irascibility about him, without being loud and insensitive, a mind like quicksilver, and a warm heart.

'I don't know. Why did the hedgehog cross the road?'

'To show his girlfriend he had guts.'

I'm still laughing as he fires off the next one, and within no time the nurse arrives saying we're all done. We roll down our sleeves. With term finished, we're now off home.

'Have a good Christmas, then,' he says, bounding off the bed.

'You, too.' I smile wistfully in the knowledge that I won't be seeing him for a couple of weeks.

As I leave the unit and cross the lawn, heading back to my room, I picture Mum's turkey with all the trimmings on the large farmhouse kitchen table. I can already hear the snapping of crackers and the telling of more corny jokes. I feel utterly content. The future seems alive with possibility.

We're all back at college after the break, and I've been roped in to help behind the bar at The Swan in return for some free drinks, and of course the continued use of the pub car park. This evening I'm in the kitchen doing a bit of general tidying when Robert Freegard appears. He's in a flirtatious mood and edges up close to me. 'I'm going to make this your lucky day, Sarah.' I don't like him being in my space, so I retreat to the other side of the room and put some glasses away.

'The two of us should get it together.' Rob comes up behind me and whispers in my ear. He's still dating my flatmate Maria Hendy and his proposition makes me feel distinctly uncomfortable. Moving away, I brush him off light-heartedly, while silently cringing.

'No way. Anyhow, you're going out with Maria.'

Rob picks up a carrot and starts munching on it.

'This pub work is only temporary, you know. I've got a masters degree in psychology from Oxford University. That's a qualification that could get me a job anywhere, Sarah. I've got major prospects.'

I've heard that Rob's mother is staying in the flat above the pub while the landlord is away on holiday. I hope she doesn't decide to come down now.

'Thanks, but no. I really don't want to get into a relationship right now. I've got exams coming up next term and a dissertation to finish.'

I seize the opportunity to change the subject. A friend of mine has been wondering whether to give pyramid selling a go and I ask his opinion. 'I wouldn't touch it with a barge pole. She'll end up being conned out of a fortune,' Rob counsels.

It's good advice. Rob does seem worldly-wise and authoritative, even if he's totally out of order when it comes to chatting up his girlfriend's friends. He's six years older than me and has obviously been around the block. I feel I can trust his judgement.

Chapter 2

Recruiting John

The Swan, end January 1993

The last of John's student friends swung lazily out of The Swan in high spirits.

'See you back at Blue Door,' Jim Cooper shouted.

'Yeah, catch you up shortly,' replied John, a big grin plastered across his face. He returned to the serious business of finishing off his pint, one arm propped against the bar. Weekend at last, time to chill. There was no other thought in his head apart from that.

'Good crowd tonight,' John remarked casually to Robert Freegard as the latter emerged from the other side of the bar. Freegard busied himself tidying the empty beer glasses and filling the dishwasher. He didn't reply. He stood with his back to John, then turned abruptly to face him.

'It'd be a mistake to believe everything you see and hear, John,' he said.

'What do you mean?' John's face creased into mild surprise.

Freegard paused before continuing. 'Your friend Garry, for instance.'

This touched a raw nerve. Garry McCullough was an Irish lad who'd been in John's tutor group. John liked him, although they had never got close. To everyone's dismay and shock, four weeks ago on New Year's Day, Garry had killed himself with a shotgun. It was put down to girlfriend trouble.

'What about him?' John asked quietly.

'Well, how do you know he committed suicide?' said Freegard, bringing a troubled look to John's face.

'It's common knowledge. . .' John stopped short. As he did, Freegard moved towards him, right up close to his face, with his eyes narrowed and his mouth turned up at the corners.

'How many students at this college are Irish, John? Don't know? Let me tell you. One in every five, that's how many. And why do you think they're here at an agricultural college in the middle of bloody Shropshire?'

Freegard started pacing slowly back and forth along the front of the bar, eyeing John up. 'Penny not dropped yet, John?'

'I've no idea what you're talking about.'

'Fertiliser.' Freegard let the word fall between them. 'And what's one of the main constituents of bombs, eh, John?'

John reflected for a moment. He knew the answer to this one. 'It could be fertiliser, but. . .'

'Hallelujah,' Freegard raised his hands heavenward. 'Nitrogen fertiliser.' He paused. 'So who bombed the Ternhill army barracks just down the road?'

'The IRA.'

'Right again. We are doing well. And who was the suspect, the "Irish Legend" shot dead by the SAS aged twenty-one?'

'Kevin Barry O'Donnell?'

'And where was O'Donnell a student?'

Slowly realisation was dawning on John. 'He was a student here at this college.'

'Bingo! Congratulations, John.'

'But you're not saying Garry was in the IRA?'

Freegard sneered. 'You're so typical, just another member of the public walking around with your eyes shut. You can't see what's right under your nose. Do you think they walk around with signs around their necks saying, "IRA Bomber"? Course not. They look just like anyone else; they try to blend in; they go deep undercover. Like O'Donnell. But do you think he'd be acting alone?'

He paused. 'You have no idea, have you? Not a clue that some of your other so-called friends are actually working for the IRA. You just can't see it. You're in your own little world, a carefree bubble where everyone around you is good and everything's cosy and safe. But the world doesn't work like that, John. There are plenty of the bastards out there. It's all a front – you have no idea at all what's going on behind closed doors.'

Freegard suddenly lightened up and looked at his watch. 'Anyway, time to go.' He made as if to leave the room, but John caught him by the arm.

'No. Hang on, don't go. What are you saying happened to Garry?'

Freegard didn't answer, but freed himself from John's grasp. He marched up the stairs behind the bar, making his way to his flat above the pub. John followed briskly, his steps quickened by curiosity. Moments later they were in Freegard's flat.

'You think I would choose to live in a dump like this?' Freegard waved his hand in front of him and snorted disdainfully. John cast his eye over the place. The sofa and chairs were under cellophane, unused; pictures lay on the floor waiting to be hung; the kitchen was empty, there was nothing in the cupboards. To John it looked as though Freegard was just passing through, waiting for the next train out.

'You think I would lower myself to live in such a backward, out of the way town? This is nothing like I'm used to. It's only temporary,' he said, wheeling round on his heels to face John. He took a letter out of his pocket. John could see it was an official notice of some sort from Nottingham Crown Court.

'This is a summons for one of your close friends, one of your sweet, innocent, fresh-faced friends. But this nice friend is a Provo through and through. He'd shoot you without thinking twice. He's been using you and your mates as cover for his covert operations. He's not the only one either.' Freegard paused. 'No, Garry wasn't IRA. He just found out something he shouldn't have done and they got rid of him.'

John was appalled and terrified. 'How do you know all this?'

Freegard walked over to the cellophane-wrapped sofa and threw himself onto it, opening his arms wide over the back.

'You really think I'm a barman?' Freegard laughed with contempt. 'You think I'd live in a hole of a town like this? Do you think this is my idea of fun, working in this dead-end pub serving these idiots?' Freegard sniggered. 'Give me a break. Christ Almighty. Can you really not work it out? You want to know why I'm really here? Well I'll tell you.' Freegard locked onto John's gaze. 'I'm an undercover cop.'

Snow lay on the ground outside as Freegard led John across the icy yard at the back of the pub and into the cellar. Wine barrels lined the walls of the damp, dreary space, the wet concrete floor adding to the chill.

Over the past four days John had been weighing up the validity of Freegard's claims. At first, Freegard's disclosure that he was a cop seemed incredible, but the more John thought about it, the more it seemed not only plausible but probable. It explained why Freegard was such an outsider, why he was so desperately trying to break into the college social scene. The flat above the pub hardly looked lived in, exactly as though Freegard had been moved in on a job and was only there temporarily. Was the IRA operating out of Harper Adams? It was feasible. It was also undeniable that a former college student had been an IRA member. So if one student had been involved with terrorists, why not others? And then, Garry. His suicide had seemed completely out of character. What on earth could Freegard gain by lying about Garry? This wasn't a business deal; there was no money involved. There was nothing in it for Freegard, so what reason could he possibly have to invent such a tasteless lie? No, it had to be the truth.

The more John thought about it, the more the facts, as he now understood them, were borne out. He was in no doubt that Robert Freegard was who he said he was – a member of Scotland Yard's Special Branch.

'How many IRA people do you reckon there are at Harper?' John had asked.

'Look. Everything I'm about to tell you is top secret, right? Just knowing it could be a death sentence, so don't go blabbing about it to any of your mates. Clear?'

'Absolutely. Not a word.'

Choosing his words carefully, Freegard had laid out the situation for John. He reckoned there were a minimum of three students at Harper who were from the IRA. Typically, he had told John, a cell would have five or six members. He and his bosses were sure of two and thought they had identified one of the others, which possibly left another two or three to be flushed out.

'That's where you come in. You're going to help us flush them out.'

John was aghast. So this was what it was all about.

Freegard went on to explain that John was already surrounded by suspects and therefore in a perfect position to help the police. He was extremely sociable and well liked, the last person the IRA might suspect as an informer. Whether he liked it or not, John was already involved. The quickest, safest and only way out of the situation was to do as he was told. Freegard had instructed John to think carefully about all the people he knew at college. He must assess whether they were acting at all strangely and he must report to Freegard any student whose actions he couldn't explain.

John instinctively recoiled at the idea, but Freegard insisted he had no choice. Besides, if there were IRA activists at the college, then surely it was John's duty to help round them up. Not to assist would be sheer cowardice. All things considered, there really wasn't a choice. So by the end of the weekend, feeling increasingly overwhelmed by paranoia and no longer sure whom to trust, John had drawn up a list and handed it to Freegard.

Now here he was, in a cold damp cellar, ready to move on to the next stage.

'Have you ever punched anybody?' Robert asked him nonchalantly, laying his leather jacket on the ground and unbuttoning his sleeves.

'No. I'm not a violent person,' said John candidly.

Freegard shook his head in disgust. 'Have you ever taken a

punch?' Freegard's lower arms were exposed and he clenched his fists.

'No, not really.'

Freegard reached into his pocket and pulled out a length of cloth. 'Right, we need to act quickly. There's no time to sort out full police training, so I'm going to give you some myself.' He tied the cloth around John's eyes, blindfolding him. 'You need to toughen up, John, and I'm going to show you some techniques. Any moment now I'm going to punch you, and the trick is not to react. You have to just stand there and take it. You ready?'

'Yeah,' said John, trying to sound brave. He couldn't see anything through the blindfold, but was aware of Freegard moving around the room, treading quietly. John clenched his abdominal muscles in anticipation of the onslaught, but nothing came. What the hell was he doing here? Suddenly doubt tempered John's resolve.

'Look, Rob, I don't think I want to be involved in this. I have other plans, you know,' he said in a voice hopeful of a last-minute reprieve and desperate for a way out.

Freegard hovered between disbelief and scorn. 'You don't have a choice, mate,' he said flatly.

'Why can't you recruit somebody else to help you instead of me?'

'We've tried other people, but they haven't worked out. We've been through this already. Like I said, you're a social kind of guy. You know lots of people. What you do will have more effect. Are you telling me you don't care about more people being murdered?'

'But I'm not a trained policeman. I'm not a trained anything,' protested John.

Freegard took a step backwards, then, with a mixture of amusement and contempt, delivered his trump card: 'John, for the last time, we're not *asking* you do to this; we're *telling* you.' With that, Freegard landed a punch on John's chin.

As he staggered back, John felt pain shooting through his head like a hot flame. If John had doubted that Freegard would physically attack him, the shock jolted him back to reality. He would do as Freegard asked. He was resigned now, resigned to whatever lay ahead.

'I want you to keep your eyes and ears wide open, be aware of where your friends are, who they're seeing, what they're doing.' Another punch. This time John held his ground, though he was seeing stars.

'Watch out for those you think are traitors. You won't have time to go to college, so I want you to work with me behind the bar for a while. From there you'll do some work for us in another part of the country as well.'

Freegard punched John again. 'My superiors at Scotland Yard tell me this is what they want you to do. You'll be paid, of course. The police always take care of their own. I want you to draw your fellow students to the pub, so I can penetrate their social circle. Objective: expose the terrorist network.' Freegard hit John on the side of the head, knocking him sideways. Involuntarily he let out a small gasp.

'You're not going to tell me you can't hack it are you?' sneered Freegard.

'Like I have a choice,' said John with resignation. Freegard followed up with a punch to his stomach.

'We think we know the ringleaders. Actually, we're on the brink of some major arrests. In a matter of weeks this will all be over, and some of your friends will be going to prison. You're in for a real surprise when you see who we're going to put away.' Freegard laughed menacingly. 'And you know what happens then, don't you?'

'Yes. I can tell everybody what's been going on, and I'll get my life back,' answered John.

'Excellent. You're starting to get the gist of this,' enthused Freegard, continuing with his blows. 'Plus all the money you've earned,' he added. 'Don't forget that! We're not talking peanuts, John.'

John was beginning to hurt. His head was spinning; his face felt like one huge bruise. He wondered how long Freegard would keep this up. He knew that if he was to speed up the end of the ordeal, he must avoid showing any weakness. That was the point of all this, wasn't it? So he continued to stand his ground, trying hard not to flinch as Freegard hit him again and again, choking away the pain and trying to appear unbothered by the whole thing.

'Before we move in on the suspects, we want to make sure we've got everybody; that everything is known about who is connected to whom.'

Freegard stopped and stood back for a moment, as if to observe his handiwork.

'We call it "shaking the tree".' Freegard wiped his eye with a knuckle.

'We need some dramatic gossip that will make people talk to each other. So, John, I want you to tell everybody you're gay.' As he uttered the last syllable, Freegard delivered his stiffest punch yet. John swayed, almost stumbling to the ground, and not because of the punch.

'You're kidding. No way!' John mumbled through the pain.

Freegard ignored the objections and added triumphantly, 'Let's see who talks to whom, then.'

A collection of images formed in John's mind as he imagined telling his friends he was gay. They'd be astonished. For sure, the news would make very good gossip, but the thought of conjuring up such a tissue of lies filled him with dismay. He weighed up his options, but came to the same conclusion. What choice did he have? He felt a sense of a duty to his country. Of course he did. And if some of his fellow students really were terrorists, then what did it matter if he told them he was gay? Not at all, he concluded, if it meant saving lives. Besides, if this was the quickest way through this and he could put the record straight in a matter of weeks, then he had to do it.

'Your housemate Jim Cooper. He's one. He's involved with the IRA up to his neck,' announced Freegard coldly.

The weight of this revelation dropped on John like a stone. 'But he's not even Irish,' he protested.

Freegard scoffed. 'How dense can you be, John? Do you seriously think that everyone in the IRA is Irish? You must know they have any number of sympathisers in America, and I can tell you there are plenty on the British mainland as well.'

John felt embarrassed and stupid, lost in front of someone who obviously had greater experience and understanding of these things.

'If you've missed something so obvious, how can I trust anything you said in your report, John? I told you to think carefully about *everyone* you know at college. Jim's not on the list. So you fouled up, John. Look, you're not getting it yet. You have to keep your eyes open for inconsistencies.' Another jab, this time to the nose, provided punctuation.

'Let's look at Jim Cooper. He sticks out like a sore thumb. One, you can see a mile away that he's far too confident and intelligent to be slumming it at a place like Harper. Two, if he's your big buddy, why is he so aloof all the time? Three, why doesn't he look anything like his brothers? And four, if dear old Jim is studying marketing, how come he's been getting up in the middle of the night to help one of our mates on a dairy management course when he's openly declared he doesn't even *like* the guy! Do cows really need their hooves dipped at that time in the morning? Come on, he's been *using* you, John, to cover for his IRA activities. If anyone deserves a punch it's Jim.'

As John withered under the continuing onslaught, he struggled to cope with the mass of revelations about his friends – people he thought he had known well for several years. It occurred to him that he knew nothing at all.

Freegard carried on talking. His bosses at Scotland Yard insisted they must manufacture a reason for John to involve Jim in a fight because the resulting furore would allow them to find out who Jim was connected to. Provocation, his bosses said, always worked well. Freegard would provide John with appropriate clothing and douse him in foul-smelling aftershave, then John must put on his best camp act in front of Jim and everyone else in the pub. The whole incident, predicted Freegard, would create a tremendous amount of gossip that would directly affect the IRA cell. It would be a huge success on two counts: in 'shaking the tree' and in toughening John up.

John groaned audibly. It was all too much and it was all happening too fast. He felt completely out of control of a situation that he had no choice but to see through if he was to get back to normal again. In fact, he was already beginning to forget what 'normal' meant.

'One other thing,' said Freegard. 'I've already warned you about this, but let me say it again. The whole situation is very sensitive. Talk to anyone and you'll not only endanger us but jeopardise the whole operation, so keep it zipped.'

Chapter 3

Entrapping Sarah

Sarah, Harper Adams, early March 1993

Walking past John's room I notice the door is locked – a sure sign he's not there. Three weeks ago we all moved out of Blue Door and into halls of residence, so we can save travelling time in the run-up to our finals. Ever since then, though, John hasn't really been around. He seems to spend all his time back at the pub; he must be working at least twelve hours a day there, time when surely he should be preparing for his exams.

The others are as nonplussed as I am about this sudden change in our friend's behaviour. On the odd occasion when he has come back to his room, he shuts the door, making it clear visitors are not welcome.

He looks distracted all the time and has effectively dropped out of college. He's not going to lectures, not writing up his dissertation, nothing. He's just given up. We don't understand why. Of all of us, I would say John stands the best chance of getting a first. The rest of us need to cram if we're to get a decent result in the finals, but to John it seems to come naturally. Even so, he has always worked like a dog at his studies; he's driven. After a career as a supermarket buyer he wants to move into diplomacy, possibly be involved in economics in Brussels. But now everything's changed, and it's so sudden that I'm deeply concerned.

Arriving at The Swan, I pull into the car park and enter the gloomy interior by the small side door.

John is wiping down the bar. He's altered beyond recognition. His dark brown hair is dyed a shocking white blond and he looks sickly and pale. There's a bruise on his chin. I recall my dismay when I heard how he recently let fly at Jim Cooper. It doesn't make sense. Jim and John have been best friends all through college, yet according to gossip, Jim and a group of friends turned up at the pub the other day in high spirits, only to be confronted by the sight of John sporting a flowery shirt and waistcoat. He reeked of aftershave and was acting as camp as a cabaret act. His appearance sparked disbelief, ridicule and gales of laughter, at which point John turned on his old pal and punched him so hard in the face that he pushed one of Jim's teeth clean through his top lip. Jim had to be driven to Telford hospital for stitches.

Now John has openly declared he's gay, which has stunned us all.

'Hello stranger,' I say gently.

'Sarah, hi.' He pauses, looking slightly uncomfortable, implying he doesn't want to face an interrogation. He carries on cleaning. Suddenly he stops, his face shifts and lights up into that broad familiar smile.

'How are the radishes?'

'Good. Should have the final results soon, so I'll be able to write up my dissertation.'

John looks directly at me. He knows what the next question is going to be and he cuts in before I have a chance to ask it.

'This is my choice, Sarah.' His tone has a finality about it. The smile has disappeared, but I press on:

'But why? You're so close to finishing your degree.' I move closer to him, as if by doing so I might win him round. He turns away, and his voice is a monotone. 'Suddenly the idea of being a buyer for a supermarket doesn't seem so appealing. I want some time and space to rethink what I'm doing. Please don't ask me about it again.'

I sigh out of total incomprehension. It makes no sense, to drop out like this so close to graduation. I feel wounded that he's turned his back on me and his other friends, cutting us all off, but there seems little point in pursuing things.

I go back to the halls of residence, feeling troubled. Further down the corridor I hear Hannah and Maria Hendy arriving back. They sound tired.

'We've driven to Sheffield and back today; it's hundreds of miles,' complains Hannah.

Why on earth would they want to go to Sheffield at a time like this?

'Robert said he had to go to court. Said he'd killed his former girlfriend's dog.'

I raise my eyebrows, and from the expression on Hannah's face I can tell she's finding the whole episode a little strange too.

'We just spent the day shopping, waiting to pick Robert up again. On the way back he showed us where his old girlfriend used to live.'

Hannah yawns, unable to disguise her weariness, and we say goodnight. As I get ready for bed I think back over the day, particularly to my conversation with John and the story of Rob's court appearance. I shake my head. Fragments of stories with missing bits of text. Everything feels a little weird right now. I close my eyes, grateful for some sleep.

The Swan

Sunday lunchtime and the pub was crowded with drinkers noisily enjoying their day off. For John, their jollity only added to his sense of wretchedness. A couple of students sat at the bar chatting, but their presence made him twitchy. By now, in his mind, everybody was a possible IRA suspect.

Freegard's line that he didn't have time to go to college had quickly evolved into 'It isn't *safe* for you to go to college at all now that you're associated with me.' So John had isolated himself from his friends. But he knew that people were talking about him, glancing at him sideways, and he heard their whisperings. He tried to ignore them, believing that arrests were due to be made soon and then it would all be over. He would be able to tell people what had really been happening and they would understand the reason for his strange behaviour. How he longed for that day.

For now, though, he felt totally exhausted. Every day he worked twelve hours non-stop behind the bar. Then, after closing time, Freegard talked incessantly about the IRA situation, sometimes giving him more 'training'. On occasion, Freegard drove him to Banbury where he said another IRA cell was being investigated. John had hardly slept. In truth he was quite miserable. The only consolation was that he felt he was doing something fundamentally worthwhile; morally courageous even.

'Feeling blue are we?' Freegard patted John on the back as he rang money into the till. 'You need some female company.'

'Yeah, right.'

'I'm serious. Let's see . . .' Freegard mused for a moment, rubbing his chin. 'What about Sarah?'

'Sarah Smith?'

'The very one . . . you know she fancies you.'

John conjured up Sarah's fresh bright face, her straightforward good nature and her honesty. He could certainly do with being comforted by her right now.

'Sure, I like her, but . . .'

'Do something about it, then.'

John considered this for a moment, running over the scenario in his head. 'No, I don't think now is such a good time. If things are as bad as you say they are, I really don't want to involve her.'

Freegard nudged John's shoulder conspiratorially, saying quietly, 'Well, you know I'm going out with Maria.' Freegard looked around as if to make sure no one else was listening. He took a step back and slapped John on the back again, his voice intimate and cordial. 'My bosses have ways of making sure people are looked after, you know.'

John was finding Freegard's familiar tone irksome. Indeed, despite his awe at what he understood to be the man's 'responsible job', he couldn't say he'd ever warmed to him. Freegard seemed capable and authoritative one minute, cold, calculating and arrogant the next; at other times he was matey and over-familiar. John, along with some of the others at Blue Door, had found him to be over-friendly to the point where they were wary of him. John dearly wished he didn't have to be involved with him, but he had made a leap of faith. He believed Freegard was an undercover policeman. He suspected undercover police work had its unsavoury side, and this explained Rob's many unattractive traits. John's conclusion: he didn't have to like Freegard but he trusted him implicitly with his own safety. There was no going back. Indeed, he felt trapped in a situation out of his control and beyond his understanding. Because of this, and for no other reason, he would force himself to push on with the prescribed course of action.

'Go on, ask her out. Give it a whirl. It'll be OK, I promise,' chirped Freegard.

John was still reluctant, but right now he was going through such purgatory that he felt he deserved a little affection. If what Freegard said was true, what harm could it do?

Sarah, Harper Adams

John and I are strolling through the college grounds, past the banks of daffodils that are starting to peep through. Out of the blue, he asks me to be his girlfriend. I am completely taken aback. Given all the strange things that have been happening, his question is slightly disconcerting.

'I thought you said you were gay?'

'I'm not sure. I'm confused about my sexuality. I want to go out with you to prove to myself I'm *not* gay.'

I chew over his response. It's an odd reason for wanting a girlfriend, and I'm not sure I like the idea of being used as some kind of social experiment while he does his soul searching. But I'm flattered, too.

Does he really fancy me? I would never have guessed. My self-esteem around men is so low I can't quite believe it. I wrestle with my feelings, but my delight at being asked wins out. I've always found him attractive, right from the early days at Blue Door. He may have lost his sparkle and wicked sense of humour since then, but I'm sure that's only temporary; he's just going through a rough patch. The prospect of having a boyfriend again is exciting, and perhaps the companionship will lift John's spirits. With a bit of help he'll soon be back to his old self.

'OK. Why not. Let's give it a go.' I smile warily, clutching a couple of books to my chest, surprised at the new direction my life has just taken. John gives me a small smile in return.

Chapter 4

On the Run

The Swan, 15 March 1993

'Listen up. We've got trouble.'

Freegard's voice was low and urgent, his mouth pulled tight and his eyes flickering restlessly. He peered out of one of the small front windows of the pub, glanced quickly up and down the busy street, then shifted back into the shadows of the dim interior.

'The IRA are on to us,' he said in a harsh whisper. 'Me mostly, but we have to assume we're both in danger.'

John's face already had the hollow look of a vagrant. Now, hearing of this new threat, the blood drained from his head and his mouth turned dry.

'Here at the pub it's not so bad. We've got things in place and people watching our backs. But outside, forget it. Going out would be suicide,' said Freegard, his eyes darting back to the window.

John felt his heart beating faster. He struggled to maintain his composure as he saw his life disintegrating in front of him. What had he got himself into? He sat down at one of the dark wood tables, moving as if underwater. Freegard snaked into the seat opposite him.

'Listen, you're not going to like this either.' Freegard leaned over the table throwing John a sharp look, his dark eyes pencil points, his mouth a thin line of blood red. 'Sarah is in danger, too, and Maria. Because they're our partners, they're on the hit list as well.'

'But you said . . .' started John. He'd only been going out with

Sarah for a week and now he was being told that she was in danger because of him. He slumped back in his seat. In the vanilla light John had the look of buttery pastry, thin and dry, ready to crumble.

'Never mind all that.' Freegard seized the moment. He raised himself up, higher and taller. His face darkened. 'We've got to get out. All four of us. We have to leave college, the pub, and just get the hell out of the area for a month.' Freegard paused, measuring the impact of his words, then continued with slow deliberation, 'After Easter we'll be making arrests. Then you can all return to your studies.'

John scanned Freegard's face, his pale eyes full of stress as he tried to comprehend. 'When are we going to tell the girls you're a policeman?' he asked, his voice faltering.

'We're not. It's not safe for them to know that yet. The less they know, the better. We have to keep them ignorant of the IRA situation, for their own safety and for the security of the operation. It's too dangerous all round for them to know the truth.'

John supported his head in his hands, his long delicate fingers taut across his forehead. In place of his smile, once so alive and carefree, there was now just a wince, an apology. 'There's no way we're going to be able to persuade the girls to leave college for a whole month right before their exams. They won't buy it.'

Freegard was silent for a moment. He observed John with satisfaction. 'My superiors have told me how they want us to play it. They know about these things, you know.' He walked over to the bar and squirted himself a glass of carbonated water. 'But you won't like it,' he said, coming back, settling the glass firmly on the table. 'You won't like it at all.'

Sarah, The Swan

Maria Hendy and I have received an urgent message from Marie telling us to go to The Swan. It's the middle of the day and it means leaving our lectures. We have no idea what's going on. As we walk in, we see John working behind the bar, looking pale and withdrawn. He looks up and motions for us to sit down at a table in the corner of the room. The bar is empty. We tell him we're in a hurry, we have work to do, we're in the middle of things. He calls upstairs for Rob, but Rob doesn't answer. It seems an effort for John to walk over to us. He takes a seat. The air is still. It smells of stale beer and wet blankets. John moves his hands sluggishly in front of him on the table. He stares at his nails as if trying to decipher a code.

Then, with almost theatrical exaggeration, and still examining his hands, he announces, 'It is with deep regret that I have to inform you . . . I'm dying.' There's a long pause in which he looks straight at me and adds impassively, 'Liver cancer.'

Everything stops. Everything turns monochrome. The words seem to be crushing my chest, making it hard to breathe. Can he be serious?

'Liver cancer?' I ask, stupefied.

'It's too far advanced for them to do anything about it. They say I've only got a few months left.' John's face is a blank, as if all the oils have run off the canvas. 'I've known for a while. I'm OK with it,' he says with a wan smile.

The hairs on my arms stand on end. I'm struggling to make sense of what John is telling me. The silence weighs heavy, as if a great tree has been felled; all that's left is a giant hole, a dusty clearing and a deathly hush. Is that why John has been looking so ghastly? Is that why his behaviour has been so very strange?

John's eyes glisten. 'Listen, I have a favour to ask,' he says. 'I want you both to come away with me for a month's holiday, a kind of final fling around the country.' He pauses, coughing lightly. 'I know the timing isn't great with the exams and all, but it's my last chance.' He turns towards me. 'I'd like us to go as two couples; you and me, Maria and Rob.'

There's a bewildered look in John's gaze which I'm sure is echoed in my own face. I've lost elderly relatives in the past, but I simply can't take in the thought of somebody as young and vibrant as John not being there any more. I feel as though I am suddenly sightless, desperately groping for some contours to cling on to, something familiar to guide my uncertain steps.

'Please don't tell anybody about my illness,' he says. 'I don't want anybody to know.'

Warrington, 20 March 1993

A huge IRA bomb, planted near a shopping mall in Warrington, Cheshire, kills two young boys on the day before Mother's Day. It injures more than fifty people.

Sarah, Harper Adams

It's just over two weeks since John's devastating news. My college room is looking decidedly bare. Gone are the knick-knacks, the walls are stripped of their pictures, the photos stored away. My room, and those of my friends, will be let out to fee-paying visitors over the Easter break. Someone else's space until I return.

I've tossed a jumble of shoes, tops and trousers into a small bag; it should be enough for the time we are going to be away. All the rest of my stuff I pile into the Scirocco. There's just one last call to make before leaving.

I picture home with its trees and bushes swaying in the breeze, tipped with the feverish renewal of spring, the red-brick farmhouse sitting like an enormous egg in the middle of a nest of fields. I've rehearsed the conversation in my head already, how I'll disguise the real reason for my trip. My mother answers the phone, asking if I'm coming back for Easter. I tell her I've decided not to this time. I'm going on a mystery tour round the country. She thinks this is a splendid idea, a break for me before exams, but warns me to take care because of 'all these IRA bombs.'

I replace the receiver with a heavy heart. Dissimulation does not come easily because I've always been totally straight with my parents, but I'm so churned up. Poor John. Poor, poor John.

I dip my head round the door of Hannah's room to tell her I'll see her after the break, and with that I walk away, hiding my heartache. My college friends think nothing of my packing up, because they've all done the same.

There is no reason for me or anyone else to think I won't be back after Easter, back to write my dissertation, sit my exams and finish my degree.

Sarah, on the road

The last ten days have been a total blur. We've travelled by rail from one end of the country to another, overnighting in the cheapest bed and breakfasts we can find. At other times we've journeyed by car; mine, John's or Maria's. The whole experience is completely disorientating. I wasn't at all sure about leaving college, dropping my experiments, leaving my dissertation up in the air, but in the end Rob persuaded me and Maria to go. Rob says there will be no problem putting my studies aside. I'll be able to get a compassionate extension for my dissertation and catch up when I get back. I'll still get my degree. This is some comfort. I'd hate to let Mum and Dad down. Mostly, though, I am worried sick about John.

We arrive, worn out, in Bournemouth. It's sunny and not too cold for the time of year, and the crowds are out in force in this seaside town. I can hear the excited clamour of children urgently building their sand castles, their tiny forms silhouetted against a sea lit by bright sun. However, the carefree, festive atmosphere jars with my own bleak mood.

We freshen up before regrouping downstairs and heading off to the front, where we walk along a beach laced with a fringe of seaweed. A stiff breeze pinches the ends of my fingers. Normally we'd be laughing at one of John's terrible jokes, but no one has the appetite.

We've just passed the end of the pier when Rob says, 'Sit down. There's something you need to know.'

As we crouch down on the sand, dread grips my stomach. What's coming now?

'Things are not what they seem,' says Rob in a matter-of-fact voice. 'I've got to tell you what we're really doing. You are here for your own protection and safety. Things are very serious, very serious indeed.'

I am fighting to keep calm, but my mind is in turmoil, thoughts racing around, colliding in my head. I look at the others. Maria's face is a picture of startled confusion. As for John, he's just looking away into the distance, his attention caught by a lone seagull.

'There's a reason I've been placed at The Swan. You know all the IRA activity that's been going on around Shropshire recently? Well, we've identified an IRA cell at Harper Adams and it's my job to root it out. The college is thick with Provos. We don't know who all of them are, so I've been trying to get close to students, get friendly with them, find out what's going on.'

Images of Rob serving behind the bar flash in front of me. Is he telling me that all this time he's just been playing a part?

'And John has been helping me.' Freegard pauses, making sure our attention is completely focused on what he's about to say.

'You see, I work for the British government. I'm a secret agent.'

I feel dizzy, as if I'm standing at a cliff-edge.

Freegard continues, 'We're not here just because of John's illness, but because we need to lie low for a while and keep on the move. Our cover has been blown. Mine and John's. Unfortunately, by being associated with us there are contracts out on your lives as well. You may not know it, but you've seen things you shouldn't have done. Going home won't be allowed – perhaps one last visit to reassure all your families, but that's it until some arrests have been made. We hope this will happen in the next few weeks.

'It's best if your families don't know where you are, don't know what you are doing and don't know you are on the run from the IRA. Any contact must be sanctioned, otherwise it will put *them* in danger as well. I can't stress this enough: you need to be ultra careful who you talk to and watch out at all times, because they might be following us.'

I picture armed men in black balaclavas positioned around my home while Mum busies herself with the church calendar and Dad examines his cauliflower seedlings. It doesn't seem possible. In fact, I'm more than a little sceptical.

'Show me some ID,' I challenge.

'You think we carry round ID?' Rob scoffs. 'Slightly counterproductive, don't you think, since we're supposed to be undercover?' He lobs a stone into the sea. 'But I know all about you, Sarah Smith,' he says, poised to throw another stone. 'Let's see. Quite apart from your age, details of your family and background, I know all about your finances. Yes, that surprises you, doesn't it?' He lets the stone fly, and I watch uneasily as it skims across the water and disappears into the murky depths.

'In terms of ready cash, you've got your savings account as well as a current account. Total balance between the two, at the last count, twenty thousand pounds.'

He's right, but I don't let on. I make a point of never disclosing to anyone how much money I have, so how does he know? This can't just be guesswork. It's too accurate.

'And then there's your trust account, too.'

I hear the blood pounding in my head.

'I know your family has land at Cliffs End and Westwood. Frankly, I could go on all day. There's nothing we don't know about you, Sarah. Get used to it.'

I look towards John for confirmation and sympathy. Wearily, he raises his head and nods slightly. 'Sarah, I'm so sorry this is all happening to you. It's all because of me. But now we just have to do what Rob says and everything will be OK.'

I sit down heavily, trying to absorb this latest twist. It's as though I've slipped into some kind of dark room where the world that was previously so safe and familiar to me is now no longer visible. Lines have to be redrawn; new images appear, but they're ghostly, as yet only shadows, their true shapes and forms still to be revealed. The moment seems to mark some kind of new beginning, but it's not one that is hopeful or cheerful. It has startled me, spun my emotions into chaos. No, this new beginning is full of foreboding.

part two
Cat and Mouse

April–June 1993

Chapter 5

Family Farewells

Bishopsgate, London, 24 April 1993

An IRA bomb rips through the heart of the City of London, killing one and injuring more than forty. It wrecks a medieval church and causes massive damage to other buildings. The police were still evacuating the area when the bomb exploded.

Nether Hale, 25 April 1993

At Nether Hale, Sarah Smith's family home in Kent, lunch was going cold on the table. Sarah's father was striding about the farm driveway in his khaki shorts, fleece and open-toed sandals looking for anything that might signal his daughter's arrival. Peter Smith's healthy red cheeks, lean frame and boyish good looks belied his sixty or so years. He had been farming cauliflowers all his life and was fiercely proud of it. There was nothing he loved better than gazing down his microscope at young seedlings and trying to judge when they would be ready to harvest. In his world, everything came down to logic. There wasn't a problem that couldn't be solved. Not a man known for mincing his words, Peter was forthright in his views. Still, his heart was warm and open, especially where his children were concerned, and as he paced he scratched his head, wondering where Sarah could have got to.

Returning inside, he was greeted by the family's five dogs. The farmhouse sprawled off in all directions from both sides of the entrance; the interior decor was old fashioned; books, papers, souvenirs, ornaments and photographs covered every surface, testament to a full and busy life.

In the kitchen, Jill was putting lunch back in the oven. Also in her early sixties, her old-school accent reminiscent of vintage Ealing films actress Margaret Rutherford, she had, like her husband, spent her life immersed in farming. But unlike Peter, Jill was defined by her emotions. Her large round eyes would always give her away. That day they were alive with expectation and tinged with mild disappointment. Sarah would normally have spent the entire Easter break at home, but instead she was on some kind of 'mystery tour' and could only call in briefly. Never mind. Peter and Jill weren't the kind of parents who would deny their brood the chance to spread their wings. They accepted that their daughter was under exam pressure and were actually quite pleased she'd been able to enjoy herself travelling around the country. They were sure the break would do her good.

They had also heard that Sarah had a new boyfriend, and were looking forward to meeting him. But now they were anxious. It was very unlike Sarah to be late, and Jill hated the thought of the hard work she had put into Sunday lunch being wasted.

'Jolly frustrating she hasn't called to say where she is,' remarked Jill.

'There's nothing to be done,' said Peter emphatically. 'They'll be here in their own good time.'

All afternoon Peter and Jill waited, watching the hours tick by. They read the Sunday papers, which were full of the latest IRA outrage, the massive fertiliser bomb at Bishopsgate in the City of London. Talks between SDLP leader John Hume and Gerry Adams of Sinn Fein had been taking place, and the two politicians had made a joint statement saying the Irish people had a right to self-determination. Hume was convinced the republicans could be persuaded to leave violence behind, but the editorials didn't hold out much hope of an imminent solution.

It was half past midnight before Peter and Jill heard the crunch of car tyres on the gravel outside. Reflections of headlights bounced around the walls and were extinguished. The dogs barked in the blackness. Sarah had finally arrived.

In his pyjamas, Peter made for the front door, with Jill bleary eyed in her dressing gown behind him. Sarah apologised sheepishly for their late arrival, avoiding eye contact. Peter surveyed the group as they filed past him, his face stern but with the hint of a smile around his eyes. Sarah introduced Maria and John.

'And this is Rob.'

Peter nodded and shook hands with Robert Freegard.

Everyone was too tired to talk, they just wanted to turn in. They'd catch up in the morning. As Peter climbed into bed he remarked to Jill on what he saw as John's rather limp personality. 'As for the dark-haired one, he's a real smoothie. Thinks an awful lot of himself.'

The following morning over breakfast Sarah fidgeted uneasily. She seemed tense and unable to relax. They had to leave again that morning, she announced.

Bewildered, Jill urged her daughter to stay another night. Sarah hesitated, looking at Robert for guidance. She seemed unsure of herself and despondent. Peter and Jill couldn't understand what had got into their daughter, her behaviour was completely out of character. Peter could see his wife was unhappy at the prospect of being abandoned so soon, and was determined to set things right. With some coaxing, he persuaded Sarah and her three friends to stay another day.

The following morning, with their bags loaded in the car, the foursome prepared to leave. Sarah was still not her usual carefree self, but Jill tried gamely to compensate for the subdued atmosphere and insisted on getting them together for a photo. She shooed away the dogs, which had sauntered up curiously, and ordered the group into position like a sergeant major. They stood in the driveway with their backs to the garage, Sarah wearing a bright red sweater and brown cords and the necklace her parents had bought her for her twenty-first birthday, John beside her, then Maria.

'That's it. Come on, Robert, you as well,' Jill cried. Freegard joined the end of the row wearing a Harper Adams College rugby shirt and holding a red baseball cap in his right hand. Sarah was trying to smile, but it didn't reach her eyes.

'Super. One more for good luck.' Jill was hugely pleased with her handiwork.

Inside the house the phone rang. Peter marched off to answer it.

'It was the head of studies at Harper Adams wondering where you all are,' he said, stepping back onto the driveway. 'I've reassured him you're on your way back.'

Sarah

As the car drives away from Nether Hale Farm I glance back wistfully and catch a look of uncertainty crossing my Dad's face. Feeling scared, I close my eyes and say a small prayer. This might be the last time I'll see my parents for a while, but John, Maria and I realise how important it is to follow Rob's instructions, to do exactly as he says, if we and our families are to get through this alive.

Rob has stressed that the only way to protect our loved ones is to try to reassure them, appear to carry on as normal but tell them nothing. If they are to be safe from the IRA then they must not know where we are and we must keep away from them.

The lie that I'm colluding in makes me feel deeply uncomfortable and I long to tell Mum and Dad what I'm caught up in, but I just daren't. Whatever Rob says about maintaining an air of normality, I find it impossible to act naturally. My parents must have realised something isn't right.

Eight days later Peter and Jill pulled into the driveway at Nether Hale. They had just returned from visiting their youngest son in Holland. Guy was also a student at Harper Adams College, but was currently working for an engineering firm in the Netherlands on his sandwich year.

Scarcely had they unloaded their suitcases when their other son, Ian, appeared. The college had rung again; they were concerned about Sarah and her friends, who hadn't returned after the Easter break.

Jill was suddenly alarmed, normally Sarah was so good at keeping in touch with her parents. Apparently Sarah's room was still empty and none of her college friends knew where she was. Trying to calm his wife, Peter reassured her that there must be a perfectly good explanation.

A shrewd and honest man, if Peter Smith caught even the slightest whiff of dishonesty or impropriety, the terrier in him surfaced and he'd go to any lengths to uncover the truth. He didn't want to worry his wife with his own uneasiness, but agreed that this wasn't at all like Sarah. Normally a very dependable girl, she had been behaving quite erratically of late. Even he had to admit that.

Sitting down at his desk, he shoved aside the piles of bills, thinking ruefully about the amount of time he had to spend processing paperwork, when all he really wanted to do was walk his fields, feel the soil between his fingers and marvel at the growth of his cauliflowers. He jotted down a list of names, then picked up the phone.

First, he called Maria Hendy's parents and spoke with her father, Gordon.

'So Maria says she isn't going back to college or taking up her VSO work afterwards. Did she say why?' Peter listened avidly. 'But what did she mean: "One day you'll understand"?'

Peter then telephoned John Atkinson's parents.

'He was fine at Christmas, but things have gone off the rails since then,' said John's father Russell. 'He was being extremely evasive about everything, and then he just announced he was dropping out of college. He said he wanted to defer his finals until next year. I have to say we're both very concerned and most perplexed by what's happening.'

Next Peter rang Sarah's college friends Hannah Wilson and Marie Gilroy.

'No, we haven't a clue why Sarah and the others aren't here. Everyone was expecting them back after Easter,' Marie said. 'The thing is, though, Rob said John is dying, which is a bit of a stunner.' You're telling me, thought Peter to himself, if it's true. Hannah had suggested ringing The Swan to see if the landlord could help further, so he put a call through to the pub.

At The Swan a new landlady had taken over. She didn't think much of Robert Freegard; in her book he wasn't to be trusted. Money had gone missing and he was suspected.

Did she know if Freegard had said anything before he went off with Sarah, John and Maria on their 'mystery tour'? Peter wanted to know. No, he hadn't; he just wasn't around. He had been off sick towards the end of March and nobody could get hold of him. The next thing they knew he'd taken off with three students.

This information left Peter feeling deeply disquieted. The landlady gave him a forwarding number for the previous pub landlord, John Sims, since he had apparently been on good terms with Freegard.

'You might try ringing the mother of a former girlfriend,' said John Sims. 'He drove me past her house once and appeared to be obsessed with her.'

Thanking Sims for his help, Peter put the phone down and mulled over the information he had gathered so far. His consternation had rapidly turned to suspicion. He made for his wife's office where Jill was distracting herself on her computer with work for the local church. She looked up expectantly, eager for news.

'I don't believe for one moment John's dying,' exclaimed Peter. 'It's an excuse.'

'But what if Sarah believes it? She'll be heartbroken. And why hasn't she mentioned it to us?' Jill pondered quietly. 'She's always told us everything before.'

The more Peter thought about the situation, the more troubled he became.

Chapter 6

Safe Houses

Sarah, early May 1993

He walks me to a telephone box and then stands inside with me as I dial the number. Everything's going wrong. Rob says there's been an operational hitch, so the arrests haven't been made yet. Because of the threat hanging over us there seems no hope of going back to college now, no chance of finishing my degree. I'm devastated. I know my parents will not accept this unless I can come up with a watertight explanation.

Rob's solution is for me to invent a story about an amazing job offer that is only open to particularly gifted agricultural students. Since I'm hopeless at spinning lies I've asked him what I should say and he has dictated my script.

Now he's standing over me, watching my every movement like a hawk, as though he doesn't trust me. At the other end I can hear the phone ringing. I glance down at my crib sheet as Dad picks up.

'Listen, Dad, I've got some really good news for you. I'm going to postpone graduation for at least a year and take some time out on another sandwich.'

'That's all well and good, Sarah, but what's this I hear about John Atkinson dying?'

The question takes me by surprise. It's off script. Rob's told me to end the call as soon as I've said my piece, but now I'm not sure what to do. I hesitate, looking over my shoulder at Rob, but decide to carry on.

'You know the Commercial Union, the large insurance company? Well, they're looking to take on a couple of pre-graduate students.'

'Your mother and I just want to understand what's going on, Sarah. What are the symptoms? Surely he should be having some sort of treatment, however serious it may be?'

'I'm going to be earning twenty-four and a half thousand a year with a car, and I'll get commission on top.'

'Why don't you tell me?' Dad ploughs on. I'm floundering. It's obvious that he isn't really listening to me.

Rob is making signs at me to end the call.

'I spoke to John's father and he never mentioned it. Odd that, don't you think?' Dad is on a roll.

'Look, Dad, I don't want to talk about that, OK?'

Rob looks furious and jerks his finger across his throat, mouthing, 'Hang up', 'Kill it', ' Now!'

'Dad, I've got to go,' I say weakly.

My father starts to ask more questions, but I don't give him the chance. 'Look Dad, I've really got to race. I'll call again soon, OK?' And I put the receiver down.

'What was all that about, then?' asks Rob, as we leave the call box. I tell him that Dad has found out about John dying but that he doesn't sound at all convinced.

I can't read the expression on Rob's face.

I know my dad. Once he's got the bit between his teeth, there's no stopping him. I just hope he'll buy into my story about the Commercial Union, for all our sakes.

We've covered hundreds of miles today. Rob hired a van in Sheffield, and we've been driving all over the place picking up the stuff we cleared out of our college rooms. Mine was in Oxfordshire, sitting in my Scirocco in Watlington, where I spent my sandwich year. Rob had told me to dump it there during the 'mystery tour'. God knows what will happen to the car.

Rob has organised a house in Peterborough, near Cambridge, to be rented in my name for six months. He tells us it's effectively a 'safe house'. It has already been swept for bugs, and another operative would be based in one of the houses opposite to keep watch over us and make sure we come to no harm.

'Why do I have to pay for it. Why not the police?' I ask, still not taking anything simply on trust. If someone's going to mess with my life, even at gunpoint, I want to know why.

Rob replies that it's all about safety: 'Look, Sarah, you have to be *seen* to be paying for the house. Remember how important it is for your parents to be reassured that nothing's wrong? This way they'll see you're still going about your life; they won't suspect that we or they are in any sort of danger. But what you said about the police paying for it? Well, they are, indirectly. You'll get it back later. The whole thing's just a cover, really.'

As far as the landlord of the Peterborough house is concerned, we are agricultural students on our sandwich year, working down the road at Perkins Engines. He seems to have bought our explanation without a problem, but the lie leaves me feeling uncomfortable again. I've been told I really don't have any other choice, though.

I know practically nothing about Peterborough other than that it's the home of Perkins Engines and the final resting place of Catherine of Aragon, Henry VIII's first wife – strange how a fact like that sticks in your mind.

It is early evening when we finally draw up in front of the small, mock Tudor-style house in Martinsbridge Road. We are exhausted. Except for Rob, who is like a cat on hot bricks, completely uptight about something.

'There's a big problem,' he hisses. 'Someone's been following us.'

He orders me to go outside and discreetly walk up and down the streets around the house, writing down car registration numbers. This is so he can verify if there are any cars around that he has been warned about. It's for our own safety, he says. He will send the details off to HQ to be checked out.

Warily, I sneak out with a pocketbook and a biro and start noting the number plates of all the cars I can find. The idea that someone is watching *me* is horrible, so I rush through the task as quickly as I can. Back inside, I hand the details to Rob. I'm so tired, I just want to get my head on a pillow before I fall asleep on my feet. Stress distorts the tiredness and makes me feel wired and drugged at the same time.

We're unzipping our bags when Rob suddenly storms through the front room telling us we have to leave this second.

'But we've only just arrived,' I protest.

'You think this is my fault? It's your bloody father, Sarah. He's a madman. He's only given our address to Jim Cooper.' Freegard glances towards John. The mention of Jim Cooper seems to terrify him.

'Shit!' says John.

'Shit is right,' Rob shouts. 'Detective Dad – he's so bloody stupid, poking his nose in. Now the IRA knows exactly where we are and they'll be on their way. We're in huge danger, and it's all thanks to you, Sarah. There's no choice, we've got to leave. Immediately!'

'But I don't understand. It's only Jim Cooper.' I look helplessly at John.

'Sarah, Rob's right. Your dad couldn't have told a worse person. Come on, we've got to get out of here.'

I'm completely terrified and thoroughly confused – what on earth has Jim Cooper got to do with any of this? But there's no time for explanation. I look down at my belongings, snatch a small bag of clothes and my jewellery and we bolt out of the door into the night.

Chapter 7

On the Trail

Nether Hale, 11 May 1993

After Sarah had told her father about her insurance job, Peter had telephoned the Commercial Union to check it out. They had assured him that his daughter was not working there. What's more, they would never accept anyone who hadn't graduated, and even if they had employed her, the starting salary for a graduate would be half the amount she had claimed.

When the landlord of the house in Martinsbridge Road had phoned Peter for a reference, he told Peter he thought the students would be working at Perkins Engines, not the Commercial Union. Nothing was making any sense to Peter. He felt angry and misled.

Back at his desk Peter thought over the conversation with the former landlord of The Swan. John Sims had mentioned how Robert Freegard regularly boasted to him about his ex, Alison, and how important she was to him. Freegard had even taken Sims on a drive past her old village home in Derbyshire to show him what a nice house she had. The landlord had described the area. Peter had another lead.

He dialled the number. The voice at the other end of the line sounded middle-aged. It was probably the girl's mother.

'So sorry to trouble you. My name is Peter Smith and I wonder if you can help me. I'm trying to track down my daughter. She's with a man called Robert Freegard, who I believe you know.'

Peter listened carefully to the story of how Freegard had

insinuated himself into the family home and done his best to create divisions. He learned how Freegard's former girlfriend Alison discovered he'd stolen £600 from her bank account. It appeared he'd taken it in order to pay back money he'd borrowed from her in the first place. Shocked by his deception, her daughter had decided to end the relationship, but he refused to let her go. After pleading and cajoling failed, he turned to violence.

Freegard invited a friend round to his home in Worksop. The friend thought he was there to help Freegard sort out a relationship problem, but when he heard Freegard outline a plan to kidnap Alison using a hammer and a rope he realised Freegard's idea of persuasion was startlingly aggressive. The friend fled and headed straight to the police station. 'You might want to give the Worksop police a ring,' said Alison's mother.

Peter lost no time in following this up. He told the police switchboard that he was trying to find his daughter who he believed had fallen in with a bad lot, including a young local man called Robert Freegard, and the operator put him through to an officer called Ivan Stallworthy. Peter explained his concerns.

'Ah, yes, Mr Freegard. Not someone you can easily forget,' intoned Stallworthy in a broad, flat Nottinghamshire accent. 'Lives in a fantasy world, that one,' he continued in short, careful sentences, taking his time. 'Whenever we asked him a question he wouldn't stop talking. Likes young ladies with money. Used to reside in Worksop with his mother Roberta. Due in court later this month for theft and incitement to kidnap a former girlfriend.'

Peter's heart skipped a beat. Incitement to kidnap? This was becoming more serious than he had thought. He pressed the officer about what he could do to safeguard Sarah.

'You can report her missing from home, of course. Other than that, there's not much you *can* do, I'm afraid. Freegard's not doing anything to break the law. Sarah is of age, and obviously she's with him by choice. If I were you, though, I'd keep an eye on her bank accounts and keep the lines of communication open.'

Peter digested this disturbing twist. Freegard had been charged only a matter of days after Sarah began her final year at Harper Adams, just around the time the students began parking their cars at The Swan.

'What a peculiar way to try and win your girlfriend back,' he thought out loud. 'Who on earth has Sarah got herself mixed up with?'

*

Sarah, Scotland

In a lay-by next to Loch Ness we all climb out to stretch our legs when Rob's mobile phone rings.

'Hello? Yes, Ma. When was this, then?' Freegard's face blackens into a mask of hatred. I have a sinking feeling that this conversation does not bode well for me.

'Peter Smith. Right. Now there's a surprise. What did he say he was doing? He said he was trying to find Sarah. I see.'

Rob fizzes like an angry wasp. He ends the call and his head swivels, thunder in motion.

'Your father's a great big fucking nuisance, Sarah. Stirring things up like this he's more of a threat to our safety than the bloody IRA.' By now he is shouting. 'Do you realise how deeply your lunatic father is jeopardising this operation? I'm really not happy. And my *bosses* won't be happy, which is much more serious. At the very least this is going to prolong things. The more that bloody man digs, the longer it will be before you all see your families again. And the longer we'll all be in this shit. Do I make myself clear?'

I nod, feeling utterly wretched. Rob turns to John, who's been listening to all this with a worried expression on his face. Maria has walked away from the car, but I can tell she knows something is going on.

'John, you're going to have to ring Peter Know-It-All Smith, and tell him you're not dying of cancer, you've got AIDS, all right? Maybe that'll get him off our backs.'

I'm not sure that telling my dad John has AIDS will make things any better. If anything it might make things worse as he'd just have another bone to gnaw at. 'That's not going to work.'

'What do you mean?' asks Rob.

'I know my dad. As I've said before, once he's got his teeth into something he doesn't let up. It's a recipe for trouble.'

'You!' Rob spits, suddenly turning on me and jabbing his finger in front of my eyes. 'You're the cause of all this. You're so high profile now we might as well have put an advert in *The Times* telling the whole world where we are. There's nothing for it. You need a disguise. You're going to have to change the way you look. Somehow we have to make you stick out less like a sore thumb.'

He flexes his fingers, thinking. 'Get your hair chopped to within an inch of your scalp and bleach it. That'll be a start.'

Brushing my protests aside, Rob paces slowly back and forth, his mouth set, eyes cold. 'Don't you want to keep yourself and your family safe from the terrorists?' I fall silent, the words drying up even as they form. There is nothing I can say to this.

Satisfied, Rob grabs John by the arm, and together they walk off towards the loch, leaving me by the car, processing these latest twists and turns. At first I don't notice Maria. Looking uncertain, she mutters something I don't immediately catch. It's another bombshell to top off the day.

'Are you sure?' I ask her.

Yes, she replies, she is almost certain. She's pregnant, and the child is Rob's.

Nether Hale, end May 1993

Jill Smith's office had been turned into a war room. On the wall hung a huge map of England, Wales and Scotland, with coloured pins scattered the length and breadth of the country. Each marked a place where they knew Sarah had drawn cash – mute echoes of her life on the run.

Tracking Sarah had become an almost full-time occupation, a campaign executed along military lines. Sarah was spending wildly on her Access credit card, and since the account was held at the farm, Peter and Jill received all the bills. They sat scrutinising the latest one, trying to understand Sarah's movements through the credit-card transactions while fixing a new pin on the map for each new location.

'They've been all over the place in the last four weeks, darling, take a look at this,' said Jill, handing the Access statement to her husband. It revealed the group's passage through Newcastle-upon-Tyne, Sheffield, Banbury, Rugby, Warwick and Leamington Spa, along with the hotels they had stayed in. It looked like Sarah had funded the lot.

The phone rang. Peter wondered if it was the call he'd been expecting. Ever since John Atkinson called with his story about having AIDS, Peter had been busy trying to check it out. He had already discovered that both John and Sarah had given blood at college a few months before the 'mystery tour'. To Peter it seemed patently obvious that someone who was HIV positive would not volunteer his own blood, and so he had been making discreet inquiries. His daughter was missing, could they please help him?

The voice on the end of the phone was one of authority. It was the call about John Atkinson's blood test, and it was exactly as Peter had predicted: John's blood was perfectly normal.

Peter's anger spilled over. 'What do they take us for? Complete fools!'

Jill looked crestfallen. She felt protective towards her daughter and couldn't help wondering whether Sarah's behaviour was down to something they had done wrong as parents. She knew Sarah had always been unhappy about being sent to boarding school. Was all this perhaps a delayed rebellion. She wanted to talk to Peter about the way she felt, but her husband was a man who dealt in facts, not emotions: life was built on certainties, not imponderables; science was about proof. So Peter shut out anything that wasn't tangible, and Jill talked to her computer instead, taking comfort in voicing her troubles out loud, even if no one could hear them.

A few days earlier she had written to Sarah, sending the letter to Maria Hendy's parents, in the hope that they would pass it on:

You have made your decisions for better or for worse, and taken a house. We will stand by you whatever has happened (although that would be much easier if we knew the truth, and what you yourself want to do). We grieve to think of you there in an empty house in Peterborough while all your possessions are here. We would dearly love to see you and talk to you, but if you cannot or will not talk to us you may come and get your furniture while we are away. You can have one of the beds from the roof and any mattresses you like from the further attic. We shall probably be away during the first two weeks of June.

In the wake of his call to Worksop police, however, Peter was now utterly certain that Robert Freegard was up to no good. What he couldn't understand was why Sarah and John were playing along with Freegard's lies, and why Sarah would not tell them where she was. He had to be missing something.

Sarah

The Lloyds Bank clerk is counting out the money, all seven and a half thousand pounds of it, the notes flashing past my eyes in a rainbow haze. I have never seen so much cash at one time.

In the last few days we've driven from one end of the country to the other – again. From Edinburgh to Winchester, via Banbury in Oxfordshire and Poole in Dorset, hundreds of relentless, joyless miles, with Rob constantly intoning the need to cover our tracks. It has become his mantra, against the interminable background of Duran Duran's 'Ordinary World', which he plays all the time.

He declares that we need the money to pay for our living expenses. Although he receives a budget from his department for day-to-day costs, he says we have dramatically overspent and blames this on my dad for blowing our cover in Peterborough. Ever since then, we've been clocking up huge debts as we travel around the country, staying in one hotel after another, trying to throw the IRA off our scent. 'Don't worry about it. You'll get the money back later,' he promises.

So here I am, standing in a branch of Lloyds Bank in Winchester, England's ancient capital, the former seat of King Alfred, watching bleakly as the entire remaining contents of my savings account are counted out in front of me. So much paper; fuel for flight. I've managed to circumvent a block my parents put on the account by going to the bank in person and persuading the bank clerk to lift it. 'I am Sarah Smith,' I tell him. 'This is my account. You can check my signature against your records.' The bank can't argue with me.

Clutching my bundle of notes, I retrace my steps to the car, where Rob is waiting. 'You succeeded, right?' He demands curtly. I thrust the money in his direction, but he stops me, reaching a hand into his inside jacket pocket.

'Here's what we do. I want you to put the money inside this envelope and sign it all along the edges of the seal.' Rob produces a pen. 'It's just to make sure no one tampers with it. Now we know it belongs to you, and when this is all over, you'll get it back with interest.'

'Are you absolutely sure I'll get this all back?' I ask quietly.

'Sure. Stop fretting and trust me for once, will you. We'll be paying you handsomely for all the trouble and danger you're going through.'

I do as Rob says, putting the money inside the envelope, licking the seal, closing it and signing it. Finally I pass the envelope over to him. I have no choice but to trust him on this. He is a government agent after all.

According to Rob, we will be placed in a witness protection programme, and in due course, he says, we will all be given new identities and new lives. In the meantime, it is imperative we erase all sign of our old selves. A large component of that is to address the matter of the money trail. It would be mere child's play, he says, for the terrorists to trace us through bank transactions, so we must gradually disappear from their financial radar – not all at once, or it might precipitate action, but in stages. To make this possible, his department has set up secure, untraceable police accounts. They want me to transfer all of my savings into these accounts. So, we are to keep moving, never stay in one place, withdraw small amounts of cash as we go and hand it over to Rob.

Once again a warning bell sounds in my head. Rules are one thing, money quite another. The idea of drawing out my entire savings and handing it over on trust seems ridiculous. Despite Rob's continuous reassurance that it's only a short-term measure and that his department will give us our money back with interest when we receive our new identities, I am not completely convinced.

'I'm not happy about handing over money to anyone, especially people I've never met,' I say flatly.

Rob and I are alone. 'Do you want the Provos to find you, Sarah? Because you know that if they do, it's not just you that's at risk, they'll go straight for your family as well,' he reasons, trying to keep me calm. 'They're not going to leave anything to chance. If they take you out because of me infiltrating their network, then they'll take your family out as well, just because you're their daughter. That's how it works.'

His tone is at once reassuring and apologetic. 'Is that what you want, Sarah?'

I sigh wearily, unable to untangle the alarm, confusion, panic, distress and fear paralysing my mind. The prospect of not being able to see my family, of them being in mortal danger, of John dying of cancer is all too much to cope with. Added to which, I'm exhausted by the sheer number of miles we have covered and the hours spent on the road.

'Do me a favour, just co-operate, will you,' he continues. 'Have we travelled all these miles around the country and put up with all this shit just so you can get hung up about what's in your piggy bank? I'm doing my best here to protect you.'

I listen sullenly but don't say anything. I think longingly of Nether Hale, of being at home. No, of course I don't want to give our location away. Deep down I'm very reluctant to agree to any of this, but I don't feel I have any choice other than to go along with what Rob is telling me.

Suspended between suspicion and terror, we spend the next few days being driven by Rob to different cashpoints all over the country. He is constantly in call boxes, receiving instructions from his bosses in London about where to go and what to do next. I have just withdrawn the last of the cash from my current and deposit accounts. Now they are empty too.

Were the students simply stupid to believe what Freegard told them? One could be forgiven for thinking so, but these were three very different young people; the deception of one might imply stupidity in that individual, but the deception of them all suggests a pattern. Sarah, John and Maria were the victims of cruel, unusual and powerful but subtle manipulation.

Freegard had a supreme ability to lie and deceive convincingly. He claimed he was almost thirty when he was just twenty-one. He claimed to have a Masters in psychology from Oxford University when he didn't. He grossly exaggerated the number of Irish students at Harper Adams College. John Taylor of Duran Duran was not Freegard's brother, and Jim Cooper was not a member of the IRA, yet Freegard could make people believe these things were true. When he showed John a summons from Nottingham Crown Court, it was in fact his own.

The most successful lies are often based on truth, and this was one of the strengths of Freegard's deception. The IRA bombing campaign in the UK and recent events at the college connected with the Troubles were a real-life threat that lent plausibility to Freegard's espionage fantasy. Subsequent lies, by extension, would appear all the more believable.

By inventing an identity as a secret agent working for the British government, with responsibility for public safety, Freegard, wittingly or unwittingly, elevated himself to a commanding position of authority and, in a masterstroke, put himself beyond scrutiny. As an agent, his identity and credentials were effectively closed to investigation. The students had little experience of the real world, and conditioned by their middle-class upbringing to respect authority, Sarah, John and Maria had no reason to disbelieve his claims, and gave way to his 'expert advice'.

Freegard's 'special knowledge' of Sarah's personal circumstances was another uncannily accurate ace. Did he or did he not have intimate knowledge of her trust fund and bank accounts? No one knows. This 'inside information' was probably no more than a smoke and mirrors deception, a combination of minute observation, accurate recall and artifice, but it all lent credibility to his claims. Freegard had an astonishing memory for facts. He would pick up small details in the course of conversation, squirrel these nuggets of information away, dig them out and use them as and when he needed to – and long after people had forgotten what they had told him.

Freegard's skills were not unique. He was already displaying many of the classic traits of a cult leader – a David Koresh-type figure – who uses intelligence, charisma and intuitive ability to spot vulnerability in others for purposes of control. In Sarah's case, Freegard quickly detected an insecurity about her relationship with men, so he set up John as the unwitting instrument of her entrapment.

Whether he realised it or not, Freegard then swiftly played another classic card: he disoriented them. John's apparent illness, and the 'mystery tour' created a deep sense of chaos and confusion, and made the students easier to control. Once he'd lured them away from their familiar surroundings he could pile on the pressure, and exploit their fears of the IRA. Although Sarah and John experienced and expressed doubts about the situation, they had become sufficiently intimidated not to question Freegard's authenticity too deeply.

Freegard probably realised that if he was to succeed in keeping his victims under his control, he had to stoke their fears. When Sarah's father threatened to become a thorn in Freegard's side, he cunningly turned this to his advantage by creating a new bogeyman: Peter Smith. Freegard never suggested to the students that Peter Smith was evil or meant them any harm. Instead he made them believe that Peter was completely out of control, and that his interference could end up putting everyone in jeopardy, Peter included. In this way Freegard turned Peter into a threat without challenging Sarah's love for her father. It was a significant moment. Without this sleight of hand the whole deception could easily have collapsed, and Freegard continued to use the threat of Sarah's father to create a sense of urgency and imminent danger. In this way he could keep his victims in a state of disorientation by moving them on at short notice.

It is unlikely that Freegard had a master plan, or even knew where this was all going. Rather his method was to experiment, to probe and test, to see what worked and then measure cause and effect. If his suggestions were met with incredulity, he would turn them around, saying he was only joking, or 'testing' the students. In this way he learned very quickly what worked with his victims, and what did not. The students' behaviour, for example, had changed significantly following Freegard's revelation that he was 'a spy', but the confidence to progress to a more sophisticated level of manipulation was the result of one particular gambit. Freegard had taken each of his victims in turn to see their parents – not individually but as part of the group, and the group was never separated. This was a breakthrough point for Freegard, the sudden realisation of the extent of his control over the students: he had proved he could break the link to the strongest bond they had – their families. From this moment on he began to abuse his newly discovered power.

Importantly, he became their only point of reference, their only security. As the students became more dependent on him, his hold over them increased.

Having defused the immediate threat from Sarah's parents, Freegard now set in motion a sequence of events that would allow him to consolidate his hold over the students still further. For this he would need a permanent base for himself and Maria, a controlled environment in which he could hide Sarah and John and dominate them all – in effect his 'lair'.

Leaving Peterborough, Freegard returned to the part of the country in which he felt most at home, the north of England. On 17 June 1993, he made a telephone call. He had spotted an advertisement in the Sheffield Star for a 'luxury flat' in the city's Hillsborough district – barely half an hour's drive from his home town, Worksop.

The landlady showed him around. The apartment occupied the top two floors of a terraced house in Dorothy Road. Freegard decided to take it straight away, signing a six-month lease and handing over £840 in cash for two months' rent.

When the landlady and her husband asked what he did, he told them he worked for British Nuclear Fuels (BNFL) and that he planned to live in the flat with his girlfriend. He didn't mention either Sarah Smith or John Atkinson.

With a safe location from which to operate, Freegard was now poised to tighten his grip on Sarah and John.

part three

Brainwashing

June 1993–March 1994

Chapter 8

Wage Slaves

Sarah, Sheffield, 19 June 1993

We've arrived in the North Yorkshire town of Sheffield. The small terraced house in Dorothy Road sits on a gently inclining street in the suburb of Hillsborough. Rob tells us it's a safe house for him and Maria, and that the bottom part is occupied by someone from security ops who'll be watching over us. For the time being we'll all be living under the one roof, but soon we'll each be transferred into separate safe houses for our own protection.

Row upon row of identical terraced homes – how I envy all these people with their 'normal' lives. I wish I could go back to college. I can't believe the turn of events things have taken; it feels like I'm occupying someone else's life. I long to wake up from this nightmare.

In the bathroom mirror I see a young woman I don't recognise. This stranger has tightly cropped hair that has been expensively dyed blonde. It isn't attractive, it's ugly and demeaning. Sickened, I turn away. The visit to a hairdresser's in Edinburgh was a deeply distressing experience. My long, rich, brown hair lay in a dark puddle on the floor. They had to use so much bleach that my scalp burnt and I'm still in pain.

The flat consists of the top two floors of a house, one of which is a converted attic, which I'll share with John. The room is completely bare of furniture, apart from a couple of fitted wardrobes – no bed, no drawers, no cupboards. Rob takes me to buy a duvet and two pillows on my credit card, but there's no mattress to lie on, only a hard floor, and the room is cold. There's no heating up here, in contrast to the rooms below where Rob and Maria will live. Rob says Maria is entitled to special privileges because she's pregnant. 'Be easy and be careful around her,' he tells us. 'Don't upset her.'

Rob explains unsympathetically that John and I are not supposed to know the location of the Dorothy Road safe house – I was meant to have been in the safe house in Peterborough, not here in Sheffield. Splitting the group of four was always part of the plan, since it makes us more difficult to find. However, my father has put paid to that plan by telling Jim Cooper of our whereabouts. I now understand why we have to be wary of Jim. Rob explained during our travels that our former flatmate is an IRA operative. So John and I are to stay with Rob and Maria until HQ has sorted out other places for the two of us. In the meantime our movements will be strictly controlled by him.

Having to keep us together in one place has ratcheted up the risks, so Rob briefs us on living undercover, and draws up a list of rules that we will have to adopt. If anyone calls at the house, for example, we must never answer the door. If anybody turns up claiming to be from the police it will certainly be a trap, since no other authority knows anything about the covert anti-terrorist operation at college, or that we are involved with it by our association with Rob.

I glance around the bare room and shudder. It's such a long way from my colourful bedrooms at college and at home. Sharing the room with John is going to be a strain because we're not getting on that well. He keeps siding with Rob over this business with my dad – in fact, over everything. I can't seem to get through to him and anyway, there's not much chance to talk as he's out on operations with Rob during the day and most evenings.

I have to hope that Rob is serious when he says this is only temporary and that everything will soon return to normal.

I look fondly at the small sparkling heap of jewellery in my lap. The flower-shaped opal and diamond ring is one of my favourites. I treated myself to it in Canterbury just three years ago, with the money saved from working on the farm during the holidays. It was so pretty and delicate I just had to have it. It cost me a small fortune – seven hundred pounds – but I saw it as an investment and really treasured it. The rest of the jewellery includes some family heirlooms, handed down from my grandparents and parents: a couple of gold rings, a pair of opal earrings, a pearl snowflake necklace and a diamond brooch pin. They are of great sentimental value, but Rob says I have to get rid of them.

'You've got to pawn them, they're just too distinctive,' he insists. 'No matter how much you change your appearance, Sarah, you will always be recognised by this jewellery. If it was cheap high street crap I wouldn't be so worried, but they're individual pieces. They keep records of this kind of thing, and if a friend could recognise you just by looking at the rings on your finger, then so could an IRA sniper. You're risking all our lives by keeping them.'

I am at once devastated and outraged. 'Why do I have to do this?'

'Stop shouting, will you,' he snarls.

Lowering my voice, I continue to argue back. 'Why can't I just hide them?' At first he ignores my question, staring out of the windscreen, then he says in a cold and emotionless tone, 'Look, Sarah, you don't have a choice. You *will* do this. Do I have to remind you again that you and John aren't even supposed to be here? *You* should be in Peterborough, but thanks to your stupid father we're now all in Sheffield, all in the same boat, and because we're all together the risks are multiplied. If one of us is found, we may as well all come out waving. How many times do I have to keep drumming it into you that we are being hunted by IRA terrorists, Sarah? They're ruthless. If the IRA comes looking for me, they'll know immediately that others are involved, not because you're in the house, but because you've left your precious *jewellery* behind!'

I start to cry.

[69]

'In any case, you'll get these things back. They'll be held by the police until this is all over.'

'How do I know I'll get them back?' I say between tears. He sighs in irritation. 'I have to telephone one of my colleagues. As soon as you've left the shop he'll go in and buy them back.' He pauses a moment. 'You know, I'm just following the rules here. This is in your own interests.'

The tears start to flood down my cheeks at the thought of parting with such dear pieces of my life, the last reminders of relatives I'll never see again.

Then, unexpectedly, Rob laughs in my face. 'Pull yourself together.' He snaps, 'Get on with it. It's not an option; this is an order from my bosses.'

Rob's reaction to my distress turns my tears into fat choking sobs. I've become used to the verbal abuse that follows any resistance to his instructions – I'm sure I must have inherited some of my dad's cynicism – but his cruel pleasure at my loss is more than I can bear. I feel utterly defeated. In the end, though, I have no choice but to give way. It is an order.

Another battle won, Rob drives me into the centre of Sheffield. He parks up, and I watch as he goes to the phone box to make the call to his colleague to confirm which shop I should go to. He says he won't go with me as it's too dangerous for us to be seen together.

'Make it snappy now,' he says, 'otherwise I'll get it in the neck.'

I set off. Shoppers crowd the streets, happy with their purchases. They'll return home and share the fun of having bought something new with their loved ones. I can't help feeling wretched, by comparison. There is no joy in this transaction. I am about to part with my most treasured possessions, and I'm not at all certain I'll ever see them again, whatever Rob says.

'I'll give you a hundred and fifty pounds for the lot,' says the man in the cardigan behind the counter.

'What about the stones? Why can't you pay me for them?' I ask, shaken by how little I'm being offered.

'We pay only for weight of gold, not for stones,' he says gruffly.

I am too upset to be shocked and nod a silent acquiescence. He takes the jewellery and I scarcely register as he hands me the cash. I get out of the shop as quickly as I can.

Climbing back into Rob's car, still sobbing, I hand over the money.

'What are you crying for? Haven't I told you you'll get it back?' He looks at me with contempt as he slips the cash inside his jacket pocket. At that moment I hate him, but I take pleasure in one small victory. Unknown to Rob I've managed to keep hidden a black opal necklace that my parents gave me for my twenty-first birthday. I'm determined he'll never, ever take it away from me.

'Get in the car!' I'm not sure why Rob looks so agitated, but this is clearly no time for argument, so I do as I'm told. It's a car I haven't seen him drive before, a Vauxhall Astra GSI. He puts his foot down on the accelerator and we race off through the streets of Hillsborough.

'Whose car is this?'

'Quiet!'

Rob's face is dark and serious. He glances frequently in his rear-view mirror, which makes me nervous. He reaches down to the console and turns the CD up full blast. It's Depeche Mode who, along with Duran Duran, are his favourite band. I cling to the handle on the passenger door, trying to focus on the road.

In the city centre he pulls up sharply next to a small park and gets out of the car motioning for me to do the same. He's fuming.

'How many times do I fucking well have to tell you?' He practically spits the words out as he paces up and down between the flower beds. 'Are you stupid or what? It's a works car and it's bugged.' He stops pacing and his eyes drill into me. 'HQ is listening, Sarah. If you carry on complaining all the time, they're going to think I'm not doing my job and I'll get it in the neck. So, for the umpteenth time, no talking in the car,' he growls.

'I just want to know what's going on,' I protest. 'It's my life, you know. Why me?'

'Listen up, Sarah. My bosses are not pleased with you. They reckon you need bringing down a peg or two, that you have an unrealistic view of what life is really like.'

I absorb this latest piece of information, not at all sure what he's talking about. It can't be good. It isn't.

'So you've got to call yourself Betty Smith. It's an alias, OK? You know what one of those is? On no account must you let them know your real name. Tell them to pay you in cash. That way neither your father nor the IRA can trace you.'

I raise my hands. What on earth is he talking about?

'You're to start right away, over there.' Rob nods in the direction of a row of shops.

'Over where?' I ask, bewildered.

'The fish and chip shop,' he barks.

'The fish and chip shop? Why? Why do I have to work there?' I shout over the top of the car at him, pounding the roof with my fist. He's about to drive off and abandon me here, but I want some answers.

'How long do I have to do this for? When are we going to get our new identities?'

Rob glares darkly in my direction and I'm frightened.

'Now you look, I'm the one who's under pressure here. I'm the one who has to answer to the department. If my boss tells me you have to do this job, then you have to do it. You know the deal, Sarah. Make my life miserable and I'll make yours hell.' With that he jumps in the car, slams his foot down and speeds off.

I glance across the road, shuddering at the thought of crossing this, my own Rubicon.

The Option Fish and Chip shop is owned by a rotund Greek woman in her mid-forties with hair the colour of coal. 'Over here is where we keep the haddock and the cod,' she says, a heavy Greek accent laced with a northern twang. 'Then you've got the kebabs and the southern fried chicken.' She guides me round the tiny shop, pointing out the L-shaped counter where all the food is kept on hot plates.

'We're right next to a nightclub and we get real busy in here after eleven o'clock at night, especially at weekends, so we need a fast and efficient system. You'll be standing here wrapping up the fish and chips and ringing up the till. I'll be cooking the food over here. We'll work it between us.'

I wonder what the hell I'm doing in this alien environment. Again I feel as if I've crashed into somebody else's life or a parallel universe. This isn't who I am. I'm supposed to be graduating right now, with a hard-earned BSc in Agriculture. But I remind myself of the danger we're in and the threat to my family and decide I'll have to cooperate with these orders from London for now.

'Out here is where we cook the mushy peas.' The proprietor is continuing her guided tour. She points to a little gas stove with an enormous saucepan on top. 'And everything is kept frozen in these freezers until we're ready to cook it. If you need a smoke, the back door opens up and you can stand outside.'

'That's fine,' I say. 'I don't smoke.'

A handful of customers have crammed into the shop, all of them looking impatient to be served. One of them, a swarthy man who seems far more at home here than I do, barks an order. The Greek owner gets to work, all plump tanned arms, hairnet and sizzling oil. I try to look as if I know what to do, but nothing here is familiar. Detachment is the only way I'm going to be able to get through this. My mind may be running in neutral in this strange world, but I can't block out the sounds and smells. Up to now, all strong smells in my life have been associated with a farm. I can muck out a horse any day, and I've never worried about dirt on my clothes and in my hair, but the odours in this chip shop are unfamiliar, the air reeks of fried fat, and even before the smell has had a chance to disperse another batch of fish hits the fryer. The stench builds up in layers until it's so thick it's like a fog. It permeates my clothes, my hair and my skin. It invades my nostrils and my mouth; I feel sick, but there's no escape.

'Two cod and chips, love, don't be stingy w'it vinegar!'

I can't get a handle on this. I try not to think of home.

'Kebabs and mushy peas.' 'Got any saveloy?'
Void.

'It's late, I'll drop you home.' Words spoken in a Greek accent start to take shape somewhere within my brain. It's one o'clock in the morning. Rob said I should get a lift back but ask to be dropped off at the end of the street. I accept the offer, grab my bag and inhale lungfuls of night air as my boss locks up.

'Where do you live?' she asks.

'Hillsborough.'

'You a long way from home?'

Tears spring to my eyes. How can I begin to explain to her what's happening to me. No one would believe me even if I could tell them. It's just too bizarre. I turn away. The houses melt into each other through my blurred vision.

My employer drops me off at the bottom of the hill, a couple of streets away from Dorothy Road, and drives off. I don't have a key to the house, Rob says it would compromise security, so I knock and wait, and knock again and again. It's really chilly out here despite the time of year.

After twenty minutes Rob opens up. He doesn't say anything as I slip in and make my way up to the attic where a hard floor awaits.

Today will be my fifth day at the fish and chip shop. My shift doesn't start until two, but Rob says if I want a lift into the city centre the only time he can manage it is eleven o'clock. That'll mean hanging around for three hours.

'Why don't you just give me the bus fare?'

'Bus fare? You've got to be kidding. We're already living well beyond our means. We don't have any spare cash, Sarah.'

And so I'm sitting in the Peace Gardens in the centre of Sheffield, killing time until two o'clock. Since emptying all my bank accounts for safe keeping, I don't have any money to buy a drink, otherwise I could have sat inside somewhere out of the cold. It looks as though rain is on the way.

'Betty Smith, Betty Smith,' I repeat my new name like a mantra. Sure enough, the first raindrops begin to fall. There's a doorway with an overhang in a quiet alleyway near the chip shop, and I edge up as close as possible to the door as it starts to rain harder. My watch tells me it's twelve forty-five. I hate the job but being warm inside has to be better than this.

As usual I zone out the moment I walk through the door. I'll get through the next twelve hours or so by cruising on remote, taking it one minute at a time.

I place a piece of fish inside a polystyrene dish, wrap a soggy mountain of chips in paper, ring up the amount on the till. Next customer; same again. It's a production line, and I perform the job mechanically, numb to all feeling. At the end of my shift I gather up the rubbish thrown on the floor by customers – empty boxes and paper, squashed chips trodden into the lino, some still with plastic forks stuck in them. My boss is trying to get rid of a drunk who's refusing to leave the premises. He's turning physical and hurling abuse at her. She looks as though she's used to it, and he's soon out on his ear. The end of another day.

The Hillsborough flat

The alarm tingled into life, waking John from his deep, exhausted sleep. Levering himself off the floor, he padded across the loft space and started down the stairs.

Just then he heard Freegard open his bedroom door and go into the bathroom, locking the door behind him with a sharp snatch of the bolt, claiming the territory as his. It was the same every morning. No sooner had John taken two steps downstairs than Freegard emerged. Every morning John had to wait for Freegard to finish before he was even allowed in for a pee. His brain hummed with humiliation. Such a petty, conceited act, he thought.

Thirty minutes later John left the house, posting the door key through the letterbox. He took the bus to work, utterly dependent on Freegard for the fare. Wages were something to be earned and then handed over. No problem, thought John, he was on good money from the police which he'd get as back-pay when this was all over.

And it was a relief just to be away from the house; from being told how to behave, what music he could listen to and what he was allowed to say. He loathed Freegard. Once, as he arrived home, Freegard caught him finishing off a bag of chips a work colleague had bought him. 'Where did you get those?' he'd demanded furiously. 'The bottlewasher bought them for me. Look, I need a shower,' John replied, choosing to ignore Freegard's glares. 'Smoky pub and all that.'

'Shower's out I'm afraid. Water's been turned off. Better luck tomorrow,' Freegard sneered back.

John knew his 'real' life was on hold and that what he was going through was a regrettable but necessary means to an end, so that things could return to normal, yet Freegard always had to have the upper hand. It drove John wild.

He arrived at The Stonehouse pub in Sheffield's Orchard Square. The obligatory morning greetings out of the way, he set to work. It was Freegard who had originally arranged the job interview, even telling him what to say. John had been anxious because he was ten minutes late for the interview, and he left thinking he hadn't made a very good impression. Freegard told him not to worry. 'Me and the boys have been on to the guy. He's been told to give you the job.' The surprise call to say the position was his had impressed John. Freegard really did have clout; his police credentials were reinforced.

It was eleven o'clock and, his shift over, John made his way to the rendezvous point fifty yards from the pub; a quiet back street, away from prying eyes. This was where Freegard picked him up. The waiting time varied, anything from thirty minutes to four hours, but no matter how long John had to wait and whatever the weather, he wasn't allowed to move from the spot. He sat on a doorstep of an unoccupied office unit, a living statue. Even when Freegard finally drew up John knew his day was far from over and that there was a long night ahead.

Sarah

The end of another week and my boss has just paid me in cash. It would be good to hang on to a little of the money. Heaven knows, there are some essentials a girl likes to buy for herself and not go crawling to a man for. However, Rob insists it must all be handed over to him to cover our general living expenses.

Arguing with him or refusing to obey his orders are not options. I was appalled at what he did to Maria once when she resisted: he shut her fingers in the car window. He justified himself by maintaining that *we* were the ones making life difficult, not him.

I'm not a confrontational person and I don't want to give him any excuse to make it worse, so I do as he says in the hope that our ordeal will be over as quickly as possible, but I feel a pang of regret as I watch him take the money from me and slip it into his own pocket.

Cash is really tight, Rob says, because he's had to spend our entire budget, and more, in covering our tracks after my dad gave away our location to Jim Cooper. Rob never misses an opportunity to remind everyone how much he and the rest of the group are suffering because of my dad.

Food is strictly rationed. On one occasion, John and I helped ourselves to some food from the fridge – nothing big, just a piece of cheese or ham – but Rob complained that it was something he had saved for himself and Maria and came down on us like a ton of bricks. 'That's it, you two are banned from taking food from the cupboards. You can have your cereal in the morning, but otherwise you check with me before you eat something from here.' This means that we can only eat when he says so. Maria has to come first because she's pregnant, Rob says. John and I will just have to manage on what's left, and on what Rob chooses to give us. John and I start scrounging food from work or buying bread rolls with the few pence we make in tips.

I feel resentful that we are being treated like this, especially since I've handed over so much money, and tonight I vent my frustrations on John.

'I don't understand why we have to live like this.'

'Talk to Rob about it, then. Don't get at me. Rob's the one in charge.'

'Why should we do as he says?'

'Because our lives depend on him, that's why. Do you want to go out there and face the IRA on your own?' asks John, clearly exasperated with me.

'But what's that got to do with what we can eat?'

'Drop it, Sarah. Rob said it's *because* we've overspent on the budget *because* we had to travel round the country, *because* your silly over-zealous father gave away our location. It's your dad's fault that we can't eat what we want. The longer he carries on looking for you, the longer we're going to be stuck living like this. Blame him, don't blame it on Rob. And stop getting at me.'

John turns out the light and turns away from me.

'You haven't really got cancer, have you?' I say in the darkness.

'Go to sleep, Sarah.'

'I can understand why you lied to me.'

Suddenly a voice booms up the stairs, making us flinch. 'Shut up, the two of you!' yells Rob. 'The room's bugged. Just keep quiet.'

'Go to sleep now,' whispers John abruptly.

Instead, I lie awake. I can see now that John came up with the cancer story as a ploy to pull me and Maria out of college without attracting attention. I don't think he had any choice, so I forgive him the lies. I need John. He's my only sounding board. There's no one else I can turn to for advice, and I still really care for him, despite everything we're going through. I can tell he's suffering too. He hates his job in the city centre pub every bit as much as I despise mine in the chip shop. He hasn't any money either, and he's always hungry. Amazingly for such a beanpole, he's even lost weight; quite a bit in fact. And he works incredible hours, often not coming back until three or four in the morning. From what I can gather, Rob picks him up after he finishes at the pub, then they go off together, so he's always exhausted from burning the candle at both ends. Still, none of this helps to allay my qualms.

'Why is everything always costing *me* so much money?' I whisper, hoping we're not being picked up.

'I don't have any answers for you. I'm not a policeman, I'm in the same position as you, remember.'

'I've paid for all our travelling and hotels. I don't trust this guy, John. Why's he always so mean to us? Something's not right.'

'Look, I don't like him any more than you do, Sarah, but if he were a conman he wouldn't have come back for more. If he were a conman he'd have just taken our money and disappeared, never to be heard of again. He wouldn't be living downstairs with his pregnant girlfriend, who's also our friend from college. OK, so maybe I'm no expert on typical conman behaviour, but I'm certain it's not Rob's behaviour. This is too insane to be a con, it's got to be genuine. No one would put themselves and other people through what we've been through just for money. It's far too bizarre to be a lie. Now just leave it.'

I chew over John's reasoning. He spends more time with Rob than I, so if he believes Rob then why should I doubt him? I guess Maria must believe Rob too. Feeling outnumbered, I resign myself to accepting Rob's rules and doing what he says.

The following morning, Rob collars me as I'm making my way downstairs. 'Weren't you listening when I told you the room was bugged, heh? What exactly didn't you understand? You kept on and on. I could hear every single word you said, clear as a bell. And you know what? My bosses in London could hear it too. Right now, I'm just the minder, the big decisions are being taken down there, and the word is they're not happy about your constant questioning and your ingratitude. How are you supposed to help somebody, for God's sake, if they make it so bloody difficult?'

Rob towers over me, and I feel myself wilting under his verbal attack. I lower my eyes.

'You know the deal by now, Sarah. You make life difficult for me, I'll make life hell for you. Remember, the only reason you're still here is because your fucking father refuses to leave well alone. Until things have calmed down, until the situation is under control, you do exactly as I say.' He holds me in his disconcerting stare. I'm trembling all over, on the verge of tears.

That night, with Rob standing over me dictating the words, I write a letter home.

I ask my parents to back off. I ask them to stop checking up on us all the time. If they don't we will disappear completely and they will never see me again. In my mind all I can see is the beautiful landscape of my childhood, the sea, the fields of golden wheat and cauliflowers, seagulls dive-bombing the freshly ploughed earth.

The tears fall freely. The letter is the complete opposite of what I really want to say. I seal the envelope. Rob orders John to post it from Milton Keynes.

The systematic brainwashing of Sarah and John was now underway. The term 'brainwashing' refers to the use of subtle techniques of thought control which dictate a subject's pattern of behaviour. It was first coined by a CIA operative, Edward Hunter, in 1951, at the time of the Korean war.

Freegard had altered Sarah's appearance by making her bleach her hair and obliterated a powerful reminder of her past by making her pawn her jewellery. By forcing her to use a false name, he had, at one stroke, removed her identity.

Under the guise of 'protecting' her, he had started to manipulate Sarah's physical and social environment. At the very time Sarah should have been graduating Freegard put her to work in a chip shop, a completely alien environment; he introduced 'rules' at the Dorothy Road house regulating when Sarah and John could use the bathroom and what they could eat; they were deprived of money and prevented from using public transport.

Freegard was controlling not only Sarah's environment, but also her and John's time. Without keys to the house, they had to wait for Freegard to let them in; he took them to work, often leaving them waiting hours for their shifts to start. By dictating both environment and time, Freegard gave his victims little opportunity to think through, question and challenge his actions. By denying the two proper sleep, exhaustion and bewilderment at the turn of events undoubtedly contributed to their psychological surrender

Crucially, Freegard used the IRA threat to cut Sarah off from regular communication with family and friends, thus removing any opportunity for them to influence her and any risk that Sarah might have her old beliefs reinforced or challenge new ones. The only communication she was permitted was under his supervision. This technique works particularly successfully on those who are used to an information rich environment and who are then suddenly isolated; because of their natural hunger for information it makes them more susceptible to brainwashing.

Sarah had regular communication with only two people: John, her sole sounding board, who reinforced Freegard's opinion; and Freegard himself, who made sure he denied her any opportunity to question or complain by maintaining both the house and car were bugged. Freegard effectively closed Sarah down. She was left with no one to reason with but herself. Such a bewildering environment was not conducive to rational judgement. In the same way that a cult community thrives on its relative insulation from the outside world, Freegard's isolation of his victims led them to become totally dependent on the information that he – as their 'guru' – gave them. By now they were poorly equipped to question. Although Sarah would not have been aware of it, her mind was beginning to unravel.

To maintain absolute control during the brainwashing process, Freegard regularly resuscitated the IRA threat. He even planted imaginary agents, or 'watchers', in the same building as Sarah and John, rooting the idea that there was a network of spies and that he wasn't operating alone.

At the same time Freegard continued to twist Peter Smith's dogged detective work to his own advantage, by portraying him as the real enemy.

The longer Freegard was able to maintain the grand deception, the more confident he became of the power of his own charisma and authority. The structure he had created boosted his ego and sense of self-importance. It made him feel entitled to make free use of the money raised or earned by Sarah and John. While his victims' standard of living declined, his own circumstances improved exponentially.

Freegard made copious use of rewards and punishments – another classic thought-control technique. Sarah's reward was that one day she would get her life back and an explanation for what had happened. All she had to do was stick it out. However, if she expressed doubts, Freegard threatened punishment or punished her freely. The ultimate sanction was the IRA threat to her family.

Fear was Freegard's most important psychological weapon in keeping Sarah in check. As the process of brainwashing her became more advanced, and her circumstances deteriorated, so she became more malleable and more fearful of his threat that unless she did what he said, things would 'get worse'.

For Sarah, certainty was replaced by uncertainty, control by powerlessness. She never knew what was going to happen to her from one moment to the next. It was Freegard who now managed her world. Frightened, humiliated, deprived of her liberty and isolated from family and friends, her circumstances were no better than those of a prisoner.

Having manipulated Sarah's external world, Freegard now aimed to disable Sarah mentally and gain total control of her inner world – her mind – turning her into what Edward Hunter described as a 'human robot', 'a mechanism in flesh and blood, with new beliefs inserted into a captive body'.

Chapter 9

Closing In

Nether Hale, August 1993

Peter and Jill were frantic. They had just received a letter from Sarah giving them an ultimatum: stop looking for her or she would disappear for ever. Peter was inclined to ignore it, arguing that they needed at least some idea of which town, even county, Sarah was living in. However, close monitoring of her credit-card spending had revealed nothing. They had no idea where she was and it had been almost two months since they had spoken to her on the phone.

The last solid piece of information they had received was when Peter had phoned Maria Hendy's father in July and been told that the two couples had split up and that Sarah and John might be in Leamington. Yet when Peter spoke to John's father, Russell Atkinson said he believed they were in Milton Keynes.

The contradictions were turning the search into a hopeless task. Peter and Jill started to pore over the credit-card statements again. Sarah had bought petrol at a garage in Sheffield, food at a Deep Pan pizza outlet in Derby. She had visited Langley Mill in Derbyshire, filled up with Esso petrol in Banbury, hired a car in Sheffield, spent money at The Boot and Shoe in Newark, and bought petrol from a Q8 garage in Peterborough. They didn't have a clue what it all meant. There was no logic to her erratic pattern of movement around the country and no one place she could be pinned down to. Peter felt he was always ten steps behind.

'I think we need help,' said Peter. 'You know that private detective in Ramsgate? I think I'll give him a call. I want him to find out everything he can about the movements of the gang.'

There was one entry, however, that Jill didn't quite understand. Peter studied it for a moment and let out a quiet growl. 'Interesting. Bramall Lane, do you know where that is?' She didn't. 'Sheffield United football club, it's their ground. Sarah's gone and bought two season tickets.'

'But she doesn't have the slightest interest in football.'

'Precisely. So we can hazard a pretty good guess at who's using one of those tickets, can't we?' Peter looked pleased with himself. He had an idea.

Guy Smith was only twenty-two, but mature beyond his years, a tall, broad-shouldered young man, affable, confident and self-assured. The few freckles on his open face resembled licks of caramel. Whenever he was in polite company his wide hazel-green eyes sparkled courteously, but threaten anyone close to him and the gentle, easy-going exterior slipped away in an instant to be replaced by something altogether more bullish, stubborn and angry. Guy was fiercely protective of those he loved, and not a man to cross.

'If it comes to it, you know Mum will never sanction cutting off any money,' he told his father, standing in the doorway of Peter's office with his hands stuffed into his trouser pockets. 'She thinks it's too drastic – Freegard might end up hurting Sarah.'

Peter observed his youngest son. He had always been impressed by Guy's down-to-earth, no-nonsense approach, and in later years would defer increasingly to his son's opinion. 'I know. All the more reason to get to your sister and try to persuade her to see sense. There's no way I'm scaling down my investigations, whatever she says in her letter.'

'I agree with you, Dad. There's got to be a way to get to her.'

'As soon as it's nine o'clock, I'm going to call Sheffield United and speak to the club manager, or the secretary, or whoever calls the shots up there. I'll tell him that one of his supporters has been buying tickets fraudulently on my daughter's credit card.' Peter paused, turning round in his chair to look straight at Guy, raising an eyebrow and giving his son a crooked smile. 'I want to find out which seat Freegard will be sitting in.'

Guy smiled back, nodding. He knew exactly what his father had in mind.

Sheffield, Saturday 25 and Sunday 26 September 1993

Guy Smith waited patiently, weighing up the moment to make his move. He knew the players were about to come on to the field. The manager of Sheffield United had been happy to help and made sure Guy would be sitting next to the holder of one of the season tickets that had been paid for on Sarah's Access card.

It was the second time Guy had been to Sheffield in the past five weeks. Through a process of elimination, and by following the credit-card trail, he and his parents had concluded that Sarah must be somewhere in or around the city. But despite spending hours visiting pubs and the Salvation Army, and showing around a recent photograph of his sister to jog people's memories, Guy had drawn a blank. Sarah hadn't featured on anybody's radar.

Maybe this time it would be different. Guy listened to the excited anticipation of the crowd and double-checked the seat number of his ticket. He knew that by the time the players emerged, Freegard would be seated and blocked in by the crowds. Then, and only then, would Guy walk into the stand and take up the seat next to him.

There was a deafening roar as cheers and whistles filled the stadium. It was Guy's cue. Gingerly, he climbed the stairs, checking the row numbers as he went. Finally he had Freegard cornered. This was his opportunity to find out where his sister was.

Scanning the row, he recognised the profile of his quarry. He knew it was him straight away, the slimy rogue. Guy, also a Harper Adams student, had occasionally returned from his sandwich year and met up with Sarah in The Swan, where he had been introduced to Freegard.

Slowly and carefully, Guy edged past the excited spectators, who cheered, hooted, chanted and whistled in their red and white scarves. The noise was deafening, but the adulation of the crowd was lost on Guy, who was wholly absorbed in his mission. 'Bet you weren't expecting to see me here,' he said to Freegard as he slipped into the seat next to him.

Confusion flashed across Freegard's face for a split second before he smirked as if at some awful joke. 'It's your father, isn't it? God I wish he'd stop messing with my life.'

The referee blew the whistle and the game started.

'I want to see my sister. You know where she is.'

Freegard watched intently as the ball passed between players down the field.

'She doesn't want to see you.' A Sheffield player was deliberately tripped and the referee blew his whistle. A yellow card was waved, a free-kick to United. 'She doesn't want to be involved with your family.' Freegard stopped and turned to face Guy. 'I'm the only one who cares about Sarah.'

'If you care about her then you won't mind if I see her,' retorted Guy.

Freegard's smile hardened. 'I'll see what I can do – after the game.'

For the next hour and three-quarters, Guy simmered. He would have liked to pulverise the man, beat the truth out of him. It wouldn't take long. Guy was by far the stronger of the two. Freegard wouldn't stand a chance; he'd soon be whining for mercy.

Guy clenched his fists but considered the consequences. It might mean prison, and it could also destroy any chance Sarah might have of regaining her freedom, for Guy was as sure as he could be that once he could talk some sense into her she'd want out. No, he thought, it wouldn't be worth it. Better to sit tight and try to get as much information from Freegard as possible. So Guy sat on his hands and waited.

The game had ended. Guy wasn't watching; he didn't care which team had won.

'Leave your car here and come with me,' Freegard told him. The pair had arrived at an MFI car park in the centre of Sheffield. 'It'll be safe here.' Guy locked his car and climbed into Freegard's top-of-the-range Astra, reluctant to follow instructions, but equally reluctant to miss the opportunity to see his sister.

'Where are we going?'

'I don't know where Sarah is, but John does.'

They drove in silence before finally pulling up in front of a pub, the Old Queen's Head.

'Go in, he's in there,' said Freegard.

Inside, the pub was filled with the jovial sounds of people relaxing. The flashes of red and white suggested Guy wasn't the only refugee from the match, but unlike the crowd in the pub, he felt far from cheerful. He could feel his anger building.

John was playing snooker in a room at the back and Guy came straight to the point. 'I want to see my sister.' John tensed, leaning on his snooker cue. He'd been rung in advance, briefed, and instructed by Freegard to keep Sarah's brother at arm's length.

'I'm protecting Sarah,' John said.

'I want to hear that from Sarah's own mouth,' Guy replied calmly.

'She doesn't want to see you. She doesn't want anything to do with you.' John returned to his game of snooker as if Guy didn't exist.

An hour later, Guy was being driven by Freegard to yet another location – a hotel about twelve miles north west of the city. The first thing he noticed was that the hotel had a secure car park with cameras. His suspicions were immediately aroused. 'Why couldn't I have parked my car here rather than leave it back at MFI?'

Freegard ignored the question. 'John told me where Sarah is, and I'm going to find her. Wait here.'

The car drove away, leaving Guy in the hotel foyer with no idea how long he would have to wait. As the hours passed he realised he would have to put up at the hotel for the night, and reached for his credit card.

*

The following morning, Freegard knocked on Guy's hotel room and announced that he was taking him into town to meet Sarah. Guy felt as though he was on a trail of vanishing ink, but while there was any chance of seeing Sarah, he knew he had to follow whatever leads he could.

By ten o'clock, Guy was standing at the bus station in the centre of Sheffield, and a moment later there she was, stepping off a bus and making her way over to him. He couldn't quite believe it was Sarah, momentarily confused by the short blonde hair. But he would recognise her anywhere. Surely she would want to tell him everything, surely she would want to come home now.

Sarah looked distant, disengaged and haunted, and neither of them spoke for a while.

'What do you think of my new haircut,' she finally blurted out.

'What's the problem, Sarah? Why aren't you speaking to us?' asked Guy gently.

'I'm not allowed to,' said Sarah.

'You're being fed rubbish. There's no reason to be doing what you are doing.'

'I can't come home.'

'I've heard this IRA tale, Sarah. Dad's been speaking to some of your friends at Harper who say Maria told them all about it. Look, if *I* can be at college and drink with these so-called terrorists, how come it's safe for me to go home, but it's not safe for you?'

Sarah began to cry.

'Have you actually seen these bomb-makers? If so, how do you make a bomb?'

'I have to go now,' Sarah said.

'Why can't you trust me?' Guy pleaded with his sister.

'I have to go now,' was all she would say. 'I'll come back later.'

Guy watched as she walked away, completely frustrated by his sister's failure to listen to him. Why was she behaving in this way, why did she want to remain with Freegard? He simply couldn't understand. As Sarah slowly disappeared from view she reminded him of a zombie, lifelessly going about the business of living, but with her heart beating elsewhere.

He waited around for several more hours, but knew it was useless. She wasn't coming back.

Back at the MFI car park Guy studied the damage down one side of his car. What a crap day, he thought. The back bumper was missing as well.

He phoned the Sheffield police. 'Joy rider I'm afraid,' they said, 'Chased him round the car park and finally apprehended him, but not before he'd done some right old damage.' Guy could hear the police officer sucking in air between his teeth. 'I'm sorry to say you won't be able to claim on insurance. Underage driver you see, no company will accept a claim.'

Thoroughly fed up with the weekend's events, Guy started the journey back home, but he hadn't gone far before he saw something that made him turn back. Taking another turn round a roundabout he saw it again. He stopped the car a short distance from the roundabout and walked back. Yes, he was quite positive now. There to one side was the back bumper of his car. He picked it up and looked it over carefully. The question was, if the police had chased the joy rider round the car park and apprehended him there, how come his missing back bumper was here, ten minutes' drive away? The police explanation made no sense. Guy thought he knew only too well who was behind it, but what proof did he have?

Freegard's power over Sarah had been given the ultimate test. Sarah had been closer to her younger brother than to anyone else, yet even Guy couldn't prise her away from him. Sarah's belief that Freegard worked for the government was unshakeable. She was convinced that unless she followed orders, her life was in danger from the IRA, and that by leaving with her brother now, he would be at risk as well.

In the process, John Atkinson had held firm as well. Both Sarah and John were, by now, almost completely brainwashed. They were Freegard's obedient slaves; he no longer had to be physically present to maintain his control over them. Freegard the master of lies had become Freegard the puppet-master.

But he knew he couldn't afford to be complacent. After the Sheffield United incident it was clear that Peter Smith was not going to give up without a fight. Freegard figured that it wouldn't be long before Sarah's father discovered the Dorothy Road address, so he knew he had to move Sarah on again soon.

This would also offer him a new opportunity to consolidate his control: by physically separating Sarah, John and Maria, he would cut their ties with the frame of reference they had shared before Freegard came on the scene.

Through his espionage fantasy he would continue to reinforce his influence; fleshing out the government department he claimed to work for, surrounding himself with colleagues and fellow spies – a network of control that would be invisible but pervasive. At the same time, Freegard would increasingly distance himself from his tough demands of Sarah. If she found an order unpalatable, he would blame his bosses, his superiors at MI5.

But before he could split the students up, he needed more money.

Chapter 10

Phoning Home

Sarah, September 1993

'Don't get uppity with me. Just get in.' Rob slams his foot on the accelerator and soon we're travelling northwards to the sound of Duran Duran belting out 'Hungry Like a Wolf'.

As the signposts fly by I wonder why we're heading towards Huddersfield, the place where I did my computing in business course. A short while later we pull up in front of a red call box. The traditional red box always used to be such a welcoming sight, a roadside friend, but not any more.

'Why are we in Huddersfield?' I ask, once out of the car.

'You told me you'd been a happy student here. Thought I'd bring you back somewhere you have nice memories of because, I'm sorry to say, I am the bearer of bad news.'

I can feel my face dropping and my shoulders tensing.

'We're running short of cash, Sarah. You have to ring your parents. Get them to pay off your Access bill so we can withdraw some more money and I can pay the rent.'

The thought of asking my parents for money makes me feel queasy – it's not something I've ever done before; I've always been financially independent. Besides, it's been more than two months since I last spoke to them.

'What am I supposed to tell them?'

'Say you need the card paid so that you can put a down payment on renting a house.'

'But . . .'

'No buts . . .'

Rob stands over me while I dial the number and rehearse the words in my head.

'Nether Hale Farm.' I hear my mother's deep, soothing voice. It sounds so rich and mellow in my ears, it breaks my heart. Rob hovers, his ear to the receiver.

'Are you alone, Mum? Can you talk?'

'Darling, where have you been? We're worried sick about you.' I can hear the pleading, hurt and relief in Mum's voice – a mother's love wrapped up in a single line. Her emotions overwhelm me and I am fighting to stay in control. I rest my forehead on the cold metal of the coin box and grip the receiver tightly.

'Mum, I need you to pay off my Access bill. I need to be able to draw out some money to rent a house.' My tone is beseeching, insistent, hurtful. I am unravelling.

'Please come home, love, let's talk about things properly.' I can hear the pain this is causing her, the vibrations of incomprehension and confusion course down the phone line. We've always been close. The lies I'm forced to tell her are torture to me.

'Maybe next month.'

'Where are you? What are you doing?'

'John told me I should ring you. I have to go now, please just pay the bill.' I can't stand it any more. I put the phone down, severing the link to everything I love, and race out of the phone box. The tears fall freely.

'That was horrible.'

Rob glares at me and walks back towards the car, expecting me to follow.

'You can't let people see you like this. You're drawing attention to yourself. Get a grip!' he snarls.

A few days later I visit a bank while Rob waits in the car a couple of streets away. In order to avoid detection and fulfil his bosses' instructions, he tells me, I've only got a limited amount of time to get the money. I withdraw a total of one thousand, one hundred and twenty-five pounds in cash on the Access card. Climbing back into the car he makes me count it all out in front of him.

A month later we're back at the phone box in Huddersfield. John has come with us this time, although I'm not sure why. Whatever we had going between us has simply fallen apart under the stress of our situation. He has been moved from Dorothy Road to Hathersage in Derbyshire where he's working as a barman at the Marquis of Granby. Just like me he has to use a pseudonym; he's now called Jamie. Rob pretends to be his brother and visits him every few days to collect his wages.

I don't want to go inside the kiosk, I don't want to make the call. I try to resist Rob, but he threatens me, saying things will only get worse. 'What's your problem? The money's to cover expenses, Sarah. You'll get it back, with interest, so what are you bleating about? This will all end when your dad bloody well learns to leave us alone. So stop being so wet. Make the call. Make the bloody call.'

I am exhausted. The lack of sleep on a hard floor, the perpetual waiting around, the endless upheaval and uncertainty are all taking a toll on my resources.

I pick up the phone. 'I need you to pay the Access bill, Mum,' I say robotically. Well practised now, I disengage myself from the situation, mind and body no longer together.

'We'll pay it if we see you, love. How about this weekend?'

Rob has his ear right up to the phone and is signalling 'no'. I obey his instructions. I want no part of this.

'No, it's not convenient.'

'We'll pay a cheque into the bank for you.' Rob shakes his head.

'No, it has to be cash.'

'We'll pay you five hundred pounds now and the rest when we see you.' Rob shakes his head again.

'No, that's not acceptable.'

Rob signs that I should put the phone down. I oblige. He tells me to call them straight back and tell them I have only very little to eat, that I want to buy Christmas presents and need to make other payments. If they don't pay the Access card they won't see me before Christmas. And if they ask me for my address I am not to give it.

Once again I do as instructed. There is no arguing with him. Anything I say or feel is ignored, the circumstances are simply blamed on his bosses. It's easier just to switch off and obey. I am not even aware of the tears that are falling down my cheeks, silent witnesses to my sorrow after I end the second call home.

Robert Freegard marched back to the car, leaving Sarah sobbing uncontrollably. He gestured to John to get out. 'Here's what I need you to do.' He edged up close to John and started speaking in hushed tones of collusion and intrigue.

'Sarah's father is ruining everything. This is all his fault, things would be over by now if it weren't for him. He's not helping his daughter. He's not helping himself. He's not helping you, and he's not helping me. He's a control freak, that's what this is about, and it's making Sarah really unhappy. See how upset she is? I want you to get on the phone and give it some, tell Mr Smith how badly he's behaving, tell him what you think of him and tell him to back off.'

John glanced towards Sarah. He felt suddenly protective towards her. Months of resentment and anger welled up inside him; he was ready to have a pop at anyone. Swallowing hard, he managed to rein himself in. He was normally a quiet, considerate individual, why on earth would he do this? The answer was automatic – because he was working for the police and Mr Smith was a nuisance. Justice, he persuaded himself, was on his side.

'Sarah, is that you again?' Jill asked quietly.

'Sarah doesn't want to speak to you. Put Mr Smith on the line.' Jill reeled from the abruptness.

'John is that you? Where's Sarah?' she asked, trembling.

'I've just been cradling her in my arms. You've completely blown it with her now. Just get it into your stupid head that she doesn't want to talk to you. It's finished. Like I said, put Mr Smith on the line.'

At that moment Peter walked in; seeing his wife's obvious distress he took the phone out of her hand. Completely shaken, Jill dropped heavily onto a chair.

'Arsehole!' John began to rant. At the other end of the line Peter listened calmly, remaining unruffled as the accusations flew. 'Acting like a fucking despot! Well listen up, your daughter's finished with you, she's fed up with you trying to control her, telling her what to do. You've fucked up, dickhead, and she never wants to see you again.' Peter could hardly reconcile this vehemence with the limp handshake of the lad who had visited Nether Hale with Sarah last April.

John slammed down the phone. He felt a rush of energy through his veins: outrage felt good.

Chapter 11

New Recruit

Sheffield, November 1993

Simon Young looked on as Robert Freegard eyed the Swatch lovingly, turning it towards the light and observing how its face reflected in myriad ways. An outgoing young man in his early twenties with dark hair and black eyes darting behind fine-rimmed glasses, Simon was the manager of the watch department at Goldsmith's in Sheffield's giant Meadowhall shopping centre. Freegard, a regular customer of the department, was obsessed with the panoply of colourful watches arranged on trays in front of him.

Swatch watches were the latest fashion, and it was clear to Simon that Freegard wanted people to know he had the money to keep up with current trends. Freegard tried on another one as he flirted with the assistant, a buxom young woman who would rather the customer kept his eyes to himself.

The manager tolerated Freegard's lengthy visits because he knew he would make a sale. This customer never disappointed. He had already bought several watches from the store.

'I have a favour to ask,' announced Freegard as he nodded assent for the manager to box wrap his latest purchase. 'Put someone up for me, will you? It'll only be for a few weeks.'

Simon considered the question. It was a rather extraordinary request to receive from a customer. On the other hand, he had a spare room at his terraced house in the small town of Conisbrough. Would Freegard offer to pay him? And how much?

'Tell you what,' said Freegard with a broad smile. 'I'll pay for the food for both of you. I'll cover her costs and you can eat for free.' Freegard leaned across the counter, raising his eyebrows and rocking sideways on his elbow. 'How's that for an offer you can't refuse?'

Simon Young calculated he'd save about sixty pounds a week on food bills. Without hesitation he took up Freegard's generous offer and wondered who his guest would be.

When Simon Young saw Sarah he was shocked. He both recognised her and yet didn't recognise her at the same time. The first thing that hit him was her short bleached hair, which he seemed to remember had been long and brown. Blonde didn't suit her, he thought, it certainly didn't match the rest of her – her demeanour seemed altogether down, depressed and introverted, not at all like he remembered.

Simon recalled events leading up to their first meeting some ten months earlier. It was a cold, damp night in February 1993. The scene was a Manchester nightclub. Simon was there with one of his customers from the jewellery shop, Robert Freegard, or Robert Frittori as he was also known around town. He wouldn't say they'd become friends, but Freegard would invite him out socially once in a while.

The evening was already well advanced when Freegard produced a half pint glass and challenged him to drink the contents down in one. The next thing Simon knew it was four o'clock in the morning, and he was riding in the back of a car. As he prised open his sticky eyes, Freegard looked over from the driving seat.

'Where are we?' Simon croaked, not recognising anything through the windscreen.

'Newport,' came the answer. 'Well, nearly. I tried to wake you before but you just crashed out on me. Can't hold your booze, eh? By the way, this is my work colleague,' Freegard said, pointing to a man with mousy hair in the front seat.

Simon felt Morpheus – or something with an altogether stronger grip – pull him back down into oblivion. Seconds later, or so it felt, his eyes shot open again. The car had stopped. Simon was alone. Struggling with the seat belt, he tried to sit up properly. The car was trying to wrap itself around him. 'What's wrong with my head?' he thought.

There was a clanking noise to his left and the door opened. Somebody's legs appeared, hovering above the wet, black tarmac, then a face sprang into his view, distorted, pink and unreasonably cheery. 'We're here,' said the face. 'Come on, you wimp!' Hands hauled him out of the car and propelled him towards what seemed to be a pub. It looked like a high street, but there were no cars. He was led through a door, stumbling on a step. The hands picked him up again and suddenly he was climbing steep stairs. Another door opened and a bed beckoned. This time when he slipped away the bed was there to catch him.

Simon remembered the out-of-body experience well – he never wanted to go through that again. What *had* he been drinking that night? Perhaps it was spiked, who knows? But the next clear memory he had was of waking up the following morning with a huge hangover and finding himself in bed on the first floor of a pub in Newport, Shropshire.

After gingerly making his way down the stairs, he had found Freegard drinking a glass of water, and the story started to come out. Freegard told Simon this was the pub he was landlord of, The Swan.

Soon afterwards, customers started dribbling in. Simon noticed how confident Freegard was behind the bar; it was as though he'd been doing it all his life. Since Simon had no money and no way of getting back home he had no choice but to phone Goldsmith's, tell them he was sick and resign himself to staying in Newport for the entire week.

In The Swan, he noticed the large number of students who crowded the bar area. Freegard took him to meet three of them at their university digs; John Atkinson, Maria Hendy and Sarah Smith.

Simon had spent only about an hour in Sarah's company, but the woman now standing before him in his living room at Conisbrough was definitely her.

'Hello,' said Sarah. He knew she recognised him too, but she didn't seem in the mood for chit chat, so he let it go and showed her to her room. She had few belongings, just some toiletries and night clothes.

Over the next couple of weeks Simon didn't see much of his house guest. When he did, she was usually in her night clothes. They talked about what was on the television, small talk, nothing much. Simon thought she looked like a ghost.

Chapter 12

Spreading Confusion

Nether Hale, November 1993

After the last phone call from Sarah and the outburst from John, Peter and Jill began to wonder if Sarah was seriously going off the rails. Moreover, the stories about the IRA seemed utterly fanciful, and Sarah's parents had dismissed them out of hand. Their search for her continued, but they started to ask themselves whether she really wanted to be found. Instinctively, they felt that Freegard must be up to no good – everything in their experience told them something was badly out of kilter – and yet Sarah seemed to be with him by choice, which made absolutely no sense to anyone who knew her.

Friends and family advised them not to pay off any more of their daughter's credit card or other bills, but Jill was finding it hard to ignore Sarah's pleas. The demands seemed plausible enough, and what if she really was in difficulty? How could Jill cut her own child off from money they had set aside for her?

Jill was deeply worried that Sarah had somehow got involved with drugs. Peter, though, didn't believe this was the case. Another theory was that she had joined some kind of cult. The daughter of a friend of theirs had recently become involved with the Moonies and now, according to Peter, 'the lights are out'. 'I really don't believe that's happened to Sarah, either,' Jill said, praying she was right.

*

Peter arrived at the Peterborough address his daughter claimed to be living at while working for the Commercial Union. He contemplated the various pieces of the jigsaw. He'd learned that Sarah had taken a six-month lease on the house and that the landlord now wanted to know what was happening. Over the phone, the man had told Peter that he hadn't seen the four of them since May. As Peter was attending a meeting at nearby Cambridge University, it seemed the perfect opportunity to carry on to Peterborough and check out the situation.

He craned his neck to see through the window of the mock-Tudor house, his hand shielding his eyes. Obviously nobody was in residence. He made his way to the back of the house and tried the door handle. It was locked.

Peter was convinced there would be some kind of clue inside the house that would help him find his daughter and understand what was going on. But how to get inside? After searching around fruitlessly for open windows and spare keys under mats and plant pots, he noticed that the panel in the bottom half of the back door was loose. With a bit of twisting it came away easily enough. He crawled through the gap, dusted off his hands and walked through the kitchen into the living room.

He stopped in the doorway, taken aback by the sight that met his eyes. Clothes, luggage and a variety of personal belongings lay on the living-room floor. A box containing mugs, a kettle, sugar, tea and coffee, the essentials of student life, had been discarded. It was as if the clock had suddenly stopped. Whoever had been here had obviously left in a hurry.

Peter checked the bags. All the clothes were either Sarah's or John's; there was nothing belonging to Freegard or Maria. To Peter, the abandonment of her belongings seemed to symbolise his daughter's desire to leave her past behind and start over somewhere else. He felt his throat tighten. Had he and Jill made a mistake somewhere along the way? Or was there a more sinister explanation?

His attention was drawn to a small book. Opening it, he saw that the pages were covered in what was recognisably Sarah's handwriting. He studied the notes closely, but was unable to make any sense of them – long lists of car registration numbers, makes of cars, house numbers and times of day.

Peter's brows furrowed. What could this all mean? He went through the pile once again and found a couple of sheets that were different from the rest. At first glance they appeared to be a letter from Sarah, the words seemed so familiar. On closer examination, he realised it was a transcript of Sarah's side of the telephone conversation they had had six months before, when she had told him about the Commercial Union job. There it was, word for word. Why had she written it all down?

This was a new twist. Peter gazed out of the window, feeling completely stumped.

Cumbria, early December 1993

Headlights swept the bedroom windows of Aldby Farm in the Cumbrian town of Cleator Moor. A knock on the farmhouse door caused Jean to wake with a start. Glancing at the clock she saw it was almost midnight and wondered who on earth it could be. Immediately fearing that something terrible had happened, she threw on her dressing gown. Her husband was now awake as well and together they went downstairs to see who the late caller was.

'John?' Jean was amazed to find her brother standing in the doorway with another man. It was six months since any of the family had seen him. Alarmed and concerned, they had all tried to persuade him to come home on those few occasions when he'd phoned to reassure them that everything was all right.

Jean urged them inside. It was snowing heavily and both men were coated in white flakes that melted into small puddles as they crossed the threshold into the hallway. John introduced his companion as Rob, a colleague. Jean pointed them in the direction of the front room, noticing that her brother looked nervous and frightened.

'What's wrong, John?' she asked. 'Why have you left college?' The youngest of four siblings, John Atkinson and his sister Jean had always been close, but when John suddenly bailed out of college even she couldn't get near him to try to understand why he had made such an abrupt change of direction so close to the end of his final year.

John appeared agitated. 'I can't explain anything in the house. We have to go somewhere further away.' Jean and her husband exchanged confused looks, reluctant to leave the house at such a late hour and in such inclement weather.

'What's wrong with talking here?' asked Jean. John didn't answer. Shaking and looking terrified, he took hold of his sister's hand, turned it over and wrote on the back the initials 'IRA'.

In that moment Jean realised that something was deeply wrong. The three initials were enough to send a shiver down the spine of anyone – initials associated with violent death and, to judge by her brother's appearance, the stakes must be high. She was not a person to be easily scared, but her pulse quickened and she started to imagine guns, bombs and men in balaclavas.

'OK, let's go,' she said nervously.

Slowly, two cars made their way down the farm lane, Freegard driving the lead vehicle. One and a quarter hours later the small convoy finally pulled into the Tebay service station at Shap. Inside they ordered coffee and Jean encouraged her brother to explain.

As John talked, Freegard remained silent, but watched intently. John told his sister about a fellow student at Harper, a friend of his who had gone back to Ireland and apparently committed suicide. However, there had been a lot more to the boy's death than that. He himself had become too afraid, John said, to stay in the college's halls of residence and so had moved to the pub with Rob. The IRA was a threat to him because he knew too much about their activities at college. For his own safety, he was now part of a police witness protection scheme, together with Sarah Smith, Maria Hendy and Rob Freegard. He told Jean that he couldn't disclose his address, but that he was safe, for now. He asked her to pass all this on to their parents, but to be sure to do it away from the house or cars as the police believed these might all be bugged.

Sarah, Sheffield, early December 1993

I'm working in a bar in the Forte Posthouse hotel on the out-skirts of Sheffield. At least, I don't smell of chip fat any longer, but Rob still won't let me have any money because funds are as short as ever and everything must be paid into the police account. He insists on driving me to work and picking me up again, no matter what time I finish. This usually means long hours waiting around for him.

Conversations with workmates are kept to a minimum to avoid difficult questions. If pressed, I am to say that Rob is my boyfriend. It's the only way to explain his constant presence.

To make it more difficult for my father to trace me, Rob has decreed that the hotel must pay my wages into Maria Hendy's bank account. He has given me her bank details and National Insurance number. If anyone at work queries this arrangement, I am to say that she's my sister. If I give away anything about my situation, Rob says I'll be in trouble for fraud and, even though I'm just following orders, if I blow my cover through my own stupidity, then I would have to deal with the risk to myself and my family on my own.

Since I moved out of Dorothy Road to stay with one of his colleagues, I've been completely cut off from the others, apart from Rob. It's a relief to escape the constant tension, but initially I hated the idea of living with a stranger. Rob insisted. He says it's only for a couple of weeks, though, while he sorts out something permanent.

I've actually seen my housemate Simon Young several times before. Rob brought him to my room at college. Now I understand why – they were obviously working together down there to root out the IRA cell. But Simon and I don't talk about 'the problem', unless I'm primed to by Rob. We talk about football and computers instead.

Rob keeps telling me this will all be over soon, and I have to believe him. I try not to dwell on my family or worry about what they must be thinking.

Nether Hale, Christmas Day 1993

In Kent it was business as usual. On the off-chance they might see their daughter somewhere, somehow, over the festive period, Jill had been Christmas shopping, and beneath the tree three colourful parcels lay unopened, a few fallen pine needles sprinkling the surface of the shiny wrapping paper. The gift tags read, 'To our darling daughter, Sarah, with all our love. Mum and Dad.' Jill sensed these messages might never be seen. Peter and Jill Smith still had no idea where their daughter was.

The last lead had withered and died. Peter wasn't able to get any information from Maria's father, Gordon Hendy, though he had mentioned that Maria was pregnant. Peter guessed that somewhere Maria must have a hospital record, and that the record would surely contain a home address. They begged a friend in the NHS to search the computer database for the address. Back it came, Dorothy Road in Sheffield. Peter wanted to put the house under surveillance, in the hope of tracking Sarah, but Jill refused, fearful of the repercussions such a move might have, so the search for their daughter had run into a dead end.

The Smith family bravely carried on with the festive celebrations, but the empty place at the dinner table was like a ghost at the feast. Nobody spoke her name.

That evening Jill wrote in her diary, 'It is heartbreaking.' She knew her husband coped by shutting out his thoughts and concentrating on the search. For her, though, as she switched off her bedside light, there was nothing but the sorrow that only a mother can know. Jill wept quietly in the dark.

Cumbria, January 1994

'Oh, John, this is dreadful.' Margaret Atkinson, John's mother, was on the verge of tears. 'Why don't you just stay here, love, until everything settles down?'

'No, Mum. I really can't. It wouldn't be safe.' John cast an anxious glance towards the window. Freegard was sitting outside in the car.

Russell Atkinson leaned forward, his elbows resting on the farmhouse table, his hands clasped as if in prayer, his feet resting squarely on the cold flag floor. As a young man, John's father must have moved with the slender grace of a greyhound. His skin had a youthful luminosity, his eyes were a translucent grey. Everything about the man was finely tuned.

Russell Atkinson always watched the television news. He knew about the Troubles, but they seemed part of another world. To think that his son was somehow caught up in Irish politics seemed faintly comical, like the Queen wearing jeans or a librarian performing a belly dance. It just didn't make sense. At the same time he realised that the IRA was a real threat; they were not men to be trifled with.

'Your friend Rob,' Russell said slowly, 'you seem to do whatever he tells you. Surely he's not the one running the show?' John reeled off the story Freegard had told him to tell his parents – that there was a separate handler who was in charge. 'No. Rob's in the same position as me. He does some stuff for the police, but he's just making sure I do as our handler tells us. I can't tell you our handler's real name, of course. He could be any Tom, Dick or Harry really, so let's call him Harry.'

'I see,' said his father. Russell wasn't happy about any of this, but had no reason to disbelieve his son.

Nottingham, 10 January 1994

Robert Freegard, of 111 Westgate in Worksop, walked out of Nottingham Crown Court a free man. Despite being accused of incitement to kidnap his former girlfriend Alison, he had successfully plea-bargained the charge down to simple theft, to which he had pleaded guilty in court. Freegard was sentenced to a twelve-month conditional discharge, bound over to keep the peace and ordered to pay a £100 fine. He had escaped without spending a single day in jail.

Chapter 13

Spy on a Mission

January 1994

Sarah's new landlord, Simon Young, sat contentedly on the National Express coach. He peered into his bag at the metal object that was the purpose of his mission and smiled secretly to himself. Hadn't he always dreamt of being a spy? Hadn't he always wanted to be like James Bond? Now here he was living the fantasy for real. He was actually working for the British government, on a real-life assignment to make a dead-letter drop at a London pub.

As the miles sped by on the M1, Simon reflected on how his life had changed in the course of the last few weeks.

'You could do more for yourself, you know, Simon,' Freegard had declared suddenly one day as they were examining a tray of watches. 'You could be driving a fast car, you could have a string of beautiful women, go on fancy holidays and buy whatever you want. The world awaits you. Why confine yourself to this?' Freegard swept his arm around the shop.

Simon was enchanted by Freegard's vision of an exciting future. Who wouldn't be? His job at the jewellers got him by, it paid the bills, but it was a nine-to-five job grinding on six days a week, and he felt he had the potential to do more. He was in his mid-twenties now and had already been contemplating his future. The offer to exchange a safe but routine life for something novel and exciting was alluring and certainly something he wanted to know more about.

'You're kidding me, right?'

'No, I'm deadly serious.'

Freegard had now got Simon's attention. 'What do you mean then? Tell me.' Freegard leaned over the counter and tapped the side of his nose. 'Come and work for me,' he invited, and proceeded to divulge his big secret.

In conspiratorial whispers Freegard revealed that he was actually a spy working for the British government. He described how he had been investigating an IRA cell at the agricultural college near Newport and using the students to 'flush out' the terrorists.

Simon was mesmerised. He completely forgot about watches as he listened to his enigmatic customer describe his work. He learned how Freegard's cover had been blown, how the IRA had discovered his identity along with those of the students who had been co-operating with him. They were all now on the run. Sarah was in fact staying at Simon's house to avoid detection, while Freegard's own job was to protect both her and Maria, as they were both on an IRA hit list. John was working with him on the mission and was currently on an undercover assignment, working in a pub in the Derbyshire hills.

Freegard told him that Scotland Yard was behind several operations to round up Irish terrorists. 'It's all terribly hush hush, as you've probably guessed. But you can be part of it, Simon. In fact, I'd say you're an ideal candidate to be trained to work with me for the government. What do you say?'

Simon's eyes widened in disbelief. He couldn't quite take it all in, but Freegard was confident and persuasive, and it was all starting to make sense. It would explain why Sarah was always picked up and dropped off by Freegard – he was mindful of her safety. It explained, too, why she was so guarded and depressed, as if she was living on a knife edge. Simon had long thought that Sarah, John, Maria and Freegard behaved as if they belonged to some kind of secret sect, now he understood why. Freegard was the one in charge, the one with the orders from the Yard. This was why, at the slightest nod, John would scurry away to do his bidding. Simon saw Freegard in a completely new light.

Leaning up against one of the watch cases, Simon decided he wanted in. 'When do you want me to start?'

Since that day in the jewellery department there had been no looking back. He discussed the IRA story briefly with Sarah and it appeared to check out.

The previous week, Freegard had outlined a number of 'loyalty tasks' he needed Simon to perform in order to check his suitability for the role. Simon had begun them with relish.

Mission number one involved Freegard dropping him in Sheffield city centre with a set of handwritten instructions. The brief was to run from place to place and get back within a set time. Simon was the first to admit he wasn't exactly the fittest of blokes, and indeed this task made him break out in a sweat, but nonetheless he'd passed with flying colours. Freegard was glowing in his praise, heaping compliments on him. It made Simon feel good, and he was impatient to crack on with the next task as soon as possible.

Mission number two took him to Manchester, where he'd been instructed to follow a set of clues. These led him to a department store. Once inside he had to buy a particular item and bring it back to Sheffield. No problem.

The third mission was the one he was on right now, the task being to deliver the object he had bought in Manchester into the hands of someone in a London pub.

Simon mulled over the meaning of these tasks. On the face of it they were quite bizarre, but he knew that MI5 agents in training were asked to do all sorts of crazy things – he'd read about it somewhere. Yes, he'd had a few doubts about whether this could all be real. However, the moment he was back with Freegard all his misgivings evaporated. The guy had so much confidence. Simon felt himself being irrevocably drawn in.

Determined to succeed in his mission, Simon hummed happily to himself as he gazed out of the coach window. He imagined how his new lifestyle might take shape, picturing himself sipping cocktails beside a swimming pool, basking in the warm sunshine, his feet stretched out on a lounger. No more terraced house in Conisbrough; in time he'd have the money to live somewhere palatial, exotic. Just think what his friends would say and the stories he'd be able to tell them. Good fortune had certainly smiled on him. It was like being in a movie.

This was only his second visit to the capital, and as the coach ate up the miles and his goal drew nearer, his excitement grew. The city loomed up ahead, and before long the coach pulled up at Marble Arch, brake pads hissing, engine grumbling to a halt. It was time for the next stage.

Simon got off and quickly made his way down into the bowels of the tube. Three stops later he was at Hyde Park Corner. He was enjoying this; it was giving him a real buzz. He turned into Old Park Lane, and there in front of him was the Rose and Crown pub. His heart skipped a beat, but he walked confidently inside and strode up to the bar.

Freegard had briefed him that the landlord would be expecting him. With a quick glance over his shoulder, Simon quietly confirmed to the man at the bar that he'd brought the designated object and handed it over. With no more ado he turned and retraced his footsteps to the coach station. He was ahead of schedule, so decided to catch an earlier bus back to Sheffield than was originally planned. He'd get extra brownie points, he thought, for completing the mission in a faster time.

Four hours later he was back in Sheffield, but the smile had been wiped off his face. Instead of being pleased to see him so soon, Freegard, much to Simon's surprise and dismay, was short-tempered and churlish. 'I had somebody following you to check you were obeying orders. How simple could it be, for God's sake? You were clearly told to catch the six o'clock bus back, not the five o'clock. You should have been on the same bus as your tail. As it was you ended up travelling separately.'

Simon began to understand the complexities of what he had become involved in. Freegard was watching him and keeping tabs on him. He mustn't stray out of line again. He'd remember that next time.

When he finally got to bed that night, Simon lay staring at the ceiling, thinking over the busy day's events. He briefly recalled the bemused look on the publican's face as he handed over the gleaming silver object and wondered where the tin opener was now.

Chapter 14

Accessing the Joint Account

Sarah, January 1994

'Listen carefully, Sarah. We need to get access to your joint account.' Rob is sitting opposite me in a park just round the corner from the house in Ivanhoe Road, Conisbrough. His mood is mean.

He is asking the impossible, the account is held in Guy's name as well as mine. But there's no arguing with him. He has had orders from London that *all* money in my name must be transferred into the police account, because accessing an account in my real name after I'm given a new identity would make me instantly traceable.

He barks his orders, shouting and bullying, and I can feel my defences weakening. However, Access bills are one thing; my joint account with Guy is quite another. There's almost £76,000 in that account, money that had been set aside for us by our parents while we were growing up. I know Guy will never agree to it.

'You *will* get that bank book. It's not a question of choice, you have to get it. You know you're going to get the money back at the end of all this anyway.' Rob batters home his point, crushing my will.

So we are on our way to the Isle of Thanet in Kent to collect my passport and Woolwich bank pass book. Rob assures me my parents are away; they've gone on holiday to Fiji. He has somebody watching my parents and even someone working for them. John is also in the car, but we drive in silence. Depeche Mode booms through the car stereo. Normally I hate his loud music, but for now it smothers my misery. I let my mind go numb.

I am to go on to Nether Hale by myself while the other two wait in the car nearby. Once inside, I must retrieve the documents as quickly as possible.

From the outside my family home looks warm and inviting, but my thoughts are focused on achieving my goal – I must get hold of my passport and the bank book.

The front door is open and I can see the farm secretary sitting in Dad's office, head buried in reams of paperwork. The safe is in the office where she's sitting. I fetch the key from its hiding place. My heart is racing. I feel like an intruder in my own home.

When she sees me she lowers her glasses in astonishment. 'Sarah!' I put the key in the lock. 'What on earth are you doing?' she asks, open-mouthed.

I search frantically through the documents and papers in the safe. They're not here. This can't be happening. Where are they?

'Where's Dad put my passport? I need my passport,' I demand.

'I don't know. Your father hasn't told me.'

I feel utterly crushed. I have no choice but to return to the car empty-handed.

February 1994

'Get inside that phone box,' Rob snarls. Back in Huddersfield, we've drawn up in front of a public phone box again and I can feel panic starting to well up in my throat. I know what's coming next. He wants me to try to get hold of my passport and bank book again.

'They won't do it,' I resist.

'I said get in. Stop snivelling, just hurry up and call them. Time's running out. You can't afford to fail again.' He marches me into the call box. My hands are shaking, I can hardly hold the coins that Rob has thrust into my hands. I look at him imploringly, at a complete loss as to how to handle this.

'You're old enough to know how to get round your own parents, aren't you? Poor sad little Sarah, are we afraid of Mummy and Daddy?' he mocks. I pick up the receiver, and slowly dial my parents' number, praying they're not yet back from their holiday. Please don't pick up.

'Nether Hale Farm.'

'Mum.' I feel my voice breaking.

'Sarah, darling, where are you?' I feel so much love and warmth on hearing her voice, it hurts to go on.

'Mum, please come up and see me. I need you to bring my passport, and I want the bank book for my joint account. Please come on your own.' Rob is breathing down my neck, listening to the conversation in the earpiece. I risk a glance in his direction and there is a darkness in his eyes that's more malign than I have ever seen before.

'You should come home, love. If you can come here while we're away, why not come now?' My mother's words seem faint. I force myself to get back on track and see this through. I dread to think of the consequences should I fail again.

'I have my reasons, Mum. I need some money. I bumped my car yesterday. . .'

'Send the estimate from the garage, love, and we'll pay it.'

Rob can hear the conversation and is becoming more agitated. I desperately want the phone call to end, but I'm scared of what will happen if I don't get the bank book and passport.

'Please, Mum. Just send me what I've asked for.'

'Can't we talk this over, Sarah. You're our daughter. Come home. You've no idea how worried we are.' I feel my composure slipping fast. 'Let us help you. If you're in some kind of trouble, we'll sort it out.'

Rob snatches the phone off me and slams it down.

That's not the end of it. The following day he drags me back to Huddersfield for another attempt at getting my parents to release my papers. Rob slams the passenger door in my face, gets into the driving seat, straightens his jacket and switches the Duran Duran tape back on. I'm terrified at the prospect of yet another call home. I try to find something else to focus on. Maybe this isn't real. Maybe I'll wake up soon. Perhaps they'll be out today. Please let them be out.

My Mum picks up again. I beg her to come up and see me. She pleads with me to come home. I tell her I'm short of money to pay the rent, I need £400, I'm about to be thrown out on the streets.

'I have a right to my own money,' I plead, 'that's all I want. Please let me have my passport and access to the joint account.' I suggest that she comes up to see me. She suggests I go to London. I tell her I can't afford to. She offers to pay the rent and the car damage, saying there's no point her coming up with the pass book as my brother Guy and I both need to be present to withdraw money from the Woolwich account. I tell her there's no point in her coming up to see me, then.

I'm in tears. Once again I beg her to bring me my passport and the bank book. Rob draws his hand across his throat, motioning me to abort the call.

This time I have no recollection of putting the phone down and leaving the box. Everything goes quiet around me, all I can hear is an echo of my mum begging me to wait, all I can feel is anguish at the hurt I'm causing my parents and the lies I'm having to tell.

'I never want to have to go through that again. I can't deal with any more of these conversations.'

'Get a grip,' says Rob coldly.

Nether Hale

It was seven o'clock and Jill was drawing the curtains on another day, troubled by the phone calls her daughter had made in the last couple of days. Suddenly the phone rang again. Jill had a hunch who was calling, and was reluctant to answer, despite her desperation to speak to her daughter again. She was devastated by the endless battles with Sarah over money and could scarcely believe she was the same girl who used to be so careful with her savings, so money conscious. Jill had thought she knew Sarah as well as she knew herself, but the events of the last year had shattered that illusion.

The shrill tones of the phone continued. Jill stared at it for a few moments and couldn't resist. She answered warily.

It wasn't Sarah. The caller announced herself as a friend of Sarah's, Roberta Freegard, Robert's mother. Jill was filled with a sense of foreboding. Roberta said there was a pressing issue that they must discuss. Jill asked her to call back when her husband was home.

Every twenty minutes for the next three hours, Roberta phoned back. The more the phone rang, the more Jill was on edge, until she felt she couldn't answer it any more. Peter was still not home. 'So what is it you wish to talk about?' said Jill finally.

As she listened, her whole body slumped. According to this woman who claimed to be Freegard's mother, Sarah was threatening to commit suicide. In fact, they had already had to restrain her once.

'Let me speak to her,' pleaded Jill in a hoarse voice. 'Put Sarah on the line.'

'She's not in a fit state.'

'She must come home.'

'There's no way she can be moved.' The phone cut off.

At that moment, Peter walked through the front door and into Jill's office. He was stunned by the sight that greeted him. The whole room seemed to be shaking around his wife, the atmosphere was so completely charged. He caught her as she was about to fall. Just then the phone rang again.

'Who's this? What have you been saying to my wife?'

'Well if it isn't Inspector fucking Clouseau himself!' Peter realised he was speaking to John Atkinson again; as before he decided to keep his cool.

'Sarah must come home, we want to help.'

'How can you help if you don't give a damn about your own daughter?'

The calmer Peter became the more angry John got. 'Sarah's on the point of committing suicide. Don't you care? How can you be so cruel?' Peter was certain he could hear a voice whispering in the background.

'You psycho, you control freak, I'm going to kill you! Do you hear! I know what'll happen if she comes home. You'll grab her and put a shotgun on me. Well listen up, I'm going to kill you first!'

John hung up, leaving Peter staring at the handset, quietly fuming.

In the background, standing in the doorway to the public phone box, Robert Freegard had been listening to the conversation. He walked out into the chill night air, smoothing down his hair.

At Nether Hale, Jill Smith came down with flu. Peter was now deeply worried about the effect the whole business was having on his wife's health. It wasn't just the flu; her chain smoking had intensified since Sarah's disappearance and her blood pressure had rocketed. Peter was convinced that the phone calls were putting an intolerable stress on her. From now on, he told her, she was not to answer the phone, she should let him do it.

As she went to bed, Peter disconnected the phone on the bedside table.

A week later, Sarah rang her parents again. No mention was made of attempted suicide. She simply asked them to meet her in six days' time at the Pomona pub on Eccleshall Road in Sheffield. Peter and Jill agreed.

Sarah

He says I have an objective to achieve, and that I *must* achieve it. He tells me he'll be watching, along with several other agents, to see how well I perform the task. There's a lot riding on this, he says, in terms of how soon his bosses believe I'll be ready to get my life back.

He tells me to take my Mum to the shopping centre in Sheffield, to keep her away from my father and not to leave the pub for any other reason. 'She's the softer touch and can be more easily persuaded to give you the money.'

'I can't do this. There's no way my dad will allow me to take Mum anywhere by herself, and Mum won't agree to go anywhere without Dad.'

'You must. I've got people watching. I want you back within a couple of hours.'

Chapter 15

Showdown at the Pomona

14 March 1994

It had been ten months since Peter and Jill Smith had last seen their daughter, and she was late. They had agreed to meet at 11a.m., and it was now nearly 12.45p.m. They sat clutching drinks, nervously watching the door. Jill lit another cigarette.

When Sarah finally entered the pub they barely recognised their daughter. Her hair was an unnatural shade of white blond; she was thin, subdued and wouldn't meet their eyes. She reminded Peter of a dog that had been whipped. A strained silence fell between them, and when Sarah finally spoke her voice was barely audible.

'Did you bring my passport and bank book?' Sarah's eyes remained focused on the floor.

'Can't we talk about something else, love? We haven't seen you for almost a year. It would be nice to have a conversation that isn't about money just for once.' Jill's frustration brimmed over.

'You don't know how important this is to me. My car still needs fixing and I'm about to be evicted. I really need some cash.'

'Let's go to the garage together then and we'll pay for the car.'

'I need to check with John whether that's OK; they'll only take cash.'

'Why don't you just come home?' Jill looked lovingly at her daughter.

Sarah began to cry and some of the terrible 'truth' started to spill out. 'Mum, I can't. The IRA are after us. We're on their hit list,' she said between tears. Peter and Jill didn't respond.

Sarah continued, the pleading note in her voice intensifying. 'You see, John saw some of his friends making bombs for the IRA at college. They threatened him and said his family had better watch out as well. John was worried about me, because I was in the same group as these lads, so he told me all about it.' Sarah's eyes were now fixed firmly on the floor. 'Rob was having some problems at the pub. He also had a court case to deal with. Maria was in love with Rob, so we thought it best we all left college together.'

Like everyone else in the UK, Peter and Jill were worried about a new turn of events in the IRA's mainland campaign. Over the last few days there had been a series of well-planned mortar attacks at Heathrow Airport. However, the idea that their own daughter was somehow at risk because of something she had seen at college struck them as complete poppycock.

'It's Robert Freegard you need to look out for, not the IRA,' growled Peter. 'Two separate police forces have told me that he likes young ladies with money and that he's a manic liar.'

Sarah stifled a sob, but didn't say anything.

'Where are you living?' her father asked.

Sarah ignored him and focused on Jill. 'I need to see you alone, Mum,' she said, pleadingly. Peter gently suggested they all take a walk outside. Reluctantly, Sarah agreed.

Refusing to disclose her address, Sarah pursued the line that she needed money to pay for accommodation and car repairs.

In reply to a question Peter asked her about the suicide phone call, she looked at him uncomprehendingly, shook her head and carried on relentlessly. 'I wish I could turn the clock back, Dad, but I can't, it's too late. I need the money, otherwise I won't get the car back. Please let me have my bank book. I need money to pay the rent.'

Peter was totally baffled by his daughter's inability to talk sense and their complete failure to get through to her. Throughout her life Sarah had always been easy to talk to. Had she really gone off the rails after all? He reasoned that if she was being forced into this situation against her will, then surely her parents' presence in Sheffield would give her the opportunity to break free. He couldn't make out what was going on. As soon as they got back to the pub, the phone on the bar rang. The barman gestured towards the Smiths – it was for Sarah. John Atkinson was on the other end of the line. Since she hadn't done what she was supposed to, he told her, Sarah must make her excuses and leave immediately.

Peter and Jill hurriedly asked Sarah to join them for dinner that evening and, believing that she and John were still together, invited her to bring him if she wished to. They would do their utmost to turn the clock back and make a fresh start. She would get her passport that evening. Sarah agreed.

Sarah

Rob heads for the park, expecting me to follow. There's no one around, just the faint rumble of traffic in the background. 'Do you realise what a complete and utter mess you've made of things,' he yells in my face.

'I told you before,' I cry. 'Mum would never go to the shopping centre on her own. My parents wouldn't let themselves be separated.'

'Are you so stupid you can't even follow simple instructions?' He looks at me scornfully.

I hang my head.

'No, you can't go for dinner. You didn't do as I instructed. You were supposed to take your mother on her own to the shopping centre. How difficult can that be?'

Back at their hotel, Jill and Peter received a phone call from John Atkinson. 'How can you be so cruel to your own daughter? You've treated her so badly. Why didn't you give her what she asked you for? I'm not going to let Sarah be so brutally treated like that any more. She's not coming to see you. She's not coming to dinner.' He hung up.

Feeling utterly desperate, there was little the Smiths could do but resign themselves to this latest turn of events. But the following morning John was back on the phone, ordering them to be at the Pomona at twelve o'clock. Even though John was against the idea, Sarah wanted to see them again. Bewildered by the constantly changing instructions, Sarah's parents returned to the pub. There was no sign of Sarah and the barman hadn't seen her.

At that moment a man ambled over to them. Terry Evans, he said, from Terry Evans Motors. He had a car that his garage had repaired and he had been waiting for his money for three weeks – seven hundred and fifty pounds. Peter asked to see an invoice. Evans shook his head; he had already sent it to Sarah, or Sarah Pickles as he called her.

Peter asked to see the car, but Evans said it was in his garage in Doncaster. Peter suggested heading back to the garage with him. No, he couldn't do that, Evans said; he was here with a transporter carrying cars that he was in a hurry to deliver. Evans left, angry and empty-handed, claiming he was going to contact the police.

Another two hours went by, but there was no sign of Sarah. At half past two Peter's mobile rang again. It was Terry Evans. Peter wondered how on earth the man knew his mobile number and figured it could only have come from Sarah. Evans told him to go to the Boat Inn at Sprotborough, near Doncaster. 'Sarah will meet you there at four o'clock. If you can get things sorted out, then I'll put off going to the cops.'

Peter checked out Terry Evans Motors in Doncaster. There was no such company. Nonetheless he and Jill hastened to Doncaster and found their way to the Boat Inn. Again they waited and waited. Nobody turned up. At five thirty, exhausted and bone-tired, they decided to head for home. Halfway down the M1, Peter's mobile phone rang again. This time it was Sarah.

'Where are you? What are you doing?' she asked.

'We're on our way home, Sarah. What do you expect? We've been up here for two days trying to help you. We've only seen you for two hours in a year. How do you think we feel about that?'

'Why didn't you pay Mr Evans?' Sarah persisted.

'There's no way I'm giving money to anyone without seeing an invoice, especially a chap who looks as fishy as him. Look, Sarah, just name one IRA bomber from college for me.'

'You know I can't do that, Dad. Please pay the car repairs and the rent, the landlord's about to change all the locks. I must have my passbook.'

'That's enough. There'll be no more money. You've had your chance. You've made fools of us, Sarah, so that's it.'

'You don't understand, Dad. I've got no one else to help me,' begged Sarah, sliding into tears.

'You've wasted our time. We've had enough of this chasing around, we're getting nowhere.'

'You won't hear from me for a long time.'

Peter fell quiet for a moment. His resolve had started to harden. They had reached the point where he felt it might be better if Sarah *didn't* ring any more. The thought of peace and quiet was very appealing. He looked over at his wife and considered the effect all this was having on her, the nightmare of continual pressure and constant worry. Would it be better to forget about Sarah now?

He had a stark choice to make. He might lose his daughter, but he was not prepared to lose his wife as well.

'So be it, Sarah. From now on, you're on your own.' The phone went dead.

Sarah

'How the hell did I get into this situation? I just don't understand!' I am wild with distress. 'Mum and Dad won't ever want to speak to me again.'

'Of course they will. It'll all be ironed out once they know the full facts.'

'I want this to all be over. Why can't it be over now?' I cannot cope with this any more. I might as well be dead. 'Why don't you just finish me off? Do away with me?'

Rob tries to defuse the situation. 'Sit down and shut up,' he commands. 'Don't be so stupid.'

'I might just as well kill myself then.' I am sobbing now, with fury and despair.

Later, when we arrive back at the house in Conisbrough I hear Rob go to the kitchen and remove all the knives from the drawers.

Chapter 16

The Last Friend

Sarah, 16 March 1994

'Right, which ones are your best friends?' Rob is holding my address book and cracking over each page like a whip. 'Who are the ones most likely to help you out in a difficult situation?' he demands, thrusting the small book towards me. 'Sarah you *have* to get more money!' he snarls wolfishly. 'You're way behind target.'

Rob keeps going on about the 'target', an amount that has been set by his colleagues in London, he tells me. I have to reach that magic figure, and then this nightmare will all be over. I take the address book and stare at it blankly. None of my friends has money, and I know it would be futile to ask them. Nevertheless, I go through the motions of looking at the names. Each of them is like a doorway to another world, except I'm on the wrong side of the door and can't get back. I feel cold.

'You think that saying nothing is going to help here?' Rob shouts with an air of menace, bursting through my thoughts, which are turning to yesterday's events at the Pomona and my father's emphatic refusal to give me any more funds.

'Get in the car. Right now!' he hisses, his face contorting with rage.

'My friends don't have any money,' I whisper. 'None of them.'

'You've got to get it from somewhere. It doesn't matter whether they have money or not, you've got to phone them.' I spring up, forced onto my feet by choking emotions and anger. 'I said they don't have any money.' I am shaking uncontrollably and can feel my face burning.

For a moment Rob's face is expressionless, but then amusement slithers into his eyes. Suddenly everything seems to move in slow motion. Rob is throwing his head back, his mouth opens, a bloodless laugh, thin at first, then turning louder and thicker. I feel engulfed by a tide of hopelessness and give way to tears.

'Priceless,' says Rob, surveying my distress and looking at me with a hyena's eyes.

'Jess, it's Sarah.' I try to sound cheerful, but Rob is standing behind me in the phone box, his presence filling me with a bleak heaviness.

'Jess, listen. I need your help. I'm in a bit of trouble.'

'Sarah, what's happened?'

'I've had a major bust-up with my mum and dad.'

I can hear my old schoolfriend thinking through the options.

'Can we meet somewhere?' asks Jess.

I look towards Rob, uncertain how to respond. He nods.

'OK, can you come to Sheffield railway station?' I ask, looking up towards the branches of the trees that hang like engulfing arms over the phone box.

'How about today? Can you make it?' My pulse quickens at the thought of the encounter and the lies I'll have to tell.

The disembodied voice of the railway announcer echoes across the platforms. I cannot imagine travelling to a place of my choice, the notion seems completely beyond the realms of possibility. It belongs to a past I once had and a future that seems beyond reach.

I'm waiting for Jess in the entrance hall of the station. She's driving down from Liverpool with her husband. I've known Jess since I was at Bedgebury and she is one of my best mates. Rob drifts around out of sight, but I know he's there, watching my every move.

The familiar figure of my friend hurries towards me, backlit by the sun. 'Sarah!'

'Jess!' We hug each other, but I pull away rapidly, aware of the need to keep my distance and concentrate on the task in hand. I waste no time, delivering my lines like a lizard dispatching its tongue to catch flies.

'How much money can you lend me?' I see the shock cross her gentle features at the abruptness of my request. I look at her pointedly, my face devoid of emotion.

'Oh, Sarah. I can't help you with money, we're short enough as it is, but I can offer you a place to stay for a few days if you need a break,' she says softly, looking to her husband for confirmation. I know that's no good and shake my head. I glance around uncertainly.

Jess puts her arm around me. 'Take a break, Sarah. Maybe you need to get away for a bit. Come with us. Come back to Liverpool with us now in the car.'

I want so much to go with her, but I know it's not an option – it will put my friends at risk. In any case I've been told that I must not, under any circumstances, leave the station. Simon Young and Rob are nearby, watching. The situation is irretrievable.

'I can't. I just can't.'

'Why not? What's to stop you?'

I look round for an escape route, a way out of this psychological maze in which every path is a dead end unless it leads to money. I catch sight of Rob signalling with his hand across his throat, his eyes urgent and commanding. I want to cling fast to Jess, but I feel the years of friendship slipping inexorably away in the quicksand of a terrifying force that I am powerless to stop.

'I have to go now, Jess.' I turn away, aware only of the gulf that has opened up between us, and head into the darkness.

The human mind is an extraordinary thing. It can adapt rapidly to dramatically altered circumstances. So it was with Sarah, who over the past year had suffered intolerable levels of sensory deprivation. All the familiar props that had supported her psyche, her beliefs and her sense of self had been stripped out and replaced with a new set of codes. Her world had turned upside down, yet her mind had adapted.

To the casual observer there would not appear to be anything wrong. Sarah herself was not aware of the seismic shift in her thinking, but to observers who knew her well, she could not have been more different.

By now Freegard controlled and managed every aspect of Sarah's external world; everything she experienced and was allowed to express was determined by him. Certainly, doubts remained in Sarah's mind, but Freegard was convincing in his explanations, and Sarah believed him. She was now conditioned to believe that, as Freegard worked for the government, he was the boss. 'If I stay it will be all right' was her mantra, a silent protest that justified her reason for staying and allowing herself to be pushed around against her will. Had Sarah been thrust into the same situation eighteen months earlier without the psychological conditioning, she would simply have walked away.

According to experts, Sarah's brainwashing could justifiably be described as a kind of 'mental rape'. In addition to being forced to hand over her money, Freegard had degraded and humiliated her and deprived her of her liberty. Exhausted by despair and fear and living in a constant state of stress and uncertainty, she had taken the only road open to her: obedience. Her only focus now was Freegard's instructions, and everything else was subordinate to that, even if she knew it to be wrong. His will was dominant.

To family and friends, who had no idea of Freegard's claim to be a spy or of the tortured thought processes going on inside Sarah's head, she seemed to act like a zombie. At the Pomona, her parents were unable to make any impression on her. Any challenge to her new beliefs met with the repeated mechanical response that her life was in danger and that she was on the run from the IRA.

In the altered recesses of her mind, Sarah genuinely felt that she was a hostage for her family, and believed that by keeping herself out of circulation she was in some way protecting them. Her concerns had narrowed to faithfully carrying out her immediate instructions and obtaining the money she needed to get her life back again.

After being drawn initially into the lie about John's illness, she was duped into the bigger lie: that Freegard was a spy and that her life was in danger. The cumulative effect of Freegard's espionage fantasy had taken Sarah too far to turn back. Isolated and alienated from her family and friends, she had nowhere else to go. She had become a prisoner, and the bars were in her own mind.

The brainwashing was complete. Sarah had become Freegard's human puppet.

part four

Birth of a Conman

1980-1992

Chapter 17

Mummy's Boy

Autumn 1980

At Hodthorpe primary school near Worksop in Nottinghamshire, Rita Taylor was on playground duty. A gaggle of nine-year-old boys chased a football around the yard. Scuff-kneed and dishevelled, their combined shouts smothered individual cries to create a general noisy chaos.

Rita observed a small boy standing alone. He was a sweet-faced, neatly dressed child, but she had noticed that he never joined in with the school games. The youngster was an asthmatic. Pale and sickly, not robust like the others, he just didn't fit in. The boy was Robert Freegard.

Robert's mother Roberta worked in the school kitchens, and Rita sensed she was highly protective of her son. She also suspected that the relationship between mother and son was the most important emotional element in both their lives. In fact, Rita had to cast her mind back a long way to recall any other male figure in Roberta's life, and that was before Robert was born. She and another teacher had run into Roberta at the school gates. Roberta was arm in arm with a young man, waiting to pick up her daughter Tracy. The marriage to Tracy's father had ended some time before.

'Hello, Bobby,' Rita's colleague called over. 'I see you've got a nice young man.' Roberta had blushed a little and leaned closer to the man. Rita never saw him again. After that Roberta always seemed to be on her own, except, of course, for Robert.

The school bell rang, and Robert looked relieved that the break was over. Rita made her way inside, shepherding the stragglers as she went.

'Today we're going to practise real writing,' Rita told her class. Robert sat up and opened his exercise book, his sharp pencil at the ready. In many ways, thought Rita, Robert was a model pupil. He was attentive, well-behaved and surprisingly polite; his work was neat; he always smiled at her before reading from his book, and invariably he opened the classroom door for her, his manner utterly charming.

She had hardly begun her lesson and already the other boys were fidgeting and looking out the window. Not so Robert; he was different. He listened avidly to everything she said and never took his eyes off her. Despite his winsome ways, it was precisely this aspect of the boy's behaviour that unnerved Rita: Robert's eyes never left her face, his steady gaze was constantly fixed upon her. It troubled Rita; something about Robert was unsettling. In fact, if she were honest, the child gave her goosebumps.

'Mummy's Boy, Mummy's Boy!' yelled Michael Ingram as he raced out of the school yard past Robert.

Robert looked hurt. He didn't have many friends, but counted ten-year-old Michael as one of his closest. 'Come back to my house and let's play soldiers,' he suggested.

Michael felt sorry he'd teased his pal and decided to make it up to him. 'Yeah, sure. You want some bubblegum?' Michael peeled open his packet of gum sticks and offered it to Robert. 'Thanks,' said Robert, snapping the gum in half in his mouth.

The two boys made their way by bus from the village of Hodthorpe to Worksop. A small market town on the northern edge of Sherwood Forest, nineteen miles from Sheffield, Worksop is in one of the seven districts that make up the county of Nottinghamshire. In the nineteenth century mines were sunk to exploit the town's rich coal seams, and along with the collieries, new villages sprang up to house the miners' families.

The boys arrived at Robert's house. It was a small red-brick semi-detached council house with a wooden fence around a tiny front garden.

'Wait here and I'll get my tin,' ordered Robert, unlocking the front door and rushing inside. Michael heard his friend's shoes pounding up the stairs to his bedroom. He hadn't been invited inside, so he ambled down the path to the back garden, where they usually played.

Ever since Michael had arrived from Aldershot three years earlier Robert had latched onto him – so tightly that sometimes Michael felt he couldn't move without Robert being at his side. Robert didn't seem to have a dad, and his half-sister Tracy was a lot older, so Michael often felt that he was the only friend Robert had. Perhaps that was why his pal was so clingy.

Robert swung out of the back door and threw himself down onto the grass, yanking the lid off the tin containing his soldiers.

'Here, let's put them on this card so they'll stand up straight. You can be British, if you like. I'll be German.'

Excitedly Robert divided his soldiers into two sides, relishing the forthcoming battle.

'My captain's got an awesome group of fearless men,' said Michael, lining up his eyes with the back of his soldiers.

'My captain has a plan that will take everybody by surprise,' said Robert, making staccato gun noises out of the corner of his mouth.

The boys were ready. The battle lines were drawn and the imaginary artillery sent a volley of gunfire. Already there were serious casualties, and stretchers had to be rushed onto the field by waiting orderlies. The guns got louder – boom, boom, boom! Robert and Michael winced and groaned at each devastating hit, falling back in mock anguish and pain. The battle blazed on. Suddenly Robert sounded the trumpet through a rolled-up hand, and full of self-importance announced that his special unit had arrived.

'Special unit?' laughed Michael wide-eyed.

'Yeah. They're invisible. And because they're invisible they can't be destroyed,' said Robert seriously.

Michael rolled on his back and shot a sideways glance at his pal.

'You're such a prat, Robert Freegard. I've never heard anything so daft.'

Casting a stern look at his friend, and speaking slowly, Robert announced soberly, 'I'm not a prat. You'll see. One day I'm going to be famous.'

Michael raised himself up on one elbow and challenged provocatively, 'How are you going to do that then? Are you going to rob a bank? Become a professional footballer? A very rich man? How are you going to do it?'

'I don't know, but I will become famous,' stated Robert emphatically.

Michael whistled long and low. His friend had no doubt that one day, like a great general, he'd make his mark on the world. At the tender age of nine, Robert Freegard truly believed he was a man of destiny.

Five years later

Jason Bennett and his two friends Darren and David Hancock were playing conkers at the back of the Rec, a rough patch of gravel bordered by a strip of grassland that the council had designated a recreation ground for the young people of Worksop.

'Look out, here comes Funky!' shouted Darren.

Fourteen-year-old Robert Freegard was approaching the group dressed in a wide-collared shirt and grey trousers. His taste for fashion had earned him the nickname Funky Freegard among his fellow pupils.

Robert was carrying a bag full of conkers, a remarkable haul. With a concentrated grin on his face, he seemed determined to show off his booty.

'Where did you get them from?' Jason asked caustically.

'From my secret tree,' responded Robert. He wasn't giving anything away.

Every year, no matter how impressive the other boys' conkers, Robert always produced ones that were bigger. By now they were all a bit fed up with Robert's brazen gloating over his success and his refusal to tell anyone the location of the giant horse chestnuts. It didn't stop them from trying to find out, though.

'Where's your secret tree, then?' demanded Darren, the elder of the two brothers.

'I'm not telling you.' Robert grinned smugly.

Darren's temper was spiked by the smirk on Robert's face.

'If you don't tell me I'll hit you,' he snarled.

Robert raced off across the playground, but the other three boys made chase and soon caught hold of him.

'Tell us where the tree is,' insisted the Hancock brothers.

'Never,' retorted Robert defiantly.

'Leave him be,' said Jason. 'Come on. Let's go down to Broad Lane and over to King and Queen's Wood. I bet we'll find some conkers there, even bigger than Funky's.'

'Yeah, right,' said the Hancock brothers in unison, turning away from Freegard. Leaving the Rec, the boys headed down towards the chestnut tree woods. Freegard tagged along a few paces behind, listening intently to their conversation. By now, tempers had evaporated and the lads' boisterous camaraderie had kicked in again.

'Met my girl last night,' said Jason, his lips puckering. 'Such a sweet chick, she is.' He jumped up and snapped a branch from a tree. 'Why don't you have a girlfriend, Funky?' He wheeled round to confront their persistent shadow. 'Are you queer or summat?'

'Yeah. Everyone's got a girlfriend,' joined in David Hancock. 'Even if it's the dog of the class, you've still gotta have a girlfriend.'

'You shy of girls or what?' Jason persisted, using the end of his stick to prod Freegard in the chest.

'No. I'm not interested, that's all,' said Freegard with complete indifference.

'Not interested,' scoffed Darren. 'How can you not be interested? That's all we do up at Whitwell Rec – snogging!' Darren imitated a pig's grunt and started dancing in front of Freegard, snorting, 'Snog, snog, snog, snog.'

'Leave off it, will you. I'm not bothered about a girlfriend. I don't want one. My mum takes care of me.'

The three boys fell about laughing.

'No Hanky Panky for Funky then,' roared Jason.

Freegard walked off ahead of them, uncomfortable with the taunts.

'I think I'm gonna need a nappy,' Jason gasped. 'I'm going to piss myself.'

The three boys erupted into belly laughs. 'What a total queer,' sneered Darren.

The lads walked on towards the woods, chatting among themselves.

'Where's he gone?' David asked suddenly.

The group looked about them, but Freegard was nowhere to be seen. They fanned out, circling the horse chestnut trees and calling Freegard's name.

'What a bugger,' complained Jason. 'That's just typical of Funky. The minute you think you've nailed his ass he disappears.'

The gang continued along the track when suddenly Freegard dropped down from a tree and landed right in front of them.

'Boo!'

'Ooh, I'm really scared.' Darren feigned fright. 'Cretin. Mind your shirt now, Mummy won't like it if you get it dirty.'

'Are these your secret trees then, Funky?' asked Jason.

'Course not. You're miles away,' trumpeted Freegard, thoroughly enjoying himself, despite Darren's sarcasm.

'Where are they then? Come on now, spit it out,' implored Jason.

'No chance, they're my trees. I'm not telling anyone where they are.' And with that, Freegard galloped off down the lane in the direction of Hodthorpe. A few moments later he stopped and turned round. With a heavy wheeze, he shouted back, 'It's my secret.'

January 1992

Robert Freegard was about to reach a milestone in his life. On 1 March he would turn twenty-one: the golden key of opportunity would be his. A child of the Margaret Thatcher era, Freegard's teenage years had been dominated by the message of entrepreneurial culture that had invaded every aspect of life, not just in Worksop, but nationwide, dramatically influencing the way forward for so many people.

Freegard had qualified as a carpenter and joiner after a two-year apprenticeship at North Nottinghamshire College of Further Education in Worksop, followed by a one-year course in construction crafts at West Nottinghamshire FE College in Mansfield. He was taken on as a joiner by a construction company and now travelled to fairs across the North of England and the Midlands. The job allowed him to see something of the world, though he was still essentially a Worksop lad, living at home with his mother, whom he supported financially.

It was the New Year, and Robert Freegard was going out with his mate Gerald to Josephine's, an up-market nightclub in Sheffield. The nightclub had a smart dress code and bouncers on the doors refused entry to anyone who didn't arrive properly attired. Freegard and Gerald paid off their taxi and pushed their way through the Friday-night crowds. While Gerald went off to get the drinks, Freegard surveyed the dance floor. The glittering baubles turning overhead sent out dazzling shafts of light and his eye was caught by an attractive young woman whispering into the ear of her female companion.

'Wonder who she is?' said Freegard when Gerald returned, and nodded his head in the direction of the two young women. 'Why don't you go and find out?' his friend suggested.

Taking a swig of his lemonade, Freegard approached the two girls. The blaring music made conversation impossible, so he sidled up and joined them as they danced.

'My name's Robert,' he shouted.

'Alison. This is my sister.'

Freegard soon found out that Alison was twenty-six years old and a teacher. He waved Gerald over and introduced him.

By half-past midnight Josephine's was emptying. Groups of men headed off to the nearest takeaway or Indian restaurant, and bare-legged young girls shivered in the night air.

Freegard, Gerald and the two girls walked across the car park. 'Can I see you again?' he asked Alison tentatively. The young woman smiled to herself. 'Sure,' she said coyly.

'How about tomorrow at twelve thirty at Sheffield railway station?'

'OK.'

For the next three months, Freegard and Alison spoke on the phone at least once a day and spent entire weekends together. As he reached his twenty-first birthday, Freegard appeared obsessed with his first love.

Winter moved into spring and early summer, and the construction company employing Freegard went into receivership, leaving him jobless. Another position as a joiner in Sheffield folded after only three weeks.

Freegard was now unemployed and on the dole, around £800 in debt and still supporting his mother. He began stealing from Alison, using her bank card to withdraw cash, unaware that she knew exactly what he was doing. So far he'd made three withdrawals totalling around £600. He even used some of it to pay back the money he had openly borrowed from her.

One afternoon in the coffee shop of Debenham's department store, Alison told him candidly that she thought they should have some breathing space and let things cool off for a week or two. After that she didn't return his phone calls.

Undeterred, Freegard began to stalk her. Messages left on her answer phone let Alison know that she couldn't escape him that easily. 'I know where you've been. I was watching you, but you didn't know I was there.' Freegard seemed consumed by jealousy.

Freegard confided in a friend called Graham and asked him if he'd help smooth things over. Not knowing what he had let himself in for, Graham went to Freegard's house in Worksop.

'I thought we could force her car off the road,' said Freegard nonchalantly. 'Originally I thought of using chloroform, but decided the best way would be to tie her up with a rope and knock her unconscious with a hammer.'

His friend looked at him, stupefied. 'Are you crazy? I'm here to help you patch things up, not attack her. This is nuts!' he exclaimed, bolting out of the house.

There was a knock on the door. Standing on the doorstep was a police officer. 'Mr Robert Freegard, I'm arresting you for theft and incitement to kidnap.'

Freegard was amiable and cooperative and he put up no resistance. At Worksop police station he was met by two officers, one of whom was Ivan Stallworthy. Stallworthy had never dealt with a kidnap case before and thought it bizarre that anyone should try and win back a girlfriend by knocking her out. As he listened to Freegard he noted that although the young man admitted to his crimes he didn't accept that he had done anything wrong. Stallworthy was further amazed at Freegard's volubility: when they asked him a question, Freegard would talk for twenty minutes where a one-minute answer would have sufficed. Nevertheless, he seemed very plausible and articulate. Acting Detective Sergeant Stallworthy had never come across anybody like Freegard before and concluded that the man must live in a fantasy world.

The case was to be heard first at the Magistrates' Court in Worksop before being transferred to Nottingham Crown Court at a later date. In the meantime, Freegard was released on bail with no restrictions. He wasn't perceived to be a flight risk or a danger to the community.

The young joiner landed himself a job in a fast-food outlet, but he never started it. If he had, the lives of Sarah Smith, John Atkinson and many others might have taken a completely different course.

Instead, one Friday night in September 1992, Robert Freegard walked to Worksop railway station with £85 in his pocket. He jumped on a train to Sheffield, where he bought another ticket to Stafford. The following morning he boarded a coach to Newport in Shropshire, where he knew Alison was now working as a teacher. If he couldn't have her, he could certainly be near her.

Three days later he walked into The Swan pub in Newport.

'Are there any part-time jobs going?' he asked landlord John Sims.

'You're not from these parts, right?'

'No, but I've spent time down here with my girlfriend. We've split up now, but I thought I'd come back, take another look around. It's a nice place.'

John Sims was impressed by Freegard's natural charm behind the bar and offered him a job.

Four weeks later, Sarah Smith and her friends from Blue Door arrived at the pub asking if they could use the car park.

Four months after that Freegard started to spin his elaborate spy story. His astonishing success with this fiction brought the realisation that he could achieve status among people by feeding them the right kind of stories. Within six months Freegard had conned the students into believing they were on the run and in mortal danger.

There's nothing in Freegard's early years to suggest he received any kind of formal psychological instruction. However, there are signs in his childhood that he inhabited a fantasy world, and as he grew older he displayed an absence of guilt feelings – seen most clearly when he seemed prepared to knock his girlfriend Alison unconscious with a hammer.

Although Freegard had an innate ability to understand his victims' weak spots, and through trial and error discovered what worked best on each individual, his virtuosity suggests a solid repertoire of classic techniques. It seems reasonable to assume he drew on textbooks for techniques of thought reform and coercive persuasion, which he then applied to his victims.

However, his ability to lie would appear to be innate. He was a master of deception, and this talent for convincing and consistent fabrication, enabled him to remain undetected.

By June 1994 Freegard was ready for more ambitious manipulation of his victims. In the early stages, he had tested their obedience in extreme but relatively small ways, for example, by persuading them to empty their bank accounts bit by bit and hand the cash over to him.

He was now confident of his control over them and felt he could vastly increase the scale of his demands. Now a father and still living with Maria, he would start using Sarah and John to generate much larger amounts of money, cash that he would spend wildly, but also use to massage his image and generate even more power. For money was only a means to an end for Freegard. What really interested him was power, the power to control other people and force them to give him the recognition he believed was his due.

part five

Stealing a Fortune

June 1994–October 1999

Chapter 18

Targeting the Atkinsons

Cumbria, June 1994

St Bees lies four miles south of Whitehaven in the Lake District, embedded in a deep valley and buffeted by the Atlantic winds. St Bees Head, a rocky promontory jutting out into the ocean, marks the westernmost point of Cumbria.

John Atkinson's family had farmed the fields surrounding this area for 400 years, proud of their ability to sustain a livelihood on land that during difficult times had seen other farms go to the wall. The family was generous in its hospitality, which it extended to all visitors who ventured to this remote corner of Britain.

John, his father Russell and mother Margaret, sat around the large wooden table in the centre of the kitchen. The Atkinsons' kitchen was the working hub of both domestic and agricultural activity in the farmhouse. Most of the important decisions affecting the family's everyday life were taken here.

'The document is obviously bogus and the company's a front. It's all for appearance's sake,' explained John. Russell and Margaret Atkinson examined the loan agreement between John and his father for the IXOS plumbing and heating business.

'Bloody Peter Smith's continual interference – trying to find Sarah – is making it impossible for us to lie low and start over with our new identities. As long as things remain unsettled like this then the IRA might find us, but if Mr Smith can see that the money we receive from our parents is funding solid businesses, hopefully he'll back off. Things will then calm down and I'll get my life back. I'll be able to come home.'

'We just want you to be safe, love,' said Margaret with quiet concern.

'Don't worry about me, Mum. Things *will* quieten down, we just need to get that man off our backs. He's such a tyrant.' John poured himself some water from the stone jug on the table, cooling the anger he felt welling up whenever he thought of Sarah's father. 'Just don't have anything to do with him. If any member of the Smith clan contacts you for information or help, say you're very sorry, but you have nothing to say to them. The man is obsessed.' John downed the water with a disbelieving shake of his head.

'We trust you to do what's right, lad,' said Russell in his soft Cumbrian accent. 'You say this money's going straight into a police account and that nobody will touch it, and that once things have settled down we'll get it all back with interest?'

John assured his father that they would get their money back once everything had returned to normal. Russell cast a sideways glance at his wife, who nodded. 'That sounds fair enough, I suppose. As long as we get to meet these bosses of yours we'll go along with this paper exercise, if that's what the police want. We don't want to see you come to any harm.'

'Thanks so much for all your help. I'm so proud of you, Dad. It's such a relief to be able to turn to you.'

That same afternoon John filled out the forms and opened an account at the Northern Rock in Whitehaven. His father paid £9,500 into it.

For the next nineteen days, John repeatedly withdrew cash from the account at a branch in Sheffield, in tranches of £500. He handed the money over to Rob, thinking how lucky he was to have such a supportive family, unlike Sarah, whose family seemed so untrusting and destructive.

Just over a month later Russell Atkinson transferred another £7,000 to the Northern Rock account, and more than £13,000 into a new Instant Reserve Account at the National & Provincial. On both occasions the transfer was conditional on an imminent meeting with the police. As before, John withdrew the money in bundles of £500 and handed the cash to Freegard.

The sooner the money was transferred, he believed, the sooner all this would be over.

Cumbria, October 1994

Russell answered the phone and waited for the person on the other end to announce themselves. Instead there was just quiet sobbing down the line. Whoever she was, she was in tears.

'Hello?' he asked, furrowing his brows.

'Mr Atkinson, it's Sarah. Sarah Smith.' He heard Sarah sniffing, her voice broken by emotion. 'I'm so sorry to call you, but I wonder if you can help me?'

Russell listened as Sarah explained how she needed to borrow some money. Her own parents weren't cooperating and were blocking access to her money. Could the Atkinsons help her instead?

Russell shifted uncomfortably. Nothing in his experience had prepared him for dealing with this. In recent weeks he had grown suspicious about the authenticity of the requests for money because his demands to see someone in authority seemed to have been ignored. Instead he and his wife received a handwritten letter from someone called Nigel Carter Baines, who claimed he was from the police and who gave his address as 'Kensington, London'.

Baines had written:

'You should know we look forward to finalising a situation with you and your wife just as soon as we are eligible to do so. If you can bear with us, you will know you will have done the right thing, and in the long run you will not regret it at all. I would also like to take this chance to say a big thank you for all your help, patience, time and understanding, for it, I know, has not been easy. We will look forward to better days which are less stressful, and I for one am certain they are just a step around the corner.'

The letter had caused him and Margaret some unease. Was it genuine? Could they take the risk it might not be? What would happen to John if they didn't pay the money?

So what should he do now about Sarah? He sighed deeply, knowing in his heart of hearts that he couldn't turn the young woman away when her distress was so palpable.

'How much do you need?'

Russell Atkinson made his way through the gleaming expanse of the Meadowhall shopping centre in Sheffield. The place was cool and smelled of talcum powder. He couldn't wait to leave its highly polished floor and artificial lighting and get back to the hills. He spotted Sarah sitting in the corner of the café. She looked besieged and was clearly an unwilling participant in the situation she now found herself in.

'Mr Atkinson,' the young woman said, standing up and lowering her eyes at the same time. 'I'm so sorry to drag you all the way to Sheffield.'

'We'll help you if we can,' he replied. They sat down and ordered coffee. Russell passed a brown envelope underneath the table. Inside was the £750 she had failed to extract from her parents for 'car repairs' and another £500 for 'rent' – £1,250 altogether.

'Thank you,' Sarah said. 'It's so kind of you to help me.'

Over the next two months Russell Atkinson would make out three cheques to Sarah, amounting to almost £58,000. It was all paid over at the request of his son so that she could be seen to be setting up a riding stables, a front to appease her father. Then things would settle down, John could get his life back and Sarah could go home.

Sheffield

'Nice body.' Freegard ran his hands over the sleek exterior of the Vauxhall Astra. The sign above the atrium read 'A D Scholey'. Robert Freegard was a regular visitor to this showroom at Deepcar in Sheffield.

His presence had caught the attention of the company secretary, Elizabeth Bartholomew, who found Freegard very charming. According to her boss, Freegard worked for MI5, and it was vital that she didn't discuss the cars he bought from them with anybody outside the company. The sense of mystery surrounding the tall, dark-haired customer only served to arouse Elizabeth's curiosity further. She thought he had noticed her, too.

Freegard told the showroom manager that he'd take the Astra – cash, of course.

Aberdeen, December 1995

John and Russell Atkinson waited in the hotel room, listening to the rain splattering against the windowpane. John looked at his watch nervously. 'They'll be here soon, I know they will.' He jumped up and darted over to the far side of the room to look outside. 'It'll be the traffic, or something that's cropped up at the last minute.'

Russell was silent and solemn, keeping his thoughts to himself. For some time now he had been brooding over the large amounts of money his family had paid out this year alone, all of it apparently to the police:

19 January 1995	*£16,600*
8 February 1995	*£32,600*
26 April 1995	*£60,000*
31 July 1995	*£26,400*
17 August 1995	*£27,300*
8 September 1995	*£23,700*
13 October 1995	*£12,000*
1 November 1995	*£13,000*
4 December 1995	*£13,400*

Together with the money for the bogus plumbing business, riding stables and other payments, the total over the last eighteen months came to more than £325,000. There had always been an apparently good reason for the demands: something else to do, another task, another situation to deal with. Russell pondered the stories they'd been given.

On one occasion, he and his wife were told that the police wanted to give each of them a car 'as a token of good faith', and a car for John as well. Although they protested that they didn't want cars, that they would prefer to have their money back and meet someone in authority, they were told they couldn't meet anybody until they'd accepted the vehicles. In the end they agreed to accept the cars.

However, that wasn't the end of it. The cars *were* eventually going to be gifts, but the family had to be seen to pay for them first, it seemed. The more Russell thought about it now, the more bizarre it sounded. However, since it was John who'd explained the twisted logic to them, the Atkinsons had finally agreed, more out of love, respect and concern for him than out of any understanding of what the police were up to.

And it didn't stop after they'd handed over money for three cars. 'Just one last obstacle to overcome, then everything else will fall into place' . . . 'then the situation will be over' . . . 'then you'll get your money back – with interest' . . . 'then you'll meet someone in authority'. The promises turned to extortion: 'If you want to see your money back, just pay one more time.' Had it not been for love of their son and fears for his safety, he and his wife would have walked away long ago.

Russell sighed. 'I don't think anyone's coming, boy,' he said soberly, glancing over at John, who was now pale as bone, his cheeks sunken and his eyes rimmed by dark shadows. Over the past months Russell and his wife had watched as their son became increasingly depressed.

'No Dad, they *will* come, they'll be here. This time I guarantee it. They promised me,' John entreated.

'John, we've travelled all over the place, setting up different building society accounts on promises. We've been to Poole. We waited three days there but nobody came. We've been to Aberdeen once before and were told to expect someone in authority then, but nobody showed up, and that was after we'd opened up an account at the Alliance and Leicester and transferred another £15,000. We've opened a Yorkshire Building Society account and a Clydesdale Bank account. We've been to Rotherham and waited and waited. Nobody. There's always an excuse; they got "called away on something else at the last minute".'

Russell felt enough was enough. 'Son, it's time to walk away.'

'Not now, Dad. I can't. It's still too dangerous.'

'You're falling apart, lad. Your mum and I can't stand to see you destroying yourself like this.'

'Dad, I promise. No more money until and unless we meet Harry's bosses. But I can't just walk away. Not yet.' John was wide-eyed and panic struck. He had never revealed to his family that 'Harry the handler' was none other than Robert Freegard.

It wasn't that he doubted Rob – all the financial transactions had been conducted on the basis of trust, a huge amount of trust. John had faith in Rob; he had to have faith in Rob, the alternative was too unbearable to think about. But his father had always been circumspect about Freegard, and now he was afraid to tell him just *how* much trust he had put in the man. His family had lent him so much money that he dared not let them down, and it wasn't only his family's money he had risked, it was their respect, his own self-respect and his future.

Chapter 19

Cottage Life

Sarah, mid-December 1995

I've been living in Dore, an upmarket suburb to the south-west of Sheffield, since leaving Conisbrough. On the day I arrived here I felt a sense of excitement mixed with hope, thinking that perhaps things were finally moving in a positive direction.

'So what do you think of your new abode then?' said Rob, nodding in the direction of a pretty, old stone cottage at the end of a neat row of houses. It reminded me of a cottage I had lived in during my previous life, and it brought a smile to my lips.

Rob motioned me through the door. The cottage was as dainty inside as outside. A pale floral carpet ran as far as a tiny kitchen. There were sparkling white walls, with dark wooden beams running across the ceiling. The single bedroom was large, and there was even a TV. My own place – what heaven.

'You may have to go to work by bus from time to time, when I can't collect you, but if you do I'll give you the fare,' Rob said.

'What about money and food?' I asked uneasily. Rob just said he'd call in when he had the chance – he was busy with other assignments – but that I had to stay here when I wasn't working. Sensing my rising panic, he reassured me, 'Don't worry, I'll be dropping by regularly. I'm here to look after you, remember.' With that he was gone.

That was some months ago. Since then Rob has given me a number of cheques, made out to me by John Atkinson's father. £58,000 altogether. Rob instructed me simply to cash the cheques and pay money to him. I had to finish working at the Forte Posthouse because I was told I'd be starting a new job at a riding stable. But it wasn't to be. The riding boots and jodhpurs he bought me lie untouched in the sitting room. There's no new job, just endless weary hours of waiting inside for him to turn up. His visits are infrequent and unpredictable, leaving me with only rare opportunities, those times when I'm sure he won't be back again the same day, to go outside and walk on the moors.

I live in fear of his anger, should he turn up and find I'm not there. Where would I go anyway? I can't go home, my parents don't want me. I long for a proper explanation of why all these things have happened to me, not least so that I can help my parents understand, but all Rob says is that there will be no explanations until I have my new identity. If I don't cooperate I won't get my life and my family back, and that is all I'm living for.

When Rob picks me up he takes me with him to some unspecified destination. I can't ask where because I'm not allowed to speak in the car. When we get there, he leaves me to keep an eye on whatever his latest car is while he goes off to a meeting. They're company cars, but he's obsessed with them and insists they mustn't be damaged in any way. I don't know what I can achieve by watching the cars, but I follow orders anyway. Often he dumps me at a pub afterwards because he hasn't time to take me home; he has more pressing things to do.

Today it's a pub at Catcliffe in the east of Sheffield. I don't notice the pub names any more.

'Here's a quid,' he says. 'I'll be back in an hour.' I examine the shiny gold coin in the palm of my hand. Not a good sign. He usually gives me no more than fifty pence. This could mean a very long wait. I open my mouth to protest, but a shadow crosses his face and I stop myself before I say anything. He'd only punish me by making me wait longer. I ask the barman for a lime and soda – it's the longest cheap drink I can think of – and take up residence at a corner table with a crossword puzzle.

Several hours pass. My drink is all but gone and I'm anxious.

Where is Rob? Every movement causes my eyes to dart nervously and I try not to let anyone catch me looking at them.

Someone heads towards me. I freeze. The way he's been talking with the bar staff suggests he's a regular here. 'Excuse me, Miss,' says the man. What do I say? It's too late to bolt. 'We was just wondering, as you're on your own 'n' all. . .' I lower my head deeper into the newspaper. 'Well, we was just wondering, as you've been here so long, always writing. . .' The man scratches his head and clears his throat. 'Are you a policewoman?'

I tell him I'm not, certain he doesn't believe me, certain he thinks I really am an undercover cop, but oh the irony!

Freegard examined himself closely in the mirror, turning one way and then the other, casting his eyes over the array of toiletries crowding the bathroom shelves to see if there was anything else he could splash on before launching himself on the world outside. He liked to take care of himself, and regularly spent hundreds of pounds on lotions, potions and aftershaves. He patted the sides of his face, humming to himself, and looked closely at his latest haircut.

He had reason to be in a good mood. This was a man who adored cars, and he had recently been adding to his collection: a blue Astra from Jessups Garage at Romford in Essex for almost £15,000, and a white Vauxhall Calibra from A D Scholey costing £27,000 or so, registered in John Atkinson's name. Elizabeth Bartholomew had carried out the pre-delivery inspection of the vehicle.

Still humming, he reached for some eau de cologne and splashed a generous amount into his palms. They were no longer the calloused hands of a joiner, but smooth and fresh. These same hands would soon be gripping the wheel of his latest purchase: a sleek four-door BMW M3 in special order Avus Blue that cost a mere fifty grand.

Freegard burst into song, Duran Duran's 'Rio', smiling at himself in the mirror. He glanced at his front teeth before giving his hair another flick. After Christmas he would buy another BMW, a 328i SE in Boston Green with a £41,000 price tag.

London, 9 February 1996

An enormous bomb explodes in London's Docklands. Two people are killed, many more injured and the bill for the damage runs to tens of millions of pounds.

The bombing marks the end of a seventeen-month IRA ceasefire.

Sheffield

At A D Scholey, Elizabeth Bartholomew picked up the telephone. 'It's me. Can you collect me from Chesterfield railway station?' The twenty-four-year-old car sales assistant recognised the voice of Robert Freegard. Married but soon to be separated, she had been seeing Freegard for a while now, lured by his unfaltering charm.

'No problem. I'll see you soon,' she replied with a warm giggle.

On her way to the station Liz thought about their fleeting visits to the pretty stone cottage in Dore. Freegard had told her it was a safe house where he hid people. Life with Freegard involved plenty of adventure; he himself was not predictable, that was for sure.

'Let me drive. You know I don't trust your driving.' Freegard barely disguised a look of disgust as Liz greeted him. Disappointed by the curt welcome – it hadn't been what she'd been hoping for – she nonetheless slid over to the passenger seat. It was Friday night and the roads were packed with commuters, so it was a relief not to be at the wheel.

The road signs flew by in a blur, and minutes later, instead of finding herself heading north on the M1 back to Sheffield, she realised they were travelling in entirely the wrong direction. 'I thought I'd take you away for the weekend,' offered Freegard casually. 'Surprise you.'

A couple of hours later they drew up at a hotel in Watford. After checking in, Freegard suggested they head down to the bar, where he ordered two pint glasses full of a mixture of pure spirits.

'It's a game,' he began to explain. 'The idea is to drink it before the ice cube melts, and catch the ice in your mouth.' Liz agreed to give it a go. She downed the first pint before the ice cube melted, opening her mouth to prove the point.

'Very good. Try this as well.' He pushed the second pint glass across the bar. Liz already felt a bit woozy, but bravely reached for it and started to drink, watched by Freegard. A couple of minutes later the glass was empty and again she showed him the cube, intact between her teeth.

'Do I win?' she slurred and promptly slumped across the bar.

Her head was lead heavy, her vision came and went, she was semi-comatose, but somewhere in the outer reaches of her senses she was aware of being dragged painfully along the floor by her arm, the carpet hot as it chafed her skin. She was vaguely aware of grazing and bruising to her legs. She remembered being dragged into their hotel room, and then nothing.

The next thing she knew, it was morning. The light hurt her eyes and she was having trouble piecing together the events of the previous evening.

Freegard was already up and about. She tried to focus on him, as if recognition of someone familiar would unscramble her mind and retrieve lost data. Catching her befuddled gaze, Freegard delivered his poisoned dart in short stark sentences.

'While you were asleep I shot videos of us having sex together. I've also snapped photographs of you stark naked. I won't hesitate to use the photos and the negatives. If you don't do exactly what I say, Liz, I'll show them to your husband.'

Utterly aghast, Liz struggled to take in his dreadful threat. She thought this man loved her. 'You wouldn't do that to me, would you?' she asked, quietly petrified.

Freegard approached her and sat on the bed. 'Of course I would,' he said coldly.

Manchester, 15 June 1996

A massive bomb devastates the heart of Manchester's shopping area and 200 people are injured, mostly by flying glass. The blast can be heard more than eight miles away. The IRA claims responsibility.

Chapter 20

The Prodigal Son

London, September 1996

Sitting on a crowded London commuter train, studying the vacantly staring faces of the other passengers, John Atkinson wondered if they would ever believe why he was travelling with £9,000 in cash stuffed in his pocket. He figured they wouldn't. He hoped they couldn't detect the huge bulge on his left side.

A week before, he had opened an account with the Co-op Bank in the city of London where he'd deposited another £52,000, reluctantly given to him by his parents. They had parted with the money on the strict understanding that they would very soon be met by somebody in authority who could assure them this was all legal, and that John would make it clear to 'Harry' that this was their very last payment.

Throughout the year his family has continued to part with money, marking the amounts with a blue dot in their bank books so they could keep track of what they were owed:

6 January 1996	*£24,000*
4 March 1996 transfers totalling	*£45,000*
4 July 1996	*£3,500*

By now they had paid just short of half a million pounds, a massive amount of money, all of which John had ultimately handed over to Rob in cash.

A few days ago a woman had telephoned his dad demanding another £7,000. She had told him that everything would be sorted out soon and that the family should stick with it. This time, however, his parents had refused to pay even though they accepted that she was from the police. The woman had then said that if they didn't see sense and pay up they would lose every penny they'd already handed over; their file would simply be closed. Russell Atkinson had put the phone down.

As the tube rattled on its way, John reflected on his life. He used to drive an Astra 1.8 sport, a 'gift' from the police as a 'thank you' for putting up with his current lifestyle, but it had been taken back now and he was waiting for its replacement.

He couldn't help noticing the fancy cars that Freegard drove. All Rob would say was that most of them were hired because of all the mileage he had to clock up for the job. His private BMW and Astra GSI, Rob said, were perks.

John had a mobile phone, but was only allowed to use it to call Freegard. Throughout the previous two years he hadn't been allowed to go out without Freegard's permission in case someone saw him. Instead, he had spent his days waiting in his Sheffield flat in Leppings Lane. These days he lay low at his parents' farm most of the time, except when he was sent by Freegard to meet 'someone in authority' at one location or another around the country. During his pursuit of these people 'in authority' he spent weeks sitting in hotel rooms or wandering around towns waiting for his mobile phone to ring with details of a rendezvous. John never once doubted that Freegard was part of a team. He always believed that somebody would eventually turn up. He even imagined his staying power was being tested, and that if he failed to show up he would provide 'the authorities' with an excuse to keep his money. Doggedly, he would keep the appointments, determined to get his money back.

It was always the same, though. He would wait and wait, but nobody would show up; only Freegard, with another reason why more money was required. John had never felt so helpless, wretched, isolated and alone. He had even gone so far as contemplating suicide. The only thing holding him back was the thought of causing his family greater distress.

John closed his eyes. He had spent the last week at the Cricklewood Lodge Hotel in north London, and was now on his way to meet Rob, as instructed, in a central London pub. According to Freegard, the £9,000 he was carrying had to be paid into the police account that same day so that they could 'keep their internal records straight'.

John exited the tube at Green Park and walked down Piccadilly in the direction of Hyde Park Corner. Turning into Old Park Lane he spotted the Rose and Crown ahead, went in and waited.

Freegard turned up an hour later and led him up the road to where his car was parked. There, John handed over the brown envelope. Freegard began to count the money.

'Are we going to see somebody?' asked John.

'Yes,' said Freegard, distracted, occupied with the money. 'Soon, soon.'

'I've got to see somebody before I can hand over any more money.'

'You will, you will, I just can't guarantee when.' Freegard continued to count, like a dog sniffing out a missing bone.

Sheffield, October 1996

At the Sytner BMW garage in Sheffield, Mark Endersby glanced at his watch expectantly. Half past four. Any minute now, Robert Freegard would come swinging through the door, smartly dressed, striding confidently through the showroom. Freegard always booked an appointment to view the latest cars, and Mark Endersby knew he'd be there until way beyond closing time.

This time his client wanted to trade in one of his recent purchases for a newer model. He was a man who spent hours poring over colour brochures. Everything this customer wanted was special order. Freegard ticked the accessories list as if he was checking a grocery order. Mark had seen him roll up in several different cars, each one with personal number plates – RDF, MAH or R1 P1. He reckoned that each set of plates must have set Freegard back at least £2,000.

The salesman spied his client breezing into the showroom.

'Good day, Mr Freegard,' he said, extending his hand. 'How are things?'

'Busy. But hey, I'm not complaining,' Freegard returned, smiling broadly.

'Walk this way. I want to show you our most recent model.' Freegard followed Mark across the shiny floor.

'How's your last car doing?' enquired the salesman.

'Great. Got thirty thousand on the clock already.'

Mark whistled in amazement. 'Wow that *is* a lot of miles in three months.' He quickly calculated the sums in his head. 'Crikey, it's about two and a half thousand a week, three hundred and thirty a day!'

'Yeah. I work with a consortium of farmers in Cumbria. They're the ones using the vehicles, and with all the driving around they do, I need to swap them regularly.'

Mark considered how much money Freegard was losing by trading in such high-premium cars so soon after purchase – around £20,000 on each one – and considering all the BMWs Freegard had bought so far, that was an absolute fortune. But who was he to say what the guy should or shouldn't do? When it came to cars, Freegard obviously knew a thing or two. In fact, Mark would go so far as to say his client was totally nuts about them, studying all the car magazines and memorising the spec for every new vehicle and its special options before the car was even released. Freegard was such a regular that he had grown quite pally with some of the staff at the garage and even taken a couple of the mechanics out for a drink.

Freegard paid cash up front for most of the cars he bought; the rest he put on BMW finance. If only he had a few more clients like Robert Freegard, thought Mark.

The salesman handed Freegard the latest brochures, which he

inspected eagerly before looking over the M3 Coupe. Several hours later Freegard confirmed he'd buy it. He'd have a personal number plate for Maria as well – P846 MHE.

'It's forty-eight grand, this one,' said Mark.

'No problem,' said Freegard.

'How do you want to pay?'

'Cash, of course.' Freegard had now bought nine cars in the space of one year, at this one garage alone. He'd spent hundreds of thousands of pounds on them, and lost over £150,000 on repeated trade-ins.

North London, December 1996

In the hotel room John was defiant. 'Another fifty thousand pounds? Absolutely not. My family is adamant. That's it. No more money. Not without meeting your bosses. Things have gone far enough and my parents are not prepared to budge.'

'You insignificant little worm,' growled Freegard. 'Cop out now and your family will face tax bills of at least sixty-five thousand quid.'

'I don't care any more. I'd rather be dead than live like this,' retorted John, his voice cracking with emotion.

'So you'd jeopardise all this and put your family at risk for the sake of one last payment? You amaze me, you really do.' Freegard laughed scornfully, but looked as if he'd like to punch John. The latter flinched involuntarily, accurately reading Freegard's mood.

There was a moment's pause before Freegard casually dropped another bombshell: 'Mr Smith is planning to have you arrested.'

'What? Why?' John stammered, backing away towards the wall, completely bewildered.

'He claims you're holding his daughter hostage. Says you're breaching her human rights,' Freegard said lazily, like a cat licking its paws.

'I haven't seen Sarah for over two years. It's not true!' John's eyes were wide with disbelief.

'Course not. It's just Mr Smith up to his old tricks again. You know he's already gone to the European Court.' Freegard straightened his shirtsleeves, admiring his gold and platinum cufflinks. 'He knows that the police are looking after you all really; he just wants his daughter back. He's using this excuse to get the police to step in and defend you openly, flush you all out.' Freegard smoothed his hair down, then turned on John menacingly. 'Obviously we don't want that happening. If it leaks out that you all left college because of the IRA it will compromise police operations. Your family must be seen to pay the legal costs for the defence.'

John was silent for a moment. 'I'll pass it on to my folks, but can't promise anything.'

'Do what you think is best,' sneered Freegard. 'But remember, if you mess this up, you'll have hell to pay, and we can no longer guarantee anything to you or your family. Plus you'll mess everything up for me, Maria, Sarah and everything we've worked for over the last four years. Think about it, dickhead. Back to square one for all of us.' Freegard marched out of the room, slamming the door behind him.

John curled up on the bed. He had come to the end of the line and felt completely trapped by his situation. He reached for the phone.

'Hello. The Samaritans. How can I help?'

In tears, John attempted to explain what he was caught up in. The man at the other end tried politely to get rid of him – this had to be a crank-caller, a time-waster. There was no way any of it could be true.

March 1997

Back at the Sytner BMW garage in Sheffield, Robert Freegard glanced through the pamphlet listing the various options available. He had already ticked most of the boxes, but wanted to make sure he hadn't missed anything.

His latest purchase was a silver 2.8 BMW 328i SE Touring,

ırah riding her horse Czarina in 1984.

ﾱobert Freegard as a small boy, growing up near Worksop, Nottinghamshire, in 1977.

Sarah, Jim Cooper, Maria Hendy and John Atkinson together in happier days at Blue Door in October 1992. Just two minutes away, at their local pub The Swan, Robert Freegard has just joined the bar staff.

The gang of four, John, Sarah, Maria and Robert, pose for a photograph at Nether Hale, taken on 27 April 1993. It was the last Sarah's parents would see of her for a long while.

...rah with the short-cropped blonde ...irstyle Freegard insisted she adopted to ...sguise herself from the IRA threat in ...ay 1993.

...bert Freegard outside a pub in Sheffield ... about 1995. It was during this time that ...eegard stepped up his deception, conning ...arly half a million pounds out of John ...kinson's family over a period of two years.

Not having seen her mother for four years, Sarah was allowed a brief meeting with her in Danbury in September 1998. The dog, Tyzer, was a gift Freegard had bought for her to give to her parents.

Sarah, assistant night manager at the Royal Berkshire Hotel, poses for a photo with her colleagues John Pott (left) and Alan Hume. She worked the hotel for two and a half years, before having to leave in a rush in August 2002.

eegard in a pub near Ascot in about
ly 2000. He had moved south and
gun working as a car salesman.

eegard in Scotland. In January
03, he would tell Kimberly Adams
at he had been offered a job
onitoring Russian submarines from
ighthouse on the west coast.

The snatched photo Renata took of Sarah, whom she knew as 'Carrie Rogers', in a London park in May 2003. She had become suspicious of the stories Freegard had told her, and she wanted proof of Sarah's identity.

Freegard on 23 May 2003: the day the police finally caught up with him, more than a decade after he had first persuaded Sarah and her friends to leave behind their studies.

OPPOSITE PAGE
(Above) Sarah reunited with her parents Jill and Peter.

(Below) Sarah and John after the court case, meeting for the first time in over eleven years.

Sarah with her brother Guy, who has been one of those to help her put back together her life.

Maria, Renata, Sarah and Kim on 6 September 2005, celebrating after Freegard is sentenced.

number plate PI MAH. He decided to have leather upholstery at just over one and a half grand extra, an electric sliding roof at a touch below £1,000, an electric front seat adjustment costing just over a grand, alloy wheels double spoke style at around £1,400, BMW sports seats at almost £500, graduated tinted screen, vehicle tracking system, automatic air conditioning, anthracite headlining, front seat heating, full colour bumper and side skirts, rear electric windows, metallic paint. Total cost over £40,000, paid part in cash and the rest on finance in Maria Hendy's name.

'I'm supposed to take you to a swimming pool. Lucky for you I decided to let you strip off indoors.' Freegard paced round the room at the hotel near Brentwood, Essex. John was shaking with terror as he removed his clothes. 'But I'm not wearing a wire,' he whimpered.

'Keep going, you mongrel,' Freegard snarled with contempt. 'I haven't got all day to waste in this shit hole.' John continued to undress right down to his underwear. Despite his height, he felt small and pathetic, and shrank into himself.

'You've got the money, I take it?'

'No one turned up to meet my dad. Look, I told you, no meeting, no money.' Freegard's eyes were livid as he tore into John. 'No money, no protection, no guarantees, nothing. Which part of that don't you understand? You cretin. You should know the deal by now. You want to risk your family's safety? Well, that's up to you. Buggered if I care. Christ! Look at you.' Freegard laughed at the sorry figure in front of him, then contorted his face and dropped his voice to a stage whisper, 'You walk away and you're dead.'

'I don't care,' John stuttered. 'Things can't get any worse. I don't care if the IRA shoots me. I'm dead already.'

Cumbria, April 1997

Almost four years to the day since he, Sarah and Maria had left college, John dragged himself down to breakfast in the familiar surroundings of his parents' farmhouse. He felt strangely detached. The day before he and his father had visited the landlord of his old Leppings Lane flat in Sheffield. There they learned that several months' rent and council tax were owed, even though John hadn't been living there.

A simple, insistent truth had begun to hammer inside John's mind. There was no way the flat could have been a safe house, because if it was, these things would have been taken care of. By extension, Freegard could not be who he claimed to be.

John silently took his place at the old breakfast table where his Dad was tucking into his cornflakes, and his Mum and sister Jean were discussing the Orange Juice Diet.

He inhaled deeply and, summoning up his courage, announced, 'Everyone, I have something to tell you.'

Naturally, they all expected him to start talking about money and the latest twist in the crisis.

John closed his eyes and said mechanically, 'Harry the Handler.'

'What about him?' asked Russell carefully.

John's head felt as if it was exploding. He was fighting for air. 'Harry is Rob,' he blurted.

'Eh?'

'Rob is Harry.'

Disbelief, disappointment, anger and sympathy all fought for dominance as the family stared at John in shocked realisation at the enormity of what he had just said.

'No,' his mother breathed involuntarily.

The seconds passed like an eternity for John, as if he was waiting for the executioner's axe to fall.

'You're not serious? Tell me you're not serious. Oh God, John, he's a complete idiot,' groaned his father.

John opened his eyes to face his family. 'I'm sorry, Dad,' he whispered. 'I know he's an idiot. I hate him. He knows I hate him. It all seemed to make some kind of weird sense before, but after yesterday it's been like a big black sheet has been lifted off everything. I'm seeing it for the first time, and it's just hit me that the whole thing might be a load of bullshit.' There was agony in his eyes.

'Course it's bullshit. Oh, John, no.' Russell shook his head. He realised he too had been conned, but unwittingly by his own son.

'What have I done?' John moaned. 'It means you're not going to get your money back,' he added giddily.

Russell recovered himself quickly. He knew how low John was, and though part of him would have liked to thrash the living daylights out of his son for being so naïve, he realised that this would break John completely. He breathed a heavy sigh of resignation. 'You weren't given a choice. You were ordered to get involved,' he managed to say.

'I've spent four years believing that man. I believed everything he said.' John clenched his knuckles, aghast at the implications for himself and his family.

Russell looked sadly at his wife, already resigned to the awful truth. 'So we've been conned. I always said that Rob was a rotten apple.' Russell's eyes swept over his wife's honest face, seeking solace.

Margaret put an arm on John's shoulder. 'It's OK, love. We'll sort it out.'

'I'm so sorry, Mum. I'm such an idiot.'

Jean pursed her lips and fought to stay silent. He had lied to her and everyone, she thought. Worse, he had used her to tell their parents. Like a lighted fuse, she was ready to explode. Why were her parents being taken in by his sob story again? He should be hung out to dry. She took a deep breath, trying to control her emotions before erupting, and in that split second reconsidered. This was her brother, the lies he had told were not his lies, it was just not him. Robert Freegard – none of us liked him; he was behind it all. Angry and exasperated as she was, she suddenly knew she had to forgive her brother. 'Oh, Kell,' she sighed, using his childhood nickname. 'What have you done?'

'We should go to the police,' reasoned Russell, looking round the table for support.

John's eyes widened. 'How can we, Dad? Think about it? We have no evidence. It's just my word against his. They won't believe us; they'll think we're making it up, or that we're mad or stupid. I am, that's for sure.'

'You're not the only one who got involved. What about Maria?' asked Margaret.

'She's as good as married to him.'

'But Sarah?'

'Christ! It's me who got her into this in the first place, but I just wouldn't know where to start looking for her. Rob kept conjuring her away. He's the only person who ever knows where she is.' John thought carefully about Sarah. He couldn't even remember when he had last seen her. Surely she had figured it out, too, by now – she was always the one with all the questions, always the one who was sceptical.

'No, Mum, Sarah's not daft. She'll be long gone by now, back with her family, back at college.' John looked at both his parents. 'I can't face going to the police. I just can't.'

His head slumped forward. He felt as though his lifeblood had drained away, his emotions hacked to pieces on a battlefield of lies and deception. He was now just the empty shell of a person who had not, to all intents and purposes, existed anyway for the past four years. Flashbacks crowded into his mind – of the humiliating tasks he had performed, the innocent people he had lied to, the places he had visited for no purpose, the years he had lost with no reward except shame. Above all, he had lied to the people he loved the most for somebody he hated. The guilt was crushing, the pain unbearable. For weeks afterwards he cried himself to sleep, hoping against all hope that he was wrong, and that Freegard really was a policeman after all. It took him six months to accept the truth.

Chapter 21

Rays of Hope

Sarah, March 1998

I can hear the dog barking in the distance. Being outside and feeling the wind on my face is uplifting.

It's been four years since I last spoke to my parents – we haven't exchanged a single word or letter since our meeting at the Pomona. Without warning, I have been dumped in Manor Top, another part of Sheffield, to live with someone else I don't know. Once again I'm sleeping on the floor. I've been working for the last couple of years at the Shiny Sheff pub on Manchester Road, about two miles west of Sheffield city centre. Everyone there knows me as Maria Hendy – Rob made me call myself that as well as pay my wages into a bank account in Maria's name. But my flatmate, Kieran, knows me as 'Liz'; again as instructed by Rob.

The only contact I have with other people is at work, but I avoid making friends. Rob moves me around so often that it would be too sad to get close to someone only to be torn away again. Rob is the single constant in my life. He's the one who decides how I spend my days. He and his 'bosses' hold my future in their hands. Sometimes he apologises for how long this is all taking. He really thought it would all be over by now, but because his bosses tell him he's screwed up by not keeping me in line, he's got to stick with my case until it's finished.

His superiors in London have paid a significant sum of money into my police account, which will pay for my new life. Rob won't tell me how much, just that it's been calculated according to what I'm deemed to be worth, based on my current earnings, earnings potential, the stocks and shares held in my name, the bank accounts in my name, and the trust fund that's expected to mature next year.

Rob says that before I can assume my new identity, I must reimburse his department for the target amount that's now in the police account. Even though I'll be in a witness protection scheme, the government isn't going to foot the whole bill for my future.

Once I have my new identity, I'll be able to get on with my life. So I'm working all the shifts and hours I can in order to reach my target as quickly as possible and get this whole thing over and done with. As well as my job at the Shiny Sheff, I've been made to get a second job in another pub so I can earn more money.

I keep walking, trying to make headway against the wind. I can see Rob in the distance.

He is arrogant and conceited, and thinks all women are in love with him. He is utterly vain and takes obsessive care over his appearance, which must always be absolutely pristine – not a crease in his shirt, not a mark on his shoes, no strand of hair must be out of place. He tells me he's joined the David Lloyd sports club so he can pass his regular security fitness tests.

If everything isn't just so, then I soon know about it. He has incredible mood swings. One minute he can be almost charming and kind, the next ruthless and menacing. He was most frightening when he forced me to make the begging phone calls home. I hated him deeply for that.

On the other hand, there *is* a bond of sorts between us. I wouldn't call it friendship, more a familiarity that has grown up between us because I depend on him for everything, and of course there's no one else I'm allowed to speak to. We've been to the cinema together, to see a couple of James Bond movies, and once Rob took me out for a drink and a drive in a smart, purple BMW: an M3 Evolution saloon he called it. He told me the car would cost about £52,000 to buy, and showed me how fast it could go, but he only had it to test drive. However, I can't take his being nice at face value; there's usually a catch to it. In fact, it's one of the few predictable things about him. If he's nice, it means beware, something nasty is on the way.

'Come here, Fudge,' Rob shouts at his chocolate Labrador. The young dog comes bounding towards us. Pedigree dogs are his latest obsession.

In the past few weeks, Rob has been suspiciously open and friendly. He's even relaxed the rule about not talking in the car. Today he appears to be in a good mood as we walk out across the moors overlooking Sheffield, and he starts talking about his family.

'My Dad died when I was young, but I followed him into the job. He was a secret agent as well. My real Mum lives in Kenya,' he says.

'Do you have any brothers or sisters?' I ask.

'Two brothers. My true name is Andrew, Andrew Parker, not Robert Freegard, that's only my codename, assigned to me by work. Came from death records. That's what they'll do in your case,' he remarks.

For a moment this new persona flashes across my mind, this new me, and I try to imagine the name I'll have and the life I'll lead.

'How close am I to reaching my target?'

'Ah well, that's what I need to talk to you about. The trouble is, things aren't going according to plan.'

My stomach lurches and I stop dead in my tracks.

'Your parents haven't handed over all the money that's in your name yet. Until they do my assignment won't be finished, and you won't have your new identity.'

I know what's coming and I don't want to go there. Panic begins to surface. I just want to get away from him. I quicken my pace, but in a flash he's beside me again, his features suddenly contorted by rage. He thrusts a mobile phone into my face.

'Ring your mother.'

I'm unable to contain my despair. 'Why is it always about

money? Why do I always have to lie to my parents? I'd rather you just chucked me off a cliff and had done with it.'

'Stop bellyaching. You can be so bloody neurotic.' Rob sounds hurt now. 'Everything you need for your new life has already been paid for. All that's needed now is for you to actually finish paying it off. Then you'll get what's coming to you. So far the money you've paid isn't enough.'

I lower my voice and try to control myself. 'I can't just ring Mum after four years of silence and ask for money. She won't want to speak to me. Neither will my dad.'

Freegard gives an irritated sigh. 'I'm just playing by the rules, you know I am. We have experts, psychologists working on these things. They know best. These are my orders. Things can only get worse if you don't get your parents to hand over everything that belongs to you financially. Come on, Sarah, stop making life so difficult.'

And so I break my four-year silence with a phone call to Nether Hale. I tell my mother I need a change of accommodation, so I have to have £3,000 of my money for a deposit on a new flat. But in four years, nothing has changed, my parents suggest paying by cheque, I say no and end the call. When I am made to call back, they suggest other compromises, but Rob signals that compromises are no good. Each time I put the phone down.

It takes six phone calls before they relent.

Nether Hale, June

Jill Smith felt a ray of hope. Sarah clearly wanted to make amends and had bought a mobile phone to keep in touch with them. Perhaps at last, Jill thought, this might be the beginning of a breakthrough. Was it too much to hope that life might soon return to normal? In a recent phone call, Sarah had told her mother that she was planning to buy a house and that her life was really taking shape. She suggested they meet soon, very soon.

Jill cast a loving look at the 'gang of four' photograph stuck on the noticeboard above her computer. She had transferred £5,000 to Sarah and also sent her the bank book for her share of the joint account she held with Guy. She addressed it to a house in Kettering, which Sarah said she was renting.

Sarah, July

I've been moved around a string of bed and breakfasts, finally ending up at this one in Penniston Road. On one side of the B&B there's Hillsborough stadium, home of Sheffield Wednesday Football Club, where almost a hundred people were crushed to death in 1989. On the other side, there's a busy dual carriageway. Curiously, it's only about 500 yards from Dorothy Road, where I used to live. I know Maria is still there, but I'm never allowed to see her.

There's a Welsh springer spaniel puppy in my room, leaping up and down for attention. Rob has decided that Tyzer, as he's called her, will be good for breaking the ice when I meet my mum. She and Dad have always had dogs on the farm and one of them, Houdi, has just been killed after running in front of Dad's Land Rover. Rob thinks the present of a puppy will act as an olive branch and help patch things up between us.

The B&B has ten bedrooms and is owned by a woman called Anna Jones, who knows me as Sarah. She's kind, but I don't tell her much because I don't want to come out with lies I won't remember afterwards.

My converted attic is small; there's just room for a single bed and a wash basin. It costs fifteen pounds a night. I have no money and I depend on Rob for food and rent.

Apart from walking Tyzer, I spend all day indoors. Rob says I mustn't go out under any circumstances, I should just wait for him to come. The trouble is, I never know when he is going to turn up – he comes at any time of the day or night, sounding his horn, which is the signal for me to leave the house. If I don't hear him and don't respond instantly he drives off and I don't eat; it's as simple as that. If I miss him, he bawls me out the next time he sees me. All this means I sit listening intently for hours on end, staring at the road to make sure I don't miss him.

Anna Jones observed her strange new lodger and thought how very little she knew about her. She recalled the afternoon when Sarah turned up on her doorstep clutching a holdall and a puppy in her arms, saying she wanted a room just for the night as she was waiting to move into a new flat. She left the following day, but came back a few hours later saying that the flat wasn't ready. She paid Anna for a second night.

The two nights had turned into several weeks and Sarah was still here, a semi-permanent figure; quite a contrast to Anna's other peripatetic clients, most of whom were working men.

Sarah was well-spoken, pleasant and polite; a 'nice girl', obviously well-educated and from a good home. Anna could tell from her accent that she wasn't local, but she had no idea why Sarah was in Sheffield.

A motherly sort of woman in her late forties, Anna had always been one to 'call a spade a spade', and was used to chatting with her clients and her girlfriends. But in all her fourteen years of running a guesthouse, she had never come across anyone quite as unusual as Sarah Smith. Discussions about Sarah's private life were off-limits; she didn't speak about her family, except to say she wasn't in contact with them. In the kitchen, the two women had swapped stories about horses and their shared love of riding – Anna had a horse stabled two miles away – but when Anna had asked her to go to the stables with her once, Sarah had refused, saying, 'I never know when I'm going to be picked up.'

Anna guessed that Sarah's plight had something to do with the mystery caller; and that because of this man Sarah was cocooned inside her own world, stuck inside the house often for weeks on end. The only time the young woman ever left the B&B was when a car turned up and sounded its horn. Then, with a look of devout urgency, Sarah would grab her coat and rush out. On those occasions she generally returned within a few hours, but occasionally she stayed away until the following day. If she was away for the night she'd ring and tell Anna not to worry, everything was fine. When she did return, she sometimes walked through the door clutching a food parcel.

Sarah's frugality surprised Anna. She never bought clothes, not like Anna's daughters, who lived to shop on Saturdays, and she seemed to ration her food to only one small meal in the evening. She was losing weight and it soon became obvious to Anna that the poor girl had no money.

Sarah mainly kept herself to herself, spending hours on end in her room, sewing or patiently piecing together the fiddly wooden parts of a marquetry picture kit. It seemed an old-fashioned pastime to have, not something that would interest today's young. Anna's eldest daughter was much the same age, but how very different they were.

Anna was used to young people who had a social life, who went to the pub, or went dancing. Sarah, however, did none of these things, nor did she seem to have any friends.

It was all very strange, yet at the same time, Sarah's lifestyle appeared to be of her own choosing. There was only one conclusion that made any sense to Anna: Sarah must be having an affair with a married man; the mystery man in the car must be her lover. There seemed no other explanation for such odd behaviour.

Anna had spoken to the car man a couple of times on the phone, but only very briefly, and although he sounded cultured he had always been curt and never gave his name: 'Is Sarah there. Could you tell her I'm outside?' Anna tried to catch a glimpse of him through the net curtains, but the car was hidden by a high wall down the side road.

From their chats, Anna had guessed that Sarah's family was a loving one, but that for some reason they wouldn't approve of the man she was seeing. Anna thought that Sarah must be waiting for the moment when her lover left his wife to present him to her parents. Only then would all be well.

Sarah didn't look the type to be in any serious trouble, and she certainly appeared capable and self-contained, not in need of any help, so Anna put the whole bizarre business down to her wanting to keep a low profile. Anyway, Anna didn't like to pry.

Still, it was strange that there was never a letter or a card from family or friends, and no telephone calls either. In fact, the man in the car seemed to be Sarah's only contact with the outside world.

Saturday, 15 August

A huge car bomb in Omagh, County Tyrone kills twenty-nine people and wounds many dozens more in the worst bombing incident in Northern Ireland since the beginning of the conflict. It's the work of IRA dissidents.

Chapter 22

The Inheritance

Sarah, August 1998

I've picked up the bank book for the joint account from the rented house in Kettering. The balance has been divided in two. My share is just over £44,000.

He makes me transfer it to a new account, and over the next few weeks he drives me to cashpoints across the country. I withdraw all £44,000 of it and hand it over to him.

I'm going to see my mother for the first time in four years. Rob has promised me I can spend the whole day with her. I am filled with trepidation. So much has been said and done that I'm not sure I'll get a lot of sympathy from her.

The locations for the meeting have changed several times already. Finally Rob has decided we can meet at a pub in Danbury near Colchester in Essex. He's adamant that this is to be a meeting with Mum only. If there's the slightest hint of Dad or my brother being anywhere near, all bets are off.

Nearing Danbury, September 1998

'Not so fast, I think we're coming up to the turning now.' Guy pointed down a country lane. Peter steered the Land Rover slowly and deliberately as they neared the meeting point.

'Jill, phone me if there's any hint of trouble,' said Peter.

'I'll be all right, honestly,' Jill reassured him.

'We'll be in the area.' Peter was grim-faced as his wife shut the door and headed off towards the garden of the Bell Inn for her midday rendezvous.

Sarah

It's four-thirty and I'm only just arriving at the pub. I wonder if Mum will still be there. 'You've got exactly one hour, then you *have* to be back,' Rob says with an acid look.

'You said I could spend the entire day with her,' I protest, my heart sinking.

'The car you're driving is borrowed from work and it has to be back by five thirty,' he counters emphatically.

Only one hour after four years to see my Mum. I am devastated.

He orders me to park the car where no one can see it, so I pull into the side of the lane, some distance away from the pub. Tyzer the puppy bounds out of the door, and together we walk the rest of the way.

As soon as I see her sitting in the garden, I am overcome with confusion. I'm not sure how to act. In order to cope this far I've shut down my emotions, so much so that I feel as if there's an abyss between us which I don't think I can bridge. There's another huge gulf as well: this one caused by all the lies I've already told, and all the new ones I'm about to heap on her. Tears spring involuntarily to my eyes.

'Let me have a look at you, darling Sarah. We've all missed you,' says my mum in a hoarse, rasping voice. I can see the tears welling in her eyes, great pools of sadness.

'Here's the puppy!' I exclaim, trying to sound cheerful. 'I know how much you miss Houdi. She's called Tyzer.'

Jill gazes down at the wriggling bundle of fur. 'Hello, Tyzer,' she says, bending down to stroke the puppy's head.

I sit down on the green plastic chair and sip my cider. Mum hasn't forgotten that it was always my favourite. I gaze blindly at the photographs and family letters she has brought and listen, as if through a window pane, to the stories of who has got married, who has passed away and who has been born. These fragments of my old life mustn't be allowed to become tangible, it would be too upsetting. They are part of a past that I have no connection with, and can only regain when this is all over. Despite myself, tears run freely down my cheeks.

For my part I trot out the lies Freegard has insisted I tell my mother.

'I've got a new boyfriend, Mum.'

'Darling, that's wonderful.'

'And I own a car. Things are going well. I'm running the restaurant my boyfriend's sister owns. It's called The Grove. I've got big plans, Mum. The Grove is doing really well, and I think I can make it even more successful, but I want to be able to share in the success. So I've been thinking: I want to buy a forty-nine per cent stake in the business.' The fiction pours out.

'And guess what?' I add happily, my final pseudo-triumphant piece of theatre. 'I want to buy a house.'

A look of joy and hope shoots across my mother's face, and I am wretched inside. There is no boyfriend, no restaurant, no house. The picture I'm presenting of my life is all fabrication, but I've gone so far down the witness protection road there's no turning back. I push on with the lies.

'Yeah, fifty-eight thousand pounds. I've been looking at paint charts. Thought I'd paint the bedroom lilac.'

'That's marvellous. Can we come and see it?' my Mum asks brightly.

I say nothing. Of course they can't see it; it doesn't exist, but I can't tell her that.

Mum reaches into her bag for her small camera. Still seated, she snaps a photograph of me with Tyzer. I manage to conjure up a big, wide smile, but inside I'm dying of misery and shame. As far as my mum is concerned the meeting is all about mending fences, building bridges, but I know there's another reason: laying my hands on the £70,000 inheritance set aside for me in my paternal grandmother's will. If I can get my hands on this money, Rob says, I'll be close to achieving my target and getting my new identity. I'll be on my way home.

I weigh my words and clear my throat . . .

Nether Hale

'I don't believe a word of it!' exclaimed Peter, appalled at his daughter's renewed claims for money.

'No, I think it's genuine this time,' pleaded Jill. 'I think she really is buying a house. She was in a much better frame of mind than the last time we saw her at that pub in Sheffield; not so tense.'

Everyone has a way of coping with their grief. Since the departure of her daughter, Jill Smith's had been to keep busy. She was a governor of the local Church of England primary school, chairman of the Royal Agricultural Benevolent Institution for Kent and a church warden. Yet despite the responsibilities brought by these roles, she still felt a gaping hole of emptiness inside.

Sarah had been the child she always got along with best. They used to go to horse shows together and share so many interests. She kept asking herself why all of this had happened; where on earth she and Peter had gone wrong with their daughter.

Peter, she knew, had shut Sarah's absence out of his mind. He coped by concentrating on the farm. He was happy when the phone was silent, because it meant they'd have some peace. But she recognised that this response also grew from a desire to protect her, to shield her from their daughter's dizzying demands for money.

The need to reach out to her daughter was instinctive, a maternal force independent of her will. Jill had persisted in trying to get through to Sarah, begging her for a phone number or an address. She wrote letters to her daughter to divert her own heartache, tapping them out on the computer. She deleted words here, tried to think of the right way to phrase a sentence there, driving herself demented as she wondered what Sarah made of them, or indeed if she ever received them. But at least the one-way correspondence made Jill feel she was reaching out to Sarah; some small consolation to heal the inner void.

Now Jill wanted her daughter to have her inheritance so that she could afford the best opportunities, buy the house she wanted, get a stake in a business venture.

'I believe her, Peter. I have to believe her.'

Peter sighed heavily, looking to Guy for his opinion. 'There have been so many lies. Why should this be true?' asked Peter cynically. 'Until there's some proof of a house purchase, some evidence of a business venture, I don't want to let her have any more money.'

'Once she's got what she wants we won't hear from her again,' Guy said with certainty.

'I'm sure Sarah will stay in touch with us now. I don't think she's lying this time,' insisted Jill.

Sarah, mid-October 1998

If Rob has something to say then it's never in a street or busy place. We make for the green zones, the parks. We blend in with the mothers and pushchairs, the dog-walkers, the roller-bladers and cyclists. Nobody thinks twice about us – two unremarkable figures.

Today we're in the Manchester area. Wispy clouds float above and a child's play area hums with their happy melody.

Rob's ugly mood jars with the warm, sleepy feel of the day. 'You have to get this money. My bosses are fed up to the back teeth with you. I want out.' His top lip curls, he looks at me like I am no more than a piece of dirt stuck on his shoes.

'I want a different assignment that has nothing to do with you and your bloody family.' He quickens his pace. 'It's your money at the end of the day, Sarah. Your parents have no right to hold it back. So what if it's been set aside for your future. This is your future now.' He throws his arms up in an expansive gesture. 'The house has already been bought, and you'll get a car. Listen, you can even choose the colours to decorate the house with if you want. Go ahead, start planning.'

I visualise a house somewhere, a paint brush in my hand. The image is so real, I want to hold on to it fast and tight. This time it will be different, it really will.

'What's the problem, Sarah, just get the flaming money, will you,' he barks.

Four weeks after Jill saw her daughter in Danbury, and much against their better judgement, the Smiths reluctantly agreed to let Sarah have her £70,000 inheritance. As Jill had already advanced Sarah more than £23,000 in various sums since communication had been resumed, she kept this amount back as repayment to herself, then they transferred the remaining £47,000 to Sarah's Woolwich account.

Three days later, on 26 October, Sarah split the sum into two accounts, then withdrew the money in cash over a period of several days.

'Count it,' ordered Freegard, wanting proof that she hadn't kept any of it for herself. 'Hand it over.' Sarah passed the money and her future to Freegard, certain that now things *would* change for the better. 'So when will I be able to move into the new house?'

'Your parents held some money back,' Freegard snapped. 'You haven't reached your target. Until you do, you won't get your life back.'

Sarah felt all her strength dissolve. The edifice of hope splintered.

'Give me back your bank book, cashpoint card and passport. You know you're not allowed to have anything that identifies you.'

On 29 October, Freegard paid a visit to the Gilders Listerdale car showroom in Rotherham, where he bought a 'fully-loaded' yellow VW Golf GTI, licence plate S1 MHF, at a cost of just over £24,500.

He paid for it in five instalments, in cash.

Sarah, Christmas Day 1998

Fairy lights dance around the edge of the breakfast-room windows and Anna has put up a Christmas tree, complete with tinsel and fairy. I'm the only remaining guest at the B&B and my loneliness is acute. Miserably, I look out at the passing traffic.

Anna comes dashing in with a glass of sherry.

'You'll join us for Christmas lunch, won't you?' She has invited some of her friends over for the festive meal. I would love to accept, but I cannot bring myself to join in with the Christmas spirit when I can't go home. That would be unbearable. I think of Nether Hale where they will be setting a place for me at the table, while my family wonders where I am. Every Christmas an extra place is laid for 'The Unexpected Guest' in case someone is passing by, and this year it will be set for me.

'I would love to, but I can't,' I say to Anna, trying to hide my distress. She gives me a knowing smile, 'As you wish, love.' And with that she trips back to the kitchen humming 'Good King Wenceslas'.

Later, when the guests arrive I escape to my attic room, the smell of turkey wafts up the stairs and I can hear the merry ripples of Christmas laughter. Time seems to stretch before me, expanding infinitely as the hours pass and the street lamps begin to glow. There are times when I feel I'm going mad, not knowing how to deal with my situation. I've had to shove all thoughts of my family to the back of my mind and forcibly close the door on memories of home. It's too painful to think about. Living my life is like being in a prison without bars; everything about it is regimented – when I go to sleep, where I go to sleep, what I eat, what I do, everything is by instruction. It's like having a prison cell that just follows you around; it goes wherever I go, and I can't leave it. There is no refuge in memories, no comfort in souvenirs. I curl up on my bed and cry myself to sleep.

Chapter 23

To the Very Last Drop

Nether Hale, March 1999

Jill Smith held a letter from Sarah, informing her parents that she now wanted all her shares transferred to her immediately so that she could sell them. In addition to her £70,000 inheritance, Peter and Jill had invested all spare savings and gifts into shares for their children.

In the letter, Sarah repeated her story about buying a share of The Grove restaurant.

Exasperated and stressed by the incessant demands for money, Jill was at the end of her tether. With a heavy heart, she persuaded the trustees to hand over everything, and the papers were despatched in the post. Perhaps now there would be peace, she thought as she gave herself up to silent grief.

Sarah, Stockport

A secretary ushers me into the solicitor's room and I am invited to take a seat. I glance at the certificates adorning the walls, testifying to the solicitor's professional qualifications. My shoulders are tense and my back feels like a coiled spring. On the desk are the share certificates and investment bond documentation relating to my trust fund. The solicitor pushes the bundle of paperwork across the desk, glancing at me over the top of her horn-rimmed spectacles. I sign for them, my signature flowing freely across the bottom of the page.

How like the tail of a kite it is, sailing up, up and away in the wind.

I sell the shares and pay the cheques totalling £47,286 into the Woolwich and two other new accounts that Rob has made me open. Over the following weeks I withdraw lump sums in cash, in Manchester, Leeds and Kettering. I contemplate the large amounts of money I've handed Rob in the last twelve months.

11 March 1998	*£3,000*	*loaned by Jill & Peter*
30 June 1998	*£5,000*	*loaned by Jill & Peter*
10 July 1998	*£44,145*	*joint account balance*
11 September 1998	*£7,400*	*loaned by Jill & Peter*
8 October 1998	*£7,600*	*loaned by Jill & Peter*
26 October 1998	*£47,000*	*balance of inheritance*
19 March 1999	*£47,286*	*value of share certificates when sold*

It adds up to £161,431. I pray that I'm getting close to my target.

But it seems I'm not. 'You need to demand the remainder of your inheritance money,' insists Rob

'What do you mean?' I ask incredulously.

'I mean, you still haven't got everything that's in your name. There's more, and you have to get it.'

I make another awful phone call to my mother, and finally in August she agrees to release an additional payment of £27,500. This brings the amount I've handed over to Rob in the last eighteen months to £188,931.

Soon after the Smiths' capitulation, Robert Freegard ordered another BMW 328i 4-door, in violet, from King's Lynn; price tag £27,500. He ticked the boxes for an additional £12,000 worth of extras so that, including VAT, the car cost almost £42,000.

Nether Hale, November 1999

The news in Kent was grim. The money paid by the big supermarket chains to farmers had fallen to less than the cost of growing the produce. It meant that the Smiths' business was under enormous financial pressure. Peter and Jill were losing five pence on every cauliflower and drastic action was needed to stave off bankruptcy.

'We'll have to sell off eight hundred acres of land and make all thirty-five staff redundant,' announced Peter, sadly. Jill stared into the distance. She couldn't believe that after all these years they would have to lose staff, some of whom had been with the farm all their working lives.

It was a devastatingly painful process. Hardly able to muster the strength, Peter and Jill broke the news to their workers. The stunned silence was shattered by the piercing tones of the telephone. The Smiths looked at each other.

It was Sarah. She claimed that a tax refund cheque they had sent her could not be cashed; she had to have cash instead.

'Your timing is intolerable, Sarah. Don't you have any regard for our own difficulties? Don't bother us with this now.'

'I'll send the cheque back.'

Peter slammed the phone down.

It rang again.

Sarah insisted on having £2,000 in cash *immediately*. Already brought low by the day's sorry events, Jill felt herself mentally collapsing.

The phone rang three more times. Jill could stand it no longer, her nerves were shot.

Peter had had enough. 'Let's pay the two thousand and have done with it,' he shouted furiously.

He lashed out at his daughter. 'That's your lot now, just don't try anything more, don't say anything more, don't demand anything more, you've had it!' Angrily, Peter thrust the phone back in its cradle and stormed out of the room.

To their dismay, a few days after sending the money they discovered the cheque had also been cashed.

Sarah, the same day

My family will never want anything to do with me again, I'm certain of it. I have deceived and lied to all the people I most care about because I want to keep them safe, but now all my bridges are burned. I have nowhere else to go. I have no home, no money, no ID, no food, no prospects, no one to turn to. I can't explain to anyone what has happened to me – no one would believe me.

It's now more than six years since I left college to take this particular road and I have travelled a very long way down it. Will I ever find out if it's the road to freedom or just a very long, very narrow dead end?

Either way, I have gone too far to turn back. I don't care now what happens to me; I only care about the risk to my family.

'When will I get my life back?' I ask Rob.

'When my bosses say it's done,' he replies acidly.

Penniston Road B&B, December 1999

Anna Jones cleared Sarah's room of its few meagre possessions. She was disappointed that Sarah had left without saying goodbye, since she had invested so much goodwill in her. Anna had taken quite a liking to the young woman, despite her odd ways.

By now, Sarah owed her about £3,500 – she hadn't paid her a penny in rent since last Christmas. It wasn't so much the money, Anna just hoped everything was all right. Perhaps things must finally have come good with her lover and Sarah was able to be with him at last. It was the only explanation she could come up with for Sarah's sudden disappearance.

So far, Robert Freegard had amassed a small fortune. Psychologists who have attempted to interpret his actions agree, however, that money was never his primary motivation, more a convenient by-product. What he really craved was status and control. He began actively to take pleasure in the process of controlling people because it engendered a feeling of real power, and in his own mind this power also conferred status.

Freegard exhibited many traits commonly associated with sociopathy, or 'Antisocial Personality Disorder'. The typical characteristics of APD include: an awareness of the difference between right and wrong but a complete disregard for the rights of others and the rules of society; an inability to empathise; antagonistic and deprecating attitudes towards the opposite sex; an inflated, even grandiose, sense of self and a tendency to be easily outraged by insignificant events. On the surface the sociopath may appear charming, but underneath he, or she, is often callous, repressive and contemptuous of the feelings of other people. Everything and everyone else are merely instruments in the fulfilment of the sociopath's own needs and desires. Interestingly, as many as seventy per cent of sociopaths are believed to come from homes without fathers.

Many of these features are shared by mind-manipulating cult leaders, of the type already mentioned in Freegard's context. Such cult leaders crave adulation, yet are unable to give or receive love. They test the beliefs and devotion of their followers with bizarre rules, punishments and behaviours, expecting them to feel guilty for their failings. Verbal outbursts and physical punishments are the norm, as is stringent sexual control of their followers – rules for dating and forced break-ups and divorces – while they themselves feel free to violate and engage in perverse sexual acts.

For Freegard the end always justified the means – he let nothing stand in his way. And so the structure of his crime fanned outwards, like an upside-down pyramid. Using the money he conned out of Sarah and John, Freegard was able to fund a lifestyle that would attract and seduce other victims. The wealthier he grew the more he could play the part of the secret agent, thus rendering himself more plausible in his victims' eyes. The easier it was for him to buy hand-stitched shirts, expensive shoes, luxury cars, Rolex watches, the easier it was to embellish his espionage fantasy and succeed at his crime. Success bred success.

Against this background he set about casting his net wider. The more people he controlled, the more pieces he had to play with and the more spectacular his manipulations. All of which fed his sense of power.

The women he now began to target were in their thirties and forties, intelligent and susceptible to a charming young man who had every appearance of being highly successful and on a par with them socially.

As his power base grew, so Freegard's cruelty increased. Sarah's life was set to become much worse.

part six

The Net Widens

December 1999–February 2003

Chapter 24

The Night Porter and the Car Salesman

Sarah, early March 2000

There's the smell of soap and dry leaves in the lobby of the Royal Berkshire country house hotel near Ascot, where I'm working as night porter. My employers and my colleagues know me as Maria Hendy.

I have a room in the staff quarters of the hotel, in a block opposite the back of the main building. Rob has a spare key to my room and sleeps in my bed while I work nights. Should anyone ask about his comings and goings, he's told me to introduce him as my boyfriend 'James'. Rob says he's working at a car showroom in West London, doing an undercover job.

I don't always make it into bed after my shift ends, though. Sometimes I get back to my room to find that Rob has locked the door from the inside. When I knock, he sticks his head round to say he has a colleague or his boss with him and I should come back in a couple of hours.

On my days off Rob takes the bed while I make do with the floor – he's never exactly been a gentleman. The hotel has been refurbishing some rooms, so I've managed to come by some old padded headboards and made a mattress out of them. Anything is better than the hard floor.

As before, at Rob's insistence, I'm using Maria's name and

national insurance number. My salary – currently around £800 a month – is paid into an HSBC bank account in her name. Rob explains that it will be withdrawn from the account in cash and transferred to the police account.

This morning Rob has the look of a wolf about him. 'I don't believe you haven't made any tips.' In fact, there are very few tips on night shifts, but I've been squirrelling away the few bits of change I have managed to accumulate in scraps of paper, in drawers, places where I think Rob won't look. I'm determined to keep some by for necessities.

'How can I possibly earn tips on a night shift?' I bluff, moving sideways, crablike.

'You've got to pay them in,' he growls, holding his hand out. 'You have to reach your target.'

He slides up close to me. My resolve is slipping. I am no match for his anger. 'The longer you're stuck in this situation, the longer *I'm* not going to get moved on, either. And I can't tell you how pissed off I am about that.' The words I need to fight back are stuck to the roof of my mouth.

'The faster you take your new identity, the better it will be for both of us.' With weary resignation I locate the small mounds of coins, and like a penitent seeking absolution, hand them all to Rob.

A few days later, there's a knock on my door. It's Jules. Living in what is pretty much a self-contained community, I have got to know my hotel colleagues quite well. There is always something going on socially, though I try to avoid getting too close to anyone because of the fear of being torn away from new friends at short notice. I've told everyone that I owe money to a loan shark and that I'm afraid he'll catch up with me, which is why no one phones: nobody knows where I am. In the meantime, I've taken a second job at a pub and explain it away as trying to pay off the debt. Of course, all I'm aiming to do is reach my target more quickly.

This relatively carefree bubble is a haven for me and I'm terrified that something might burst it, so I live in a permanent state of anxiety and react to any new development with wariness and foreboding.

'Maria, why don't you come downstairs.' Jules beams, jigging about like an excited puppy. 'Come and have a drink in Alan's room. Don't look so glum! Come on, let's go.'

I pull on a worn old cardigan, lock the door behind me and make my way downstairs behind Jules. She throws open a door and sitting in the middle of a decorated table is an elaborate fresh cream and strawberry cake with candles. The room is festooned with balloons and multi-coloured streamers and my hotel friends are all laughing.

'Surprise!' they chant.

For a moment I'm completely nonplussed. It's not my birthday. It's not the anniversary of anything. What's it all about?

'Happy Birthday, Maria,' intone the staff in unison. Then the penny drops. Of course, it's the real Maria's birthday, I'd forgotten I'd told them when I first arrived.

'Everyone, let's raise a toast to Maria,' urges Jules.

'Here, here! A toast to Maria!' shout the staff enthusiastically, and they begin to sing 'Happy Birthday'.

My mask drops. I am overwhelmed at such unaccustomed kindness and my tears run freely. I have forgotten what it's like to be loved.

Hammersmith, May 2000

In the Normand Continental car showroom at Hammersmith in West London, Polish-born Renata Kister opened the door of a Volkswagen Golf and peered inside.

The attractive young blonde was in her late twenties. Normally, cars gave her a buzz; she was an inveterate 'petrol head'. Just now, however, the prospect of buying a new one didn't even register on the thrillometer. She was five months pregnant and feeling vulnerable and tearful since the father of her unborn child had abandoned her to cope on her own. She had come to the showroom only because she would need a more reliable car when the baby was born.

Her cousin, Darius Mazurek, had agreed to loan her the money for a car – around £8,000 – and stood by as she went through the motions of checking out the Golf. In her peripheral vision, the showroom sparkled with new models, like icicles winking in sunlight.

'I'm sure it'll be fine,' she said to her cousin, with all the enthusiasm of a prisoner facing another meal of bread and water.

Just then a car salesman hove into view, a tall, dark-haired man. She couldn't help noticing how smart he looked. Everything he wore matched and he had nice cufflinks. She could smell his aftershave long before the rest of him arrived.

'Can I help you?' he intoned silkily.

'Well, I'm looking to buy a car,' said Renata wearily.

'I think you're going to need something reliable and safe.' The salesman gave her a knowing, sympathetic smile. 'You must be very happy,' he nodded towards Renata's visible bump. 'Congratulations, what a lucky man the father must be.'

The comment touched a raw nerve and tears started to well up. 'Actually I'm on my own,' she sniffed. 'Things are a bit difficult.'

'We'll soon set things right,' said the salesman reassuringly.

Freegard had recently changed his name by deed poll. He extended his hand to Renata. 'The name's Robert Hendy-Freegard by the way. Happy to be of service.'

She dabbed her eyes. What a kind, comforting man, she thought, as she signed for a brand new VW Golf 1.4.

It didn't take long for the car salesman and his vulnerable customer to strike up a friendship. Renata still hankered after the father of her unborn child, but welcomed Freegard's affections, which seemed genuine enough.

Three months after they met, Robert Hendy-Freegard invited her 'home' to the Royal Berkshire's staff quarters. He had told her that he lived in a hotel in the country, which she thought was very chic. He also revealed that he was not really a car salesman but had been placed at Normand's garage on a top-secret mission to keep an eye on someone.

Renata noted the shocking lime green and lilac walls of the L-shaped room, the single bed with matching green and lilac duvet, the desk and the wardrobe, and the small ensuite bathroom just beyond. It was all pretty basic.

'I would have expected something a little more, well, plush,' she remarked light-heartedly.

'Don't believe all you see in those Bond movies.' Freegard loosened his tie. 'That's not really how we live, you know.'

Renata smiled shyly and carried on with her inspection. Suddenly she started back. The wardrobe door hung ajar and inside she could make out a pair of women's shoes. She picked one up. 'These yours?' she asked, looking bemused.

Hendy-Freegard laughed. ''Course not. They belong to a colleague. She's based here as well. We're both working under cover. Luckily she works nights while I'm busy during the day. We share the facilities.' He swept an arm towards the bed.

'That's not very glamorous, either,' Renata cooed through bubblegum-pink lips. She rolled her hands across her by now very large bump. 'Well there's no way *I'm* sharing,' she said, stretching out her back to distribute the load more comfortably.

'You know I'd never ask you to do that. I'm a gentleman,' said Freegard, cupping her face in his hands and giving her a quick kiss. He took off his jacket and hung it carefully in the wardrobe, brushing it down with a hand to make sure it remained crumple free.

'I'm your knight in shining armour.' He smiled at her, quietly locking the door.

Sarah

I turn the knob of my bedroom door. Locked. My head drops forward in exasperation and exhaustion. I'm so tired I can't wait to get to bed.

I think I can hear voices, so I try knocking quietly. The door opens.

'I'm busy,' he says, his voice dry and cold. 'Come back in three hours.'

With that he slams the door in my face.

West London, April 2001

Renata listened to the water running in the shower. She had never met anyone who spent so long getting ready. Some mornings he was in the shower for an hour and a half.

The debris of Freegard's life lay scattered around her London flat. He had moved his things in some months ago but she never quite knew when he would be there. He often had to be away, he said, 'on business'.

Renata stared down into the cot where her baby daughter slept. Although she was relaxed about her friendship with Freegard, she was keen to keep tabs on him. By now she had lent him hundreds of pounds, which he said was for his children's maintenance. Believing him to be the perfect, caring father, she accepted this at face value, but still, she wanted to know she'd get her money back, and accommodating his things in her flat was as good a way as any of making sure she would see him again and be reimbursed.

Freegard appeared, drying off his hair with a towel. He burst into song – Duran Duran's 'Rio'.

'Not that old song *again*,' complained Renata.

'What's the matter, Ronnie? Don't tell me you don't like it? You have no taste.' He tutted at her. 'Give me a kiss.'

Renata allowed him a quick peck. 'I'm surprised you've not washed yourself away with all that showering.'

'Well, I've been giving a lot of thought to something,' he replied earnestly.

'Oh yeah, what's Einstein come up with now?' Renata joked.

Freegard spoke slowly and purposefully, like a mathematician unveiling an astonishing new proof. 'Something really good is coming up. It's nice and fast and I know you'll love it. True, it's a bit more expensive, but believe me, I can get a really great deal on it.'

At the showroom Renata fingered her purse nervously. 'Eighteen thousand pounds is an awful lot of money.'

'I wouldn't want you to go for it if it wasn't a great deal,' Freegard reassured her. 'This is the best that money can buy, a car with a kick.'

Renata smiled back at him weakly. She didn't take much persuading, though; she loved fast cars. She signed the papers for the black 1.8 Golf GTI. Her cousin Darius Mazurek had agreed to finance the deal again.

Chapter 25

End of a Brief Idyll

Sarah, October 2001

The phone echoes down the corridor of the staff block. Sleepily, I pull my dressing gown around my shoulders and push my feet into my slippers.

'Hello? Staff Quarters.' Silence. There doesn't seem to be anyone there. 'Hello?'

I'm about to put the phone down when a small voice says, 'Hello, Sarah.'

'I'm sorry, but this is Maria,' I reply.

'Sarah, don't hang up, please. I need your help. I'm at my wits' end.'

My jaw slackens, I can feel my face flush and my heart pound. I want to put the phone down, but the shock of hearing the voice on the end of the line roots me to the spot.

The distress in the real Maria's voice is palpable, but Rob had warned me that somebody might try and contact me, and that if I talked to anyone, even my old friends Maria and John, it would screw up my chances of getting my life back. For the first time in eight years I've actually had a little stability in my life and I'm terrified of losing it.

'The bills are mounting up and we have no money to pay them,' Maria continues.

'I'm sorry, I can't help you,' I cut in, self-preservation uppermost in my mind. I can't even help myself.

There's a moment's silence before Maria says falteringly, 'Please tell me you went with Rob and the children recently to the London Eye and he told them your name was Caroline?'

I don't know what she's talking about. 'I can't remember when I last saw your children, Maria. But I've definitely not been introduced to them as Caroline,' I say apologetically. Maria is agitated.

'Can I come and visit you, Sarah?' she pleads.

'I don't think that's a good idea. I'm sorry, Maria, there's nothing I can do.'

I put the phone down. I am suspended in space.

Life has been almost bearable here. For the last two years I've balanced precariously on the high wire of my existence, acutely aware of how little it would take to upset the equilibrium of this fragile tranquillity. Now, with one phone call, the wire has begun to sway. I cannot bear to look down at what might happen next.

And as soon as I see Rob approaching the staff quarters the next morning my heart sinks. His sudden appearance after a long absence bodes ill, and instinctively I know this is the thunder before a storm. He orders me out of my room without explanation.

We climb into his Golf and ride in silence down the long driveway, out along the road, past the tidy houses and clipped hedges of Sunninghill. My ears are burning and my chest is throbbing. After a few miles he pulls into a motel car park and kills the engine. There's a small restaurant adjacent to the motel, where he orders steak and chips, then he calmly tells me that he knows about Maria's phone call and everything that was said, because the phone is bugged. He orders me to repeat the conversation.

Completely unnerved, I regurgitate word for word yesterday's phone call with my erstwhile college friend. Rob's eyes are like marbles, his face expressionless. Something tells me that the peace and quiet I have known are now well and truly over.

Blyth, near Worksop, October 2001

'Phone her and tell her we've been over for the past two years!'

yelled Freegard at his common-law wife Maria Hendy.

'No!' she shouted, desperate to escape the car.

For the past two years Maria had only seen Freegard on the occasional weekend and for holidays. Trapped in his imaginary world of espionage and counter-terrorism, Maria was a virtual prisoner at the Dorothy Road 'safe house'. He told her the phones were bugged; she was not allowed out without his permission. She lived off money she thought Freegard paid into her bank account – unaware the funds were actually Sarah's wages. She had long ago given up asking him questions: it would only start an argument. She was bringing up their two daughters more or less as a single parent.

It was shortly after the birth of their first child that Freegard had hit her for the first time. Since then there had been an undercurrent of violence – threats, physical and verbal abuse – and his volatile temper scared her.

Persistently short of money though she was, Maria had been made to sign so many finance deals for cars over the years that she had lost count. Freegard's explanation was that his poor credit rating meant she had to sign the deals in his place. She never wanted any of the cars herself, but was afraid of the consequences of not doing what she was told. Privately she couldn't understand why he kept buying expensive cars and selling them so quickly. She had now built up so much debt on cars and credit cards that she felt she had no choice but to stay with him. He always told her that they were his cars, paid for out of his money. He could do what he damn well pleased, he said.

Maria had found a card in Freegard's rucksack signed 'Love C'. Earlier that evening, over a drink at a pub in Freegard's home town, Blyth, the subject of an affair had been raised and, unhappy at Maria's comments, Freegard ordered her outside. Back in his car, he drove out of Blyth along the Retford Road, stopping after a while at a lay-by.

It was completely dark. Maria tried to hide her fear.

'Phone Caroline!' he barked.

Maria lowered her voice: 'You are not being a good father to the children.'

Enraged, Freegard grabbed her hair and punched her in the face. The blow landed on her nose, left eye and cheek. Stunned, she slumped forward, her head colliding with the gear stick. She noticed something white in the footwell of the car; it was a bloody tooth.

Freegard climbed out, marched round to the passenger door, grabbed her by the hair again and tried to pull her out of the car. 'I'm going to kill you,' he threatened, his eyes full of hatred. 'I've got nothing to lose.'

Terrified, Maria begged him to stop.

'Look at the state of you,' he said with contempt. By now, as well as losing a tooth, she had the beginnings of a black eye and a swollen nose and cheek.

'Look what you've made me do,' he sniggered as Maria blotted her bloodied lips with a tissue.

A week later Maria was facing eviction from the Dorothy Road flat. She was behind on the rent and there was no hope of finding the money to pay it. Gordon Hendy drove up from the West Country to collect his daughter's furniture before the bailiffs arrived.

At the same time almost £450 was being debited each month from an account in her name to Volkswagen Finance Services for a silver Golf 2.8 V6 4Motion. The car cost £18,000.

Maria moved out of Dorothy Road and in with Freegard's mother, Roberta.

Blyth, near Worksop, November 2001

'Daddy said we're going to London.' Maria absorbed this piece of information and walked into Roberta's bedroom, where Robert Hendy-Freegard was reading his post. Despite living elsewhere he still had his mail sent to his mother's address.

Maria noticed Freegard's mobile phone on the bed. She knew her partner had two mobiles, but she didn't have the number for the second one. She picked it up, hoping to get a number in case of emergencies.

Freegard snatched it from her, so she turned to the mail on the bed instead. Suddenly she felt his arm squeezing tight around her neck; it was difficult to breathe.

'You've gone too far this time,' snarled Freegard before releasing his grip. She tried to get past him out of the room, but he pushed her hard with both hands and she collapsed backwards into a clothes rail, grabbing one of Freegard's shirts as she fell. She heard it rip.

'I'll make sure you never see your children again.' His anger was cold and controlled. Maria tried to rise from the floor, but each time Freegard pushed her down. She could hear her daughters crying next door.

Eventually she managed to slip past him, flew into the living room and grabbed the telephone. She dialled the police, but Freegard killed the connection. She tried again, but this time he pulled the cable out of its wall socket.

Freegard gathered up the children and shepherded them towards the front door. Maria tried to prevent him from taking the children, but he shoved her brutally back inside. Quickly, she turned tail and raced back to the kitchen to get her own mobile. But Freegard was behind her and snatched the phone out of her hands. She squeezed past him and dashed out of the front door, but once again, Freegard was at her back. He unlocked the car and helped the children get in.

Panicked, Maria ran back inside to look for Roberta's mobile phone. With trembling hands she locked the front door, slipped the security chain into place and dialled 999.

'Operator. Which service?'

'Give me that phone,' came a cold voice laced with menace.

Maria jumped, fumbling with the phone – she had forgotten about the back door. Shaking with fear, she carried on talking to the operator, all the while dodging Freegard's clutches. She had managed to say her name and address when Freegard gave up and walked off. Moments later, Maria heard him drive away.

At twenty-five to nine that evening a female police constable stationed at Worksop was radioed to attend a domestic incident at Greenview bungalows, High Street, Blyth. There, the policewoman found Maria Hendy in a state of extreme distress with red marks around her neck. While she was still at Greenview, colleagues contacted the WPC to let her know that Robert Hendy-Freegard was at the police station with his children.

Three days later, Maria Hendy and her daughters returned to live with her parents in the West Country. Freegard threatened he'd do anything to get the children back, so Gordon Hendy increased the security on his farm.

Sarah

In two days' time I was supposed to have been a guest at Jules's wedding in Zimbabwe. Rob always said he didn't have a problem with this and was sure his bosses would sanction the trip. For the first time in years I have let myself hope that I will be allowed a small taste of real life, but now he tells me I have to leave the hotel and forget the wedding. It's a crushing blow.

To explain my sudden absence, Rob instructs me to tell the hotel management that my father is sick. He argues that it's only a matter of time before somebody turns up looking for me and then 'who knows what the repercussions might be.' At the very least I could lose all the money I've painstakingly saved so far. We have an emergency situation, he says. End of story.

The plan now is for me to be placed temporarily with another of Rob's colleagues, who, he says, knows all about me, but in order to gauge my suitability for living in a safehouse will be testing me on my ability to role play. He gives me a choice: I can either convince an older man that I'm his long-lost daughter, or I can pretend to a younger woman I'm a non-English-speaking South American.

I blanch. It's not much of a choice. There's no way I'm going to try to convince anyone that I'm their long-lost daughter, so I'll be staying with Rob's other colleague. 'It's imperative you say absolutely nothing,' he says. 'And I mean nothing. Don't forget this is a test.'

Before long we draw up outside an Edwardian house in West London, where I shall remain until he comes to collect me.

Chapter 26

Suspicious Behaviour

West London, November 2001

Renata Kister examined the young woman with long, hennaed hair standing on her doorstep. She had no idea that this was the same girl whose room she had slept in at the Royal Berkshire Hotel. According to Rob, who had phoned her earlier, the woman had been raped by her husband, a powerful businessman; she testified against him in court, but he had been acquitted. Fearing he'd take revenge, she needed to lie low until things blew over.

The woman was from Venezuela and couldn't speak a word of English, so there was no point in trying to start a conversation with her.

Renata beckoned the woman inside her modest apartment and motioned for her to sit on the sofa. Renata's baby daughter Ola sat in a plastic car, rolling backwards and forwards, smiling and gurgling. Renata felt awkward because she didn't have money to feed and lodge Freegard's refugee, but neither had she the heart to turn the woman away.

'Coffee?' Renata asked her. The woman looked at her blankly. 'Tea?' No response. Renata shrugged and reached for a couple of mugs. The woman's complete lack of comprehension was very strange. Surely anyone could understand 'coffee' or 'tea', wherever they were from?

There was a sudden crack of bone on wood and Ola shrieked. Racing out of the kitchen, Renata found that the child had lost her balance and banged her head on the doorframe. She cuddled her little girl and scowled at the Venezuelan for not keeping an eye on her daughter.

Renata picked up the phone angrily. 'Robert, I don't want this person in my place. I don't have the money to feed her, and she needs as much attention as the child.'

'Calm down, calm down,' Freegard soothed.

'I have my own child,' shouted Renata. 'That's enough.'

'Ronnie, please. Just hang on to her for another day. She really needs your help.'

Renata sighed. Freegard knew she wouldn't throw the woman out on the streets.

'While you're on the phone, Robert, where's my car?'

Freegard had persuaded Renata to go for yet another upgrade, this time a dark green Golf V6 4Motion. On top of that she'd given him another £15,000 after he'd persuaded her to let him buy a car at low cost through the trade and sell on at a much higher price. He told her the money he would make on the deal would pay towards the loan on the Golf GTI she had bought six months earlier.

'It's coming, coming soon,' Freegard promised.

'You've been saying that for the past month, Robert. I've given you the money for this car. I'd like to have it now.'

'It's in Glasgow. I just need to find time to collect it.'

'Thanks for coming.' Renata let her friend Richard into the flat one evening a couple of days later. He was a lawyer who worked on Columbian drugs cases and he spoke Spanish. She wanted his help.

Richard listened as Renata relayed her concerns about her strange lodger: not a word spoken so far, and now she had gone to bed early, indicating she had a stomach problem. Very odd, agreed Richard. He promised to straighten the visitor out and get to the bottom of what was going on.

The woman lay on the bedroom floor pretending to be asleep. Richard switched on the light, leaned over her and put his face close to hers. 'Hey you! Listen to me.'

She blinked.

'Who are you? What are you doing in this country?'

Startled, the woman looked about her, sat up and clutched the bed covers to her chest.

'I think you can understand exactly what I'm saying. I think you do speak English. No? How about Spanish, then? Hablas español? Creo que comprendes español.'

Her eyes filled with panic. Richard continued to talk rapidly and she pulled on a jumper.

'You're trafficking drugs, aren't you?' Richard crouched inches from her face. 'You're a mule. That's why you've got stomach ache.'

The woman sat hunched on the floor, wrapping her arms tightly around her knees, her eyes darting nervously.

'The drugs are going to explode in your stomach and if you don't do something about it you'll be dead. Why are you staying here? Why are you acting so strangely? If you don't speak to me as I believe you really can, I'm going to phone the police.'

She sprang to her feet, pulled on her jeans and in two steps was at the door. Richard blocked the way, but she managed to slip past him. The sound of her footsteps echoed down the hallway as she made her getaway.

Sarah

My breath is laboured, my lips are dry. I'm confused. Have I done the right thing? The last thing I want is to have the police stirring things up – then I'll never get my life back. But was that part of the test? I fumble around for the fifty pence piece I know I have somewhere in my pocket and press it into the slot. By pure chance I have a phone number for him written on a scrap of paper. He picks up.

'Rob, you need to come and get me,' I sob, petrified of his reaction. 'It all went pear-shaped. It was a nightmare. A friend of hers became aggressive. He accused me of drug smuggling and talked about phoning the police. You've told me not to get messed up with any cops, so I left the building.' I slump into the corner of the telephone box, worried about what might happen if Rob leaves me on the streets of London all night.

West London, end January 2002

London lawyer Caroline Cowper was only a matter of days away from marrying her fiancé, Robert Hendy-Freegard. They'd been dating for the past year. In August he had impressed her with the giift of an expensive diamond ring, and over Christmas and New Year he had taken her on a lavish holiday to Rio de Janeiro in Brazil. However, in recent months doubts had started to creep into her mind.

At his suggestion, the two of them had planned to set up a car leasing business. Accordingly, just before their holiday in Brazil, he had told her he was going to buy two Volkswagen cars, together worth over £30,000. She had provided him with the lion's share of the money, although she only ever saw one of the cars, a dark green Golf V6 4Motion. Caroline had even driven this car, but since there was no room to park it outside her house, Hendy-Freegard had said he would leave it in nearby Park Royal while they finalised arrangements for their leasing business.

He had boasted to her that he had a portfolio of shares worth around six or seven hundred thousand pounds; money he'd saved up during the course of his previous career with the Secret Service. When she had asked for evidence of this, he'd always prevaricated. Instead, he'd told her about the various expensive BMW cars he had bought over the years, and he had called Mark Endersby, the car salesman at the Sytner BMW garage in Sheffield. Over the phone, Caroline had asked Mark whether Hendy-Freegard was trustworthy. 'I wouldn't trust him as far as I could throw him,' came the response from Endersby, who was still smarting from Freegard's costly failure to pick up two cars that he had ordered.

In a last attempt to find someone who would vouch for Hendy-Freegard's trustworthiness Caroline asked him to recommend another person she could speak to. The name he gave her was the mother of his first girlfriend Alison.

After phoning her, Caroline Cowper cancelled her wedding at the Richmond registry office, and contacted the police.

Nether Hale, February 2002

A stiff breeze bent the trees and shrubs backwards; the battleship-grey sky threatened rain. Fresh from a holiday in Tobago, where they had gone to recover from the stress of the last few years, Peter and Jill Smith deposited their suitcases in the hallway and quickly reunited themselves with the familiar.

Peter headed for his office nursing a mug of coffee. Letters and bills had piled up on his desk in his absence, and to one side he spotted a scribbled note from their eldest son: 'Alison's mother phoned about a lady in London who made contact.'

Peter gazed out across the fields, the violet hue of the imminent downpour smouldered in the leaden light of morning. He studied the note again. This was a surprise. It had been some years since Peter had spoken to Alison's mother. Had Freegard emerged again?

It was not the only surprise that awaited Peter and Jill that day. They had not heard from Sarah for two years, yet within half an hour of their return from holiday the phone rang. Peter braced himself. He had a strange inkling that it was his daughter and that she wouldn't be calling for a friendly chat with Dad. He was right.

Without greeting or explanation, Sarah launched into another demand for money. 'Dad, I need twenty thousand, seven hundred pounds in a hurry.'

Peter bristled with the sheer effrontery of the request.

'I've been going out with a guy called Darius Mazurek, but I've just bust up with him.' She paused. Peter waited, simmering but composed. 'He was involved with the Polish mafia and he's gone off with my car, a dark green Golf V6 4Motion. It was me who signed the paperwork with the finance company and they're now demanding that I pay the outstanding sum immediately.'

Hardly a breath had passed Peter's lips, but this fairytale was too much. 'The Polish mafia, is it?' However harsh it might appear, he wasn't going to give her any more money. 'All I can suggest is that Guy brings you home,' he said wearily. There was a moment's silence.

'That's not possible,' Sarah told her father. 'If you love me at all I must have the money.' Another pause. 'I've got to phone someone now, I'm in a hurry.' The phone went dead.

Minutes later it rang again. Peter was not surprised. 'It's worse than I told you, Dad. I forgot to mention that the car's apparently now been sold to somebody called Mrs Lucas, and *she's* threatening to go to the police because of the outstanding finance. I really need this money, Dad.'

Peter guessed that Sarah had been consulting Freegard. 'Sarah, I thought you said you had nothing to do with Robert Freegard. He's not good news . . . I believe this money is going straight to him. There is no way we are ever going to give you any more money. You can come home. As for the money, that's it. No more, never again.'

'I can't come home. I have to sort this out.'

'In that case, it's goodbye, Sarah.' Peter put the phone down firmly.

Scarcely any time passed before the phone rang yet again.

'Stop interfering with my life!' It was Freegard this time, yelling down the line. 'Things will be far worse for you if you don't stop interfering!' Peter switched on the phone's speaker, knowing that when Freegard heard the click the line would go dead. It did.

Peter sat down heavily, removed his glasses and passed his hands slowly over the contours of his face. After a minute or two, lost in thought, his old investigative impulse returned. He reached for the phone and dialled the number for Alison's mother.

She thanked him for responding to her message and proceeded to tell him about the woman in London. Her name, she said, was Caroline Cowper, and she had phoned a few days before asking for a character reference for Robert Freegard.

Peter almost choked at the implausibility of Alison's mother being expected to say anything positive about Freegard, but he didn't want to interrupt the story. She explained that Ms Cowper had been all set to marry Freegard – a date had been fixed, arrangements made – but at the last moment she had become suspicious of him. Could Ms Cowper, she wondered, have any information that might help Peter find Sarah?

Peter wasted no time in phoning Caroline Cowper. While she didn't have any information about Sarah, Caroline told him about giving money to Freegard to buy a Golf V6 4Motion. Freegard had even shown her the logbook. The car was registered in the name of Darius Mazurek, but she'd driven it only once.

'Does the name Mrs Lucas mean anything to you?' asked Peter. As he listened to the answer another piece of the jigsaw fell into place. Lucas, as it turned out, was Caroline's married name. She had reverted to her maiden name, Cowper, after her divorce.

'So that's what Freegard is up to,' mused Peter. 'Conning more than one person into paying for the same car. An old scam, an old scam indeed.'

West London, February 2002

Renata Kister's friends felt that Freegard was exploiting her and had warned her against him. He was unreliable, they said, and she would be better off without him. Before Christmas she had demanded to know where her latest car was – the dark green Golf V6 4Motion – and once again Freegard had put her off with a string of excuses: it was at the manufacturers, it was in Glasgow, it needed some adjustments, it wasn't his fault.

A natural gambler, Renata had always loved to have a flutter here and there. The excitement of the game was like an addiction, but one she could control. With Freegard, it was the same. Just one more chip on the table, he'd come good and she would get back what she had lost. Just one last bet. She'd even paid him an extra £2,500 in cash for a custom-fitted, satellite navigation system. 'Last thing you want is to be looking at maps when you've got a young kid to think about,' he'd argued persuasively. But now she'd had enough.

Renata had told Freegard she was going to the police. That got his attention all right and he promised to come round straight away.

When she ran down the front steps, disbelief stopped her in her tracks. There was Robert at the wheel of *her* car – she was sure it was her car, they were certainly her number plates – smiling broadly and telling her he loved her. 'The number plates are yours, but the car's not,' he'd said about the Golf VB.

Renata hadn't seen Freegard for weeks now, and to date she had paid out close to £60,000 for cars he had talked her into buying, raising the money either through hire purchase loans or from her cousin Darius. The repayments on the loans were crippling. At the very least she wanted her £15,000 back. She wanted to know where he was.

After hearing that Freegard had recently been sacked from his job at Normand Continental, Renata decided to approach his former employers. Freegard was a good salesman, the managing director told her, but he was hassling female customers and there had been complaints. She asked him for a forwarding address. The garage, he reported, had sent a cheque to Freegard's address but it had been returned. The place turned out to belong to an elderly couple; they had had a bag stolen, but had never heard of Freegard.

The man cast a sympathetic look at Renata and little Ola in her buggy. There might, he said, be someone who could help, a lady who used to pop into the showroom and say hello to Freegard. Her name was Caroline and she lived in a house nearby.

Renata made her way along the street, ringing on every door bell. Caroline lived three doors down, a woman told her, pointing her in the right direction.

A blonde-haired woman opened the door and invited Renata inside. Barely had she taken two steps into the hallway when Freegard appeared.

'I want my money back,' demanded Renata, holding her ground against Freegard's attempts to get her outside. 'Where's the fifteen thousand? I've told you before, I'll call the police.' Renata glared indignantly at the man she thought was her friend.

Freegard's face darkened. 'If you care about the life of your daughter, you will not phone the police.'

Renata momentarily lost her balance. 'Are you threatening my daughter's life?'

'Just come outside with me.'

Suddenly subdued, Renata obeyed and followed Freegard to the end of the driveway. The heavy London traffic buzzed in the background.

'I was seeing Caroline as part of a game at first, but I've become emotionally involved,' Freegard looked straight at Renata. 'I'm in love with her.'

Renata observed Freegard coolly. She realised she had no idea who he really was.

Sarah, February 2002

'I'm going to France for a bit. Can't cope with the job any more. I'm not sure whether your case is going to be allocated to somebody else.' Rob breaks this news as casually as if he's off to post a letter. I stare at him in complete astonishment.

We're walking around West London and he turns to look at me. 'Do you want to come with me?'

It takes no longer than a second for me to reply. 'What happens about me getting my money and my life back?'

'Well, you wouldn't get anything back if you came away with me now,' he says dismissively in flat tones of finality.

'In that case, I don't want to go. The whole point of this wretched situation is to get my life back and tell my family what really happened.' Nine years of loss and misery churn beneath the surface.

Rob looks tired. 'I wouldn't blame you if you went home now, that's all I'm saying.' His face is expressionless and distant.

'Home? What do you mean, home?' I demand. My family, my friends – they won't want me. I don't have any skills. I try not to think about my past. I don't know who I am anymore. 'You can't suddenly suggest something like this. You *know* I can't go home, not without a full explanation for everything that's happened.'

'I just thought I'd better say goodbye, that's all.'

'You can't just leave me. What's going to happen to me?'

'I have to go now, Sarah.'

I can't believe he's just going to walk off, leaving me at a B&B. Everything is in freefall. I calm myself with the thought that Rob will turn up again. He always does, and I'm not wrong. Within a week he phones to say he's back.

Chapter 27

A Crucial Transaction

Central London, August 2002

Elizabeth was on her way to Green Park tube station. Freegard had summoned her to meet him near Langan's restaurant.

On the tube she clutched a plastic bag in her lap. She had turned it inside out, as instructed, to hide the Debenhams brand name. She snatched a look inside to check the sari was still there, then rolled the top of the bag over it again.

About two weeks earlier, Liz and Freegard had been sitting in a car in West London when he told her, 'We're going to a wedding party with some of my colleagues from MI5. They're from Pakistan. You'll need to wear a sari; it's not respectful to turn up in English clothes.'

Liz tried to imagine herself in a sari, but somehow couldn't quite picture it. She stared at him, stupefied. This had to be a wind-up. A real sari? She thought she'd misheard or that he was pulling her leg. 'What other sort is there?' he shot back, laughing hysterically at her confusion. Then he insisted she wore the full outfit, sandals, bangles, jewellery, scarf and 'one of those spots' on her forehead.

The tube train rumbled on through the blackened tunnels, its wheels screeching to a metallic halt every few minutes as it reached another station. Liz cast her mind back over the last couple of years and the strange direction her life had taken. She hadn't heard from Freegard for quite some time when he'd phoned her out of the blue. He had been planning to emigrate to Brazil, he told her, but wanted to give their relationship one last chance. 'I'm your Richard Gere, remember? I'm the one who'll sweep you off your feet.'

Now divorced, he had asked her to change her name from Bartholomew, so that she could cut all ties with Sheffield and begin a new life, he said. Why not Elizabeth Taylor or Elizabeth Hurley? he suggested. Liz had other ideas. She went down to a phone box with her friend Karen and leafed through the telephone directory. She reached R. Richardson. Yes, she thought, I like the sound of that, and legally changed her name by deed poll.

Robert had told her he was on a deep undercover mission and had infiltrated a gang in Glasgow. He boasted that he'd had people beaten and killed, that he had a hit list and that the undercover work required him to have a string of safe houses dotted around the country. He had six mobile phones, one for each of his personae. He wanted her to help him with his job, which meant that she should take time off work.

She did a lot of travelling for him now. Once he had ordered her to drive to Hastings, on the south coast, and to keep to an exact route. It was a test, he explained, to see whether she could follow police instructions. He warned her that she would be monitored by police surveillance throughout the task and that both her car and her mobile phone were bugged.

He also asked her to prepare reports for the police on the suitability of Canterbury or Aylesbury as a place for them to live – he said he was staying in single police quarters but was trying to find suitable police accommodation for when they were married.

Freegard promised to sort out her mortgage and debts. This came as a huge relief to Liz, because there had been no money since their relationship had restarted. In fact, she had had to resort to washing in public toilets and filling a pop bottle with water to keep her going through the day. She had to meet Freegard at locations all over London and, in between times, was regularly left in places for days on end. There was never any explanation. Liz had accepted this treatment because, according to Freegard, she had to prove her suitability for marriage by doing exactly as he told her.

Arriving in Piccadilly for the latest rendezvous, she spotted Langan's on the other side of the busy thoroughfare, but could see no sign of Freegard. She hovered around the entrance for an hour, until a wolf whistle caught her attention and she saw him beckoning from further down the road. She hurried along the pavement, expecting a kiss or a hug at the very least, but without any greeting he snatched her mobile phone, scrolling through the memory to see if she had rung anybody and to check on the remaining credit.

'Did you tell anybody we were meeting?' he asked, exchanging her mobile phone for a blue metallic one he pulled from his inside pocket.

'Course not,' she replied. 'Do I get a kiss?' she asked timidly.

'I've got a colleague just round the corner and he's watching us, so we've got to be discreet. No affection. We need to keep our distance,' said Freegard flatly.

'I don't know how to use this phone,' Liz said.

'You're only going to borrow it. I want you to do something for me and then come back here. You *are* listening to what I'm saying, aren't you? It's very important that you listen to what I say,' he said condescendingly. 'Take the tube to the city and find a ladies' toilet. Take off your English clothes and put on the Pakistani ones. Put on really dark foundation, all the way down to your chest, paint some liquid kohl on your eyes and stick the little jewel on your forehead. Tie your hair back and put the scarf around you and your sunglasses on, so that all anyone can see is a bit of your forehead and a bit of your chin. When you've done that I want you go into the Halifax Building Society. Once you're inside I'll give you instructions.'

Liz quailed at the idea. She didn't know her way around London very well and the noise, the crowds, the tall buildings and the city's intensity overwhelmed her. She set off nervously.

Meanwhile Freegard boarded a train from London St Pancras to Leicester, putting distance between himself and London. From time to time he rang to ask if Liz had got to the building society yet. Why was it taking her so long?

Liz changed out of her black jeans in a toilet cubicle and put on the sari with all the accessories, finally slipping on the big dark sunglasses.

In the Halifax, with the mobile phone to her ear, she listened carefully as Freegard directed her to a television monitor on an upright podium. 'Don't ask questions, just listen and do as I say. This is a test to see what sort of relationship we have, to see how loyal you are to me.'

Liz moved up close to the electronic banking machine. Her sunglasses were in the way, so she lifted them up to see the screen better. 'Don't take the shades off whatever you do, Liz!' he ordered. He dictated a number and a sequence of pass codes. Liz typed them into the machine, slowly and obediently.

'Did you say "T" or "V"?' she stammered.

'Are you utterly stupid! Can't you listen? You're failing the test already.'

Liz bit her bottom lip. Her throat felt dry and her hands were shaking. She was having difficulty changing from lower case to capitals. The screen timed out and returned to the main menu.

'Can't you take simple instructions?' Freegard roared into her ear. 'I thought you'd used a computer for years, why can't you do a simple job like this?'

Liz felt confused. The bank, with its big glass windows, was hot and tiny beads of sweat made her sunglasses slip down her nose. She pulled the scarf over her head to hide her hair and pushed her sunglasses back. Freegard told her to try again.

He repeated the codes number by number, letter by letter. Obediently, Liz typed in each letter as she heard it. Finally the security screens relented, giving her access to an account. She noticed the name Caroline. 'Are you sure this is OK, Rob?' She knew PIN numbers shouldn't be disclosed. The whole episode seemed a little odd.

'It's a test, remember,' he barked.

With a quick nervous glance over her shoulder, she carried on. He instructed her to tap in the figure of £13,884. She obeyed again.

'Now press transfer,' he commanded.

Liz understood now. He wanted her to move money from the Caroline account into an account belonging to somebody else. Freegard gave her the name of the destination account. She wasn't sure she had heard correctly. 'Robert, are you sure we should be doing this?'

'How many times do I have to tell you? I said it's fine. It's just a test to see whether you can follow my instructions.'

Liz hesitated. She wanted to be certain she wasn't doing anything wrong. 'When is the money going to be returned to this Caroline person?' she asked meekly.

'You'll fail if you ask too many questions.' There was a finality to his voice now. She didn't want to fail him so she pressed 'transfer'. The money left Caroline Cowper's account, destined for a bank account in Robert Hendy-Freegard's own name.

Hammersmith, 14 August 2002

At a police station in the London borough of Hammersmith and Fulham, Detective Constable Mark Simpson glanced at the witness statement. In it, a London solicitor by the name of Caroline Cowper alleged that almost £14,000 of her money had been fraudulently transferred via the internet into a Halifax Building Society account in the name of Robert David Hendy-Freegard. The transaction, she insisted, was carried out without her permission.

It wasn't the first time Caroline had been in touch with the police. Six months earlier she'd repeatedly called them until they finally sent an officer to her home. She told them Freegard had been obtaining money from her by deception. They informed her it was a civil matter. Freegard did not appear to have committed a criminal offence, and so had nothing to answer for.

Frustrated by the police response, Caroline had been conducting her own investigations, discovering among other things that Freegard claimed to work for 'Classic Cars' in Mayfair, when no such company existed. She'd allowed him back into her life to try and regain some of the money she'd given him for the car leasing business, but it had been short lived. Now this – a large sum of money gone from her account.

DC Simpson picked up the phone, and dialled the mobile number he'd been given for Robert Hendy-Freegard.

'Sure, no problem,' said the friendly voice at the other end. 'Just a small mix-up. I can explain everything. Of course I'll come down to the station. I'll be there tomorrow.'

But instead, Freegard turned his car around and headed west. There was a risk his prisoner might be found, and he wanted to make sure she wasn't.

Sarah

We've just finished a staff party and I'm about to start clearing up when Rob arrives.

I've been back at the Royal Berkshire Hotel for the last five months, ever since I ran away from his colleague's flat because some guy threatened to call the police.

I have that dreadful sinking feeling again, like I'm plummeting down a lift shaft. Bitter experience has taught me that his sudden reappearance signals that change is afoot.

Rob is agitated, like a fox that's strayed into enemy territory. He practically marches me up to my room, which is now crammed with his belongings and files. I've never dared look at the files – he said he'd soon know about it if I did.

His sentences are short and harsh. 'You have exactly one hour to remove anything that identifies you. Any handwriting, any photographs, anything personal. Take a few clothes with you. Only what you can carry. Leave the rest behind.'

'What's going on?' I ask. Rob is extremely tense and I'm alarmed by this new development.

'I've been warned someone's messing with things. You're at risk.'

'Who?'

'Shut up and stop asking questions, Sarah.' He is deadly serious.

'Hurry up, will you. I'm not joking here. Just fucking shift it.'

He loads everything of his into the car, but will only let me take a small bag. In truth I don't own very much anyway.

We race down the M4 towards the West Country. Rob says he wants to see his children.

A couple of days later we're sitting in a beer garden at the back of a pub and he starts going through all the files, tearing the documents into tiny pieces. 'I don't need these any more,' he says. 'They're car sales records from Normand and that operation has fallen through. We need to be able to move around. These files are way too heavy to lug about.'

The next day the remaining files are transferred back to the boot of his car. He drives me to London, and over the next couple of weeks he leaves me to sleep in the car in various south-west London cul-de-sacs.

Hammersmith, 22 August 2002

For the past week DC Mark Simpson had tried over and over again to arrange an interview with Robert Hendy-Freegard, but every time the man failed to show up at the police station, so Simpson circulated Freegard as 'wanted' on the police national computer.

The officer had begun to take the case more seriously now, and had received some new information from Caroline Cowper, who told him she'd been in touch with a man called Peter Smith. Mr Smith also had an interest in Freegard and had sent her a copy of a letter he'd received from someone called John Atkinson. She forwarded Atkinson's letter to DC Simpson.

I am really sorry Sarah has still not been in touch. I feel I need to explain further how it was for Sarah and I.

The officer skipped through the letter.

He was very convincing and I made the personal leap of faith and believed him. From this point on I would trust him implicitly with our personal safety. It was also at this time that Sarah and I became close.

I have heard since that sleep deprivation, hunger and systematic humiliation are tools of brainwashing, and I would agree.

DC Simpson looked up suddenly.

I remember making some pretty awful phone calls to you. Rob had me convinced that we must get you to do as Sarah asked. Most of the time I didn't know what Sarah had asked for, but in retrospect I can guess. At the time we weren't allowed to talk about it. Rob would send Sarah back to the car (next to the public phone boxes we used) and I would be summoned. Rob would tell me what to say and what the consequences would be for everyone if I didn't, then he'd stand quietly by as I lied and profaned down the phone. I feel sick thinking about it. I apologise again.

On April Fool's Day 1997 I told my family everything for the first time, including the fact that Rob was my contact. They were devastated, angry and disappointed. How and why could I have lied to them all this time? What hold did Rob have over me? I couldn't answer. I had believed in Rob so completely and risked so much on my belief that I think I had been deluding myself for a long time rather than face the truth. I had no self-respect. Perhaps Sarah stays away too because the humiliation of being so wrong is just too embarrassing to face.

DC Simpson placed the letter carefully on the desk and dialled Nether Hale Farm.

'Mr Smith?'

'Speaking?' said a noticeably wary voice on the other end.

'This is Detective Constable Mark Simpson, from the Metropolitan Police.'

Chapter 28

Living Rough

Sarah, early September 2002

We're on the move again. This time heading up the M6, the signs pointing to Birmingham.

'I'm going away on a golfing weekend,' he announces when we arrive in Shirley. 'I'll have to drop you at a bed and breakfast.'

He gives me enough cash for two nights at the B&B, with an extra four pounds for food, and promises he'll be back. By the fourth day there's still no sign of him. The owner of the B&B offers to organise a lift back to London for me, but what would I do there? I have no money and nowhere to go. I know, too, that if I'm not in the place where Rob has left me he'll go berserk, and I have no appetite for confrontation.

The questions at the B&B are becoming uncomfortable and I don't want to run up another unpaid bill. I feel I've no choice but to do a runner. Leaving everything in my room so as not to arouse suspicion, I walk out while nobody's looking. The evening wears on. I can't go back to the B&B and Rob still hasn't shown. There's nothing for it, I'll have to sleep outside.

As I wander the streets, looking for a likely spot, I imagine the parks will be less well patrolled in this suburb of Birmingham than the city centre. I concentrate on the green spaces, finally settling on a clump of bushes in a dark corner, hoping the foliage will hide me from view.

It's September, but the weather hasn't been great recently and it feels more like late autumn; damp, chilly and drizzling. In preparation for sleeping rough, I've managed to snaffle some plastic bags from a late-night supermarket and spread them out on the ground to form a makeshift blanket. I fashion a kind of mini sleeping bag by making a slit in the bottom of one of the bags and slip my legs inside. The base of a tree trunk is my pillow.

I only have the clothes I'm wearing – a pair of jeans, a rugby shirt and a jumper – everything else is back at the B&B. I hunch my shoulders together to try to keep warm. It's so cold and I'm scared of being found by the police or a potential rapist. When will Rob ever come back to pick me up? How has it come to this?

The telephone number is scrawled on a scrap of paper that's been curled up at the bottom of my wallet for several months. I ring from a red telephone box. Nothing. I've spent the entire day walking around. He's given me a mobile phone but it hasn't got any credit – he can phone me, but I can't contact him. I try again from the box. I'm really not allowed to ring the number, but I'm desperate. Nobody answers. I ring again and again and again. Still no answer. I give up and walk away, dejected.

The following morning I wake to a damp sunrise, the chatter of birds, the rumble of commuter cars and the screech of early morning buses. After a second night in the park I am ravenous. Fumbling around in my pockets, I count the loose change that is left from the four pounds Rob gave me. Barely forty pence.

I find my way back to the supermarket where I got the plastic bags and scour the shelves for anything cheap. In the bakery section they're selling bags of yesterday's stale rolls for twenty pence each. That'll keep me going for a while.

If anything it's colder today than yesterday. I'm going to need a plan. There is no guessing how long Rob's going to be, and I don't fancy going down with pneumonia, so I decide to find a public library – at least it should be warmer in there, and reading books and papers will help pass the time. All I have to do is wait for the doors to open . . . in three hours' time.

*

I'm standing in the call box trying to keep warm. I've been trying over and over to get hold of Rob. No response. Just as I'm about to leave, the phone chirps behind me. I turn round and pick up the receiver.

'What the hell were you thinking? I told you never to ring that number apart from just that once. Do you never listen? I was just about to come and pick you up, but now I'll have to turn back to London and explain to the chief why you've broken protocol and called a safe number against all instructions.'

'Rob, I just need to know when you're coming. I've got no money and nowhere to stay.' But the phone is dead. I shouldn't have phoned him.

It's late and I'm tired and hungry. Trudging to the café of an all-night supermarket, I tell staff I'm waiting for my boyfriend and ask if I can stay indoors where it's safer. They kindly give me a hot drink. In the early hours of the morning, not wanting to outstay my welcome, I find shelter at a bus stop.

The next day Rob finally turns up and provides a room in a cheap hotel. He has a colleague waiting in the car, so I mustn't be seen with him; he's breaching regulations by even being here.

'You've only yourself to blame for being cold and hungry. You weren't supposed to leave the bed and breakfast. If you'd done as you were told, you wouldn't have had to sleep outdoors.' He thrusts a fiver into my hand.

He pays cash at reception for my overnight and hurries away, saying he'll collect me tomorrow morning.

Life and warmth flood back into my body as I wash away the grime of the last few days.

The following day is spent waiting in the hotel reception, but again Rob doesn't show up. At six o'clock the receptionist tells me I cannot stay any longer, so I gather myself up and walk into the hotel next door, where I tell them a friend of mine is due to be checking in but has been delayed. They let me wait in reception until six the following morning.

When Rob still doesn't appear, I walk into central Birmingham, where I buy some more knock down bread rolls at a supermarket and a coffee from a burger outlet. Sitting here with my hands around the warm paper cup feels so good; I make it last as long as possible, extracting every trace of heat from it.

Towards evening I begin the walk back to Shirley. On the outskirts there's a canal bridge with a towpath below, and as it feels like rain I climb down to investigate. The bridge will at least provide some shelter and should be safe. Nobody is likely to find me down here. This is to be my home for the next three nights.

Another cold morning and I'm up with the birds. I didn't get any sleep and I need to get my circulation going, so I set off again on foot, ending up at the bus station in the city centre. This isn't a good idea. The place is depressing with the constant coming and going of people arriving and departing. People with lives, people with a purpose, in contrast to me; exhausted, hungry and dirty. My spirits flag. I slump in one of the bus shelters with my head down.

I don't want anybody to talk to me; they might ask awkward questions. Even the simplest – 'what's your name?' – is a problem because I would have to lie. Giving anything away about myself means I might never get my life back. He'll find out somehow, his bosses won't be pleased and I'll be back to square one. How do I know who might be watching? If I want my life back I have to regard everyone as a potential snitch, ready to make a phone call to special branch should I give them the slightest hint of doubt about who I am and what I may be up to.

A wheezy, nasal voice intrudes on my thoughts. 'Spare some change, love?' A beggar holds out his hand. I shake my head and look studiedly at the ground. How ironic that someone should be asking *me* for money.

My mobile rings, making me jump. I'd almost forgotten it was there.

'Listen carefully. You've got to meet me near the M42. There's a superstore near the junction we turned down the other day. Wait in the car park.'

'But that's miles away,' I protest.

'Don't get antsy with me. This is not a debate. Just follow the signs to the M42 and wait for me in the car park. OK?'

It's a ten-mile trek from central Birmingham to the superstore. By the time I get there I'm hungry, thirsty and tired, and my feet have blisters. I needn't have hurried. The hours tick by and there's no sign of Rob. As the light goes and I start to wonder whether he's coming at all, a car finally pulls up.

We trawl around the shop looking for a snack, and he updates me on his bosses' latest orders. 'This is the situation. You're going to have to sleep in a car again for a while. Everything's busy right now.'

The motorway lights slip past in a blur as we begin the night drive back to London. At least sleeping in a car is better than sleeping under a bush.

Back in London, he points out the silver Volkswagen Polo. 'If anybody asks you, say you're a friend of Kimberly Adams.' I nod. I haven't the slightest idea who Kimberly is, but store the name away in my head anyway.

'And you're to wait here until I receive further instructions. For your own security I have to lock you in the car.' I hear the door locks thud down and watch as he puts the keys in his pocket. With that he is gone.

The car is in a car park next to Fulwell railway station in south-west London. It is now my 'home'. I am hoping this will be a temporary arrangement; just a day or two before moving on somewhere else.

Rob takes the car during the day, returning with it at night, when he locks me in again. Through my long nights of incarceration, I can't help wondering if my brother Guy still lives nearby, but I've alienated my family as well as my friends, and I can't expect them to help me now. The truth is that I have nothing left and nowhere to go. All I can do is wait. Wait for Rob and do what he tells me.

I have no idea when he will reappear, it could be seven in the morning or one o'clock in the afternoon. It's too bad if I need to go to the toilet; I just have to cross my legs. Although I can open the car from the inside, I daren't leave it in case he comes back and I'm not there – he would make my life even worse then, and that thought is unimaginable; I'm trapped in a living hell.

When I ask Rob why I have to live like this, he tells me his bosses say so, because there's no money to pay for my accommodation. There's never any explanation beyond that, and I've learned the hard way that if I argue with Rob things deteriorate, so I choose the path of least resistance and acquiesce.

However, I do succeed in persuading Rob to lend me a couple of rugby shirts, which is important, because as the nights draw in the temperature has started to plummet.

I spend the days wandering around Teddington, killing time and drinking from washbasins in public toilets.

Kimberly Adams, it turns out, is the code name for a fellow agent. Actually, she's from America, and he's hinted that he's been asked to keep an eye on her because there is some question about her loyalty. He stays with her in a safe house a few blocks from the station.

The weeks pass by, and when Kimberly is at work he lets me have a shower in the safe house. It's good to feel clean and warm.

The warm water is hypnotic and soothing, and I stand under the jets with my eyes closed. The steam rises and thickens in the bathroom, fogging the mirror. I'd like to unzip a hole in it, climb inside and disappear.

I hear Rob come into the bathroom and my eyes shoot open, suddenly alert. Blood throbs in my head. I turn off the water as he yanks back the curtain.

'Your hair needs to look like Kimberly's,' he says brutally. 'Then anyone seeing you from a distance will mistake you for her.'

A flash of steel catches the light. I drag the curtain back across me, but he tears it open again. He stands looking at my nakedness, a glint in his eyes. He lunges forward and pulls my head sideways. I hear the slicing sound of scissors, then the dull thud of chunks of my hair hitting the floor. I want to scream, but the sound is strangled by sobs.

As Freegard's feeling of power grew, so his cruelty intensified. After nine years together, Maria Hendy had finally left him, but at one stage in 2002 Freegard was simultaneously deceiving at least five other women: London solicitor Caroline Cowper; former Sheffield company secretary Elizabeth Richardson; Polish-born Renata Kister; Sarah Smith; and Kimberly Adams, an American psychologist. Dr Adams was in fact a thirty-three-year-old who had been living in London for the past year after leaving her job at the University of Minnesota in the United States. She had a teenage son from a previous marriage, who had stayed in America, and she worked for Reading Borough Council as an educational psychologist. Weary of commuting by train from West London, she had decided she needed a car. Before moving to Teddington, she had lived in Chiswick; her nearest garage – Normand Continental; the salesman – Robert Hendy-Freegard.

As she signed the documentation for the VW Polo, Freegard asked her out to dinner. Kimberly couldn't see the harm in it. 'Sure, why not?' she said, brightly. She had been seeing him regularly since then.

Sarah remained at the centre of his web, but the treatment he meted out to her was now being replicated with others, particularly Elizabeth Richardson. She, too, was being kept constantly on the move; forced to live in squalid conditions and reduced to near starvation. Other than using her as a tool in a theft, however, Freegard's primary objective here was not financial gain. Rather, this was an exercise in pure sadistic control; Elizabeth's suffering evidently gave him satisfaction.

So confident was Freegard in his hold over the women that he had felt able to bring Sarah and Renata together without either of them realising that the other was also a victim.

With the transfer of money from Caroline Cowper's account, a turning point had been reached. The police were now taking the claims against Hendy-Freegard more seriously, and were actively on his case. And by giving Caroline the number for Alison's mother, Freegard had committed a fatal error: Alison's mother was the link between Caroline and Peter Smith, and once that link was established there was no holding either of them back.

However, despite knowing the police were after him, Freegard prepared to push the stakes even higher. Seemingly insensible to the risks, he was about to embark on a more elaborate intertwining of his victims' situations, bringing strands of his fiction together into one story. On the one hand, this would minimise the pressure of having to remember the complexities of the stories he had spun for and to each of them; on the other, it would help satisfy his apparently overwhelming desire to demean and abuse his female victims.

Chapter 29

The Cottage Prison

Sunninghill, October 2002

Robert Hendy-Freegard and Kimberly Adams had rented a house in the Terrace, at Sunninghill near Ascot in Berkshire. It was a pretty little old cottage, in a neat and tidy row of houses with picket fences and well-tended gardens.

Nearby was the Royal Berkshire Hotel, where well-heeled guests dined after a day at the races and where, until recently, Sarah Smith had worked as an assistant night manager.

Freegard's relationship with the young American psychologist had blossomed, and while holidaying together in southern Spain he proposed to her on a beach in Marbella. They planned to get married as soon as possible at a small church in Wales, and had been looking at engagement rings. A couple of months earlier Freegard had also bought his future wife a Rolex watch for her birthday.

He had told Kimberly that his job at the Volkswagen garage had actually been no more than a cover for his real work. He was a spy for the British government and had been investigating illegal activity at the garage, but that was all finished with now.

Whenever Kimberly asked him about his undercover work, his reply was always the same: 'You know I can't talk about it. It's really hard for me, Kim. I want to tell you so much but I just can't.'

After they were married, he said, they would have new identities. He would be called Harry Sinclair and she would adopt a Polish name, Monica. His department would erase all record of her old life. 'It will be as though you never existed,' he added, gently caressing her cheek.

They paid one and a half month's rent as a deposit on the Sunninghill cottage, and a month's rent in advance, signing the papers in the names of Dr Robert and Kimberly Adams. Kimberly was looking forward to living there.

Sunninghill, a few days later

'Here it is, Ronnie! What do you think?' Freegard threw a winsome look at Renata Kister as she cast her eye over the little cottage with its white picket fence.

'Oh, it looks perfect,' she said happily.

Renata was tired of London with its dirt, its crowds and its pressures. The little village of Sunninghill felt like a tonic, and there was even a school for her daughter nearby. It was ideal. Yes, she would be happy here.

She'd had her ups and downs with Freegard, most especially that time outside Caroline Cowper's house, but she had forgiven him and was prepared to give things another go. He had been in and out of her life for more than two years now. Her living conditions were poor and Freegard had offered her an escape route. The cottage was rented and the deal was that they would split the bills, and he would give her a car to drive as well.

'You should move in some furniture and clothing,' he suggested. 'You know what, though, why don't you think of starting a cleaning business here, perhaps with a more English-sounding name?' He thought for a moment: 'Like Kimberly Adams.'

'Who on earth is Kimberly Adams?' Renata asked, her face aglow.

'Just an invented name. There's no such person.' He gave her a quick kiss. 'But seriously, I want you to bank money in this name. Out here you can become a new person, cut everybody else out. I even have a new ID you can have.'

Sarah, November 2002

'Lie flat,' he commands. 'Cover yourself up with these towels.'

I stretch out on the passenger seat and pile the towels on top of me, blotting out the daylight. I'm very anxious now, wondering what's going on.

We drive for about an hour but, completely disorientated, I have no idea which direction we're heading in. The air is warm and sickly in the car and I need some oxygen. Suddenly we stop.

I hear the rustling of something being pulled out of a bag. 'Put this over your head,' says Rob, in a matter-of-fact voice. I peer round the edge of a towel to see him waving the bright blue plastic bucket we'd purchased earlier. He dumps it on my head.

'As I said, you mustn't know where we are,' he says tersely. 'Remember, you'll be safe as long as you do as I tell you.' He guides me as I walk unsteadily up a short garden path.

'In here,' he hisses. 'Don't make a sound.' He pushes me inside a door and closes it behind us. 'You can take the bucket off now.' I look around. I'm in the small, unfurnished front room of a cottage.

'We're in a safe house. The guys had to leave in a hurry.' I take two steps towards the bay window and see a picket fence.

'Come away from the window! Christ Almighty! What do you not understand about the word "security"?' he yells at me.

He motions me into the kitchen at the back of the house. 'You've got to stay at the back of the house, out of sight. I want you to clean the place. Make it spick and span.'

By the end of the day my hands are sore from scrubbing and I'm ready to leave. He has other plans, however.

'There is no option.'

I wonder what he's talking about.

'I've got to be somewhere else. Now.'

Where's this leading? Anxiety floods through me.

'There's no time to take *you* anywhere else.' He motions me inside the bathroom telling me I've got to stay there. That's not so bad, I think, starting to feel relieved. It's warm, it has a bath, a shower and a toilet and is a vast improvement on the car. Then he drops the bombshell.

''Fraid I'll have to lock you in. It's for your own safety.'

'You've got to be kidding. You can't lock me in here,' I panic.

'You're not allowed to be seen by anybody. You're not supposed to be here. This is a safe house. It's the only way to ensure you can't be detected.'

'What happens if there's a fire?'

'Don't be stupid, nothing will happen.'

'What if something happens to you? Nobody knows I'm here.'

'Stop whingeing! I'll be back later.'

With that he slams the door, locks it and removes the key.

I turn around and drop to my knees, sobbing. But in the cold silence there is no one to hear me.

Drip, drip, drip . . . The bathroom tap is leaking. Apart from that there isn't a sound. The hours pass by and still he doesn't show. I could die in here and no one would know. It's a grim thought. I get up and splash cold water on my face.

There is a window, but it's small, frosted over and firmly locked. I can't see out and there's no air. It's a prison cell. There's nothing to eat. I've lost a lot of weight over the last few months, down from a size sixteen to a size twelve. I feel very alone, as if the world has abandoned me.

Night encloses the tiny space.

The key turns in the lock. 'Where the hell have you been!' I tear into him. 'Don't you ever leave me in here like that again.' Frustration and despair boil up as anger.

He seems to find my outburst amusing. 'It's work. I couldn't get back,' he says, a smirk on his face. He opens a takeaway pizza box. 'Here, eat this. Don't stress out so much.' I devour the tasty offering, despite the complaints of my stomach.

'Glad that went down well,' remarks Rob, unpacking a Dualit toaster from a John Lewis bag and placing it carefully on the kitchen worktop. He's wearing his black leather jacket, rugby shirt and jeans, he is unshaven and looks uncharacteristically scruffy. I wonder why.

'I've got to go now.' He points to the bathroom. 'Back inside.'

His words hit me like a blow and my face freezes into utter incomprehension.

'You're not serious,' I say as the panic wells up again.

'It's the rules.'

'But Rob . . .'

'It's the fucking rules!'

I'm shoved unceremoniously back into my cell. All I can hear are his disappearing footsteps and the dripping of the tap.

Sunninghill, a few days later

Renata had a spring in her step. Her friend Monica was over from Berlin and she wanted to show her the country cottage she was going to live in after she had sorted out a job for herself.

The two girls arrived in Sunninghill and drew up outside the cottage, giggling.

'Cute,' said Monica.

'Come on, I'll show you around,' said Renata excitedly.

They tripped down the garden path, heels clacking. Renata pulled out the key Freegard had given her and put it in the lock, but the door wouldn't open. She wiggled it around, becoming more and more frustrated, but finally gave up, defeated.

'I can't believe he's given me the wrong key,' she fumed. Snapping open the letterbox, she saw a light on in the hallway. Otherwise, nothing stirred.

He had a lot to answer for. Imagine giving her a key that didn't fit the lock! She worked hard for what she had, a single mother running a cleaning business. How could he do this to her? She'd tell him she'd had second thoughts and wasn't going to live in the Sunninghill cottage. She would listen to her friends now. 'Don't trust him,' they still warned her. 'He's up to no good.'

Renata banged on the door all the same, more out of frustration than any hope of there being anybody there. 'Just wait till I see that man. I'll wring his bloody neck.' Renata stomped back down the garden path.

Sarah

I can hear banging on the front door. I am terrified in case someone comes in and finds me here. What do I do then? Footsteps click away down the path and I breathe a sigh of relief.

A week has passed. I lie curled up on the cold floor. There's been no heating since a gust of wind blew out the pilot light. Outside, night after night of fireworks remind me what I'm missing. In here there is nothing but endless empty hours.

Sometimes Rob lets me out of the bathroom to clean for a few hours. Anything is better than being cooped up with nothing to do. Last time he visited, he let me put my clothes in the washing machine, but although the cupboards are well stocked with food, he doesn't let me have any. He tells me it's all reserved for the next agent who'll be living here.

I asked him to bring me a newspaper and I devour every word over and over again. Otherwise I just think about how to get through this, how to survive.

To kill time I imagine all the nice food I could be eating. I make up different meals in my mind, piecing together various food combinations into elaborate menus.

It's been three days since he last called. Hunger gnaws at my insides.

'You're imagining things,' he insists when he finally turns up. 'You're exaggerating, I've only been away for two days.'

'I know how many times it's gone dark since you were last here,' I say ruefully.

'Eat this.' He produces a takeaway Indian meal, which I tuck into ravenously, but the food just goes straight through; my stomach can't hold it.

Now he's gone again, but this time he's left the light on and I can't turn it off because the switch is outside. In place of the natural cycle of day and night, there's just one long stretch of white light.

I toss and turn from side to side, trying to catch some sleep, but it comes only fitfully in short bursts of suffocation. When I wake I lie there, haunted by my new existence. My world has shrunk to a washbasin, a bath, a shower and a toilet.

West London, November 2002

Renata Kister was at home ironing when the telephone rang. It was her cousin Darius Mazurek. He had just received a letter addressed to him from the police. They were making general enquiries and wanted to know if he had bought a car from Robert Hendy-Freegard.

'Did the letter come through the post?' asked Renata.

'No,' replied her cousin. 'Someone shoved it through the letterbox. It's handwritten on a scrap of paper.'

Renata was suddenly alert. She remembered what Rob had said about fake police. If anyone claiming to be the police should attempt to contact her, he had frequently warned her, she must deny knowing him. If they really were the police they weren't going to confirm his existence to her anyway, because of the sensitive nature of his job. Renata thought about this, along with the fact the letter had been handwritten on a scrap of paper. It sounded way too inefficient to be from the police.

'Does it say anything else?'

'It gives the names of DC Mark Simpson and DS Bob Brandon and their telephone numbers.'

'Just ignore it,' she advised.

With that, Darius Mazurek rolled the letter into a ball and threw it in the bin.

Sarah

I want to beat my head against the bathroom wall in frustration. I've been working for years towards a new life. What if it's all a lie? If it is, I've wasted nearly ten years of my life and damaged every relationship I care about beyond repair; all for nothing. If it isn't, if this *is* real, why I am still here – surely I can't be of any use to him? But if this is all there is to my life, I may as well be dead.

I stare at the ceiling. Memories flit through my mind. My childhood horse rides across Nether Hale have a mythical quality, as though they belong to another life. I've become disconnected. I remember my family and all the pain I've put them through, the endless calls about money. What will they be doing now? But my family and Nether Hale, my home, are lost to me. 'Home' and 'life' are alien concepts; I have no idea what they mean any more. My life adds up to this: nothing. All I can do is see this thing through to the bitter end. But is there even any point in that? Why not oblivion?

I look round the bathroom for something, anything . . . but there is nothing, no knife, no rope. A long, low howl bursts from deep inside me, a cry of loneliness, emptiness and grief at the realisation that I can't even take my own life.

West London, November 2002

Renata's cousin Darius Mazurek was on the line again. 'Listen, I just got another letter from the police.'

Renata padded around the flat in her bare feet, the cordless phone stuck to her ear. She cast an approving eye over the freshly manicured nails of her other free hand. 'Oh, yeah, dropped through the letterbox again was it?' she asked with a small laugh.

'It came by registered post this time, only there was no stamp on it. So guess who had to pay the postage!'

'No kidding. What a bore.' Renata dropped onto her sofa, tucking her legs underneath her.

'The letter asks if I am related to "Ronnie",' continued her cousin.

'What? It actually says, "Ronnie"?' Renata asked with mild

surprise. The only person who ever called her Ronnie was Freegard. Perhaps Robert himself was behind the letter, perhaps it was a test to see if she would contact the police.

'It can't possibly have come from the police,' she said. 'There's no way they would be so stupid as to send a letter by registered post and not pay the postage.'

For the second time in a month Darius Mazurek screwed up a letter from Scotland Yard and tossed it into the waste-paper basket.

Sarah

Three weeks have passed. It's cold and my ribs are showing. I can't seem to hold together any positive thoughts as numbness and mental apathy creep over me.

I hear my jailer at the door. This time I don't get up from the floor. I barely raise my eyes, yet I see something flicker in his: a kind of arousal.

'I've always liked you, Sarah,' he murmurs, the cold-death tone of an assassin.

'But you've locked me in a bathroom,' I say slowly and thickly, paralysed with fear at where this might be leading.

'I'd like to go out with you. Be my girlfriend?' He moves closer, his eyes intense.

I'm stunned. 'You'd need to treat a girlfriend much better than this,' I mutter.

'I want to have sex with you.' His voice is dark, a sickly treacle sliding through my consciousness.

My body pushes back involuntarily into the cold brick wall, but my mind is suddenly alert and begins to calculate, like frantic fingers running up and down a keyboard, whether there might be a way out of this prison if I give in, whether I might be able to negotiate better treatment.

He is already undressing me. My mind is fighting. This is horrible; it's really horrible.

I'm in the turgid river with him now, carried helplessly

downstream, barely clutching at survival. I let my mind go blank. I'm floating above this, somewhere outside myself. It's not really happening, it's not happening at all. Such sordid exploitation of my body is the last remaining hope that my life will get any better. Tears stream silently down my face.

Late November 2002

Metal tore against metal with a horrible screech, and DC Mark Simpson lay slumped over the steering wheel. He knew his injuries were bad. He realised he was going to be off work for some time.

His investigation into the Robert Freegard case would have to be suspended for the forseeable future.

Chapter 30

Losing It

Late November 2002

As Freegard drove northwards, he laid down the law to Kim. 'I don't want you working for Reading Council any more. You've worked your last day there. I don't want you going back ever, I want you pregnant.'

Kim said nothing.

'My mother is a model of what a good woman should be. I'm taking you to live with her.'

Kim gently nodded her acceptance. Overriding everything was a feeling of guilt that she had done something terribly wrong, that she needed to make up for whatever it was and work on their relationship. Robert was such an upstanding man, and so proud, that she felt ashamed of the couple of flings she'd had in the past. She didn't want Freegard to leave her. As long as they were together everything would be all right, things would work out. She would just have to prove to him that she was worthy of his love and that she was committed to him. She'd do whatever he asked.

He dropped her at his mother's house in Blyth, then drove straight back to Teddington to pack up her things. Stuffing Kim's clothes into plastic bags, he paused to look at a red coat, a pair of black gloves and a black scarf. Elizabeth Richardson had been complaining of needing a coat. Yes, he'd get Sarah to take it to her in Kettering. Before leaving, he shredded all of Kim's photographs, including those of her son.

Sarah, late November 2002

'You can come out now.' Rob ushers me out of the bathroom. 'We're off.'

Stumbling out of my prison cell into the fresh air and daylight, I feel my spirits lift at last. But the optimism vanishes just as quickly, as there's a dark side to every action Rob initiates.

We're going back to the house in Teddington. Rob tells me sombrely that Kimberly Adams, the American agent he had been investigating, has committed suicide rather than face trial, and that he has to clear out all her stuff.

'You can stay there for the time being,' he says, suddenly cheering up. 'It should be safe. But you'd better be on your guard. Kim's family and friends haven't been informed of the circumstances of her death yet. If anyone comes looking for her, don't answer the door, but if they won't go away, tell them she's on holiday with me. And if anyone asks why you're there, say you're a friend of Kim's and she's asked you to look after the house while she's away.'

Blyth, December 2002

'You're a whore! If you betray me in any way I'll destroy your family.' Freegard was in another black mood. Now he was accusing Kim of disloyalty on the strength of relationships she'd had before they even met.

'I've designed a special padlocked box to torture you. I'll rub your legs with lard, put them in the top of the box, and fill the whole thing with hungry rats,' he ranted while she cowered in a corner of the room.

'On second thoughts, I'll leave you to Pav. Pav is very good with a knife,' he said, smiling crookedly.

Kim was terrified when he was like this. There had been an awful incident when Freegard had been burying his mother's old dog and had dragged her out into the backyard to watch. She had looked on, cold and miserable, as Freegard lowered the dog into the hole and shovelled the earth back on top. Still carrying the spade, he had walked right up to her, his face just inches away from hers, and spat out, 'I hope I don't have to do that to your son.'

She had no money, no mobile, no bank cards, no driving licence and, since the plan was for her to change her identity after they got married, she had surrendered her passport to Freegard. She couldn't even prove who she was. She didn't dare call his bluff, in case he did have a friend called Pav who was good with a knife. She dared not risk her own safety or that of her son. She simply had no choice but to stay where she was.

The south west, January 2003

Freegard was in a violent temper. His eyes blazed with the look of someone possessed. 'You've been unfaithful to me! You've been screwing around!'

Kim had been looking forward to a quiet weekend away, but now he was accusing her of flirting with a guy in the hotel bar. 'How can you try and get off with someone else when you're with me?' Freegard paced around the room, raging at Kim, spittle forming at the edge of his mouth. 'You fucking whore. You slut. Don't you know that I could kill you right now and no one would ever know?' He lunged at her.

Kim was astounded by the about-turn in her fiancé's mood. She was truly afraid now. 'Get away from me!' she shouted, rushing to the window.

He followed her. 'I've killed a man before. Nail gun in the head.' His nostrils flaring, he pummelled the terrified woman's head and shook her by the arms. Suddenly he pushed her away. 'You piece of shit. The marriage is off.'

The room echoed with a horrified silence. Then in a low voice Freegard whined, 'You've absolutely destroyed me. Have you any idea what you've done to me? Look what you've done to me. I love you. I don't want to give you up. If it weren't for me you'd just be a whore. I want to save you from yourself. I want to make a good decent woman out of you.'

Sarah, January 2003

I'm on edge, expecting someone to call about Kimberly's death. I'm upstairs when I hear keys rattling in the lock. It can't be Rob because I know he's abroad. He's told me to bolt the door, but this person isn't going to go away and is now knocking loudly. I peer out of the window anxiously and look out onto Fulwell Road, but I can't see who's there. Perhaps it's a trap. I pad downstairs and open the door gingerly.

On the doorstep is a man I've never seen before. He's tall and intimidating and is staring at me in surprise.

'Hello,' he says warily. 'Who are you?'

As instructed, I introduce myself as Juliet Butler.

'I'm Simon Proctor. This is my house.'

Full-scale panic. I try to gather my wits as he explains that he's returned early from travelling around the world. He was expecting to find Kim here.

'What are *you* doing here?' By now he's standing in the hallway.

I fall back on the contingency plan Rob outlined should anyone close to Kim turn up. I know Kim from a bar I worked at in south London and she's asked me to look after the place in her absence. I'm in contact with her by email, I say. She's fine.

'That's odd. I've been trying to contact her and got no reply. I'm worried about her.' He throws me a suspicious look and I feel myself blushing. 'Nobody knows where she is, not even her mother. No one's heard anything from her,' he says.

He pauses, studying me, then his face clouds over and he announces that he's going to call the police to report Kimberly a missing person. He asks for my phone number and address. He wants me to be a witness.

I'm struggling to work out what to do next, since he's clearly not buying my story. I repeat that I've only been doing what I was asked to do and that I've kept the place clean and tidy.

Again he demands my contact details, but I just shake my head.

'Give me your keys and get out,' he says frostily. I snatch a small bag from the fridge and leave in a hurry. My instructions are clear in such circumstances: make for Heathrow airport, terminal four, and wait until Rob gets there.

Heathrow is about ten miles from Teddington, a fair hike on a good day. However, it's just started snowing and it's bitterly cold. My mind is in shock. What is going to happen now? Will Simon Proctor – if that is his real name – phone the police? Have I messed things up? When will Rob ring me? How long will I be at Heathrow? I have two pounds in loose change, that's all.

After a few miles I stop to buy a bag of doughnuts and a cup of tea. It's snowing more heavily now and the flakes are sticking to my hair. My shoes are almost worn through and my feet are frozen. The wind picks up, sending the snow swirling into a blizzard.

I put my head down and press on towards the airport; driven on by blind panic.

Sheffield

Elizabeth Richardson was on a National Express coach to Sheffield. She wouldn't arrive until late at night and had asked her friend Karen to pick her up at the bus station.

Elizabeth looked gaunt and smelled as though she hadn't washed for a long time. She hadn't. Her face was swollen with eczema and her ribs were showing. She wasn't wearing any make-up, but then she didn't have any to put on.

Her friend was shocked at the sight of her and started to say so, but Liz motioned for her not to talk, pulling a mobile phone from her pocket and waving it about. Karen frowned, but followed Liz's silent instructions. With the mobile safely stashed in the boot, they sat inside the car with the CD player turned up loud.

'It's so that nobody can hear us,' explained Liz.

'You look so ill. Aren't you eating?'

'The only thing I want is a bath.'

At Liz's flat they lit some candles – she was under strict orders from Rob not to switch on any lights. A sniper, he said, was monitoring her from the nearby Stocksbridge bypass. The sniper was after him, of course, but if they couldn't kill him they wouldn't hesitate to kill her as a way of getting to him. The bypass was on a level with her lounge windows, so her instructions were to duck under the windows to avoid drawing fire.

Closing the curtains to make sure the sniper couldn't see them, she turned her mind to a bath. She didn't have any money to feed the electricity meter, so it was going to have to be a cold one.

Sheffield, 31 January 2003

There was nothing Robert Hendy-Freegard and Kimberly Adams wanted to see at the cinema, so they drifted back to the car. Overhead the stars sparkled glacially in the night sky. It had been snowing hard earlier.

Kim looked pale and listless. She had lost all sense of reality and felt as though she were clinging to a cliff side which might crumble any moment.

'Kim,' said Freegard, softly. 'Look, cheer up. I've been offered something that could be a great opportunity for both of us.' He paused. 'I'm not sure if I should really be talking to you about it, but...' Freegard's voice vibrated with excitement and he puffed himself up like an exotic bird.

'Well, here goes. I was at a meeting yesterday where they floated the idea of me monitoring Russian submarines off the west coast of Scotland. We could both go up there. What do you think?'

Kim smiled weakly. She knew better than to ask too many questions.

'We'll have to go to a meeting in London, but I can try to put them off for a while so we can talk this through between us. If we go ahead we'll need some training, though, and that will cost...' Freegard's voice trailed away. Something seemed to snap. He arched his back like a horse about to buck off its rider and his eyes rolled in his head. 'What happened with Paul? I know you fucked him.'

Kim gasped. He pushed her into the car, and started the engine. 'Why won't you admit it?'

'I didn't.' Kim was struggling to keep calm.

'You're lying to me,' said Freegard through clenched teeth. 'You're just a whore, a slut. That's it, I've had enough. I'm gonna kill you.'

Freegard revved up the engine and threw the car into gear.

'First, though, I'm going to torture you. Do you hear me?' he screamed.

The wheels screeched as they raced into the countryside at high speed.

'How does it feel to know you've murdered your own son through lies? Because that's what's going to happen, I'm going to kill your son,' he rasped. In the passenger seat, Kim wept silently.

'Would you trade your life for his?' Freegard demanded.

She nodded. 'Yes. Yes, of course I would.'

'Fine, that's where we're going.' Freegard picked up speed again, and Kim closed her eyes.

'Are you scared?' he asks nonchalantly.

'Yes.'

'You'll be glad to be dead in the morning.'

Freegard drove recklessly through the country lanes. Suddenly, he seemed exhausted and pulled into a deserted lay-by. 'I need to sleep for a while. Don't get out of the car. If you do, it'll be worse for you.'

Dazed and frightened, Kim's fear of these unimaginable consequences kept her rigid in the seat while Freegard slept.

When Freegard eventually opened his eyes, blinking, it was like a man trying to grasp the threads of a fading dream. Turning to Kim, he said in a matter-of-fact voice, 'I'm not going to do it, Kim. I can't. I love you. Why did you have to lie to me? All I wanted was to give you the world. All I wanted was to take care of you. We'll be fine as long as you never betray me and never cheat on me again.'

Sarah, 3 February 2003

'You got it all wrong. You didn't give the right responses.' Rob scowls at me. His mood is foul. I feel humiliated and small.

'No. I told him I was a friend of Kim's, just like you said,' I say defensively. 'I thought I followed the instructions exactly.'

'It was all part of the programme, Sarah. The guy was supposed to turn up and start asking you questions. All you had to do was give the right answers and he would have let you stay. You failed.'

We get in the car and he throws it into first. It's two thirty in the morning. The wind tugs at the trees, each swaying movement of their branches sends showers of melted snow slapping against the windscreen. Heathrow is behind us; the planes have started flying again after being grounded for several days because of the extreme weather conditions.

We haven't gone far before I begin to recognise the shapes and outlines of familiar buildings. Even though the windows are streaked with water there's no way I can be mistaken. We drive right past it – the Royal Berkshire Hotel. Rob makes no comment as we turn left and into Sunninghill, just around the corner. We draw up outside a cottage with a picket fence and he cuts the engine.

'Don't worry. I'm not going to lock you in.' There's a note of contempt in his voice. 'I'm too knackered to go through the precaution of sticking buckets on your head again. You already know more than you should about a lot of things. I'm trusting you not to tell anyone where this place is.'

I can't believe it. I was locked up in a bathroom in Sunninghill, only two minutes from the hotel where I worked for two and a half years, where I once had good friends.

'We need to be up at four o'clock in the morning because I have to go to Gatwick airport. You're coming with me.'

My short sleep is fitful, as though I'm lying in a bird's nest of fragile twigs.

*

He pulls up outside the departure level at Gatwick's North Terminal. The forecourt hums to the mechanical rhythm of taxis arriving, unloading and leaving.

'I have to pick someone up.'

'You can't just leave me here!' I say, incensed.

'You got things wrong in Teddington.' He scans the sky, craning over the steering wheel and peering up through the windscreen. 'It's your fault you're being dropped at the airport.' His words hang in the air like a challenge, the shivering red cloth of a bullfighter.

'Rob, I need some money. I'm not budging until you give me some money.'

He sighs and digs into his pocket. 'Here's ten quid. I'll be back in a couple of hours. Just go and sit in the lounge upstairs and keep yourself out of trouble.'

He waves me out and slams the door behind me.

Somehow I know it's not likely to be just a couple of hours.

Chapter 31

Lighthouse Spies

Gatwick, 3 February 2003

Kimberly Adams's father was due in any minute from the United States on a flight from Minneapolis. After dropping Sarah at departures, Freegard circled around to arrivals and left his car in the short-term car park.

John Adams slowly made his way through customs. A proud and single-minded man, he was devoted to his daughter. Ever since Kimberly's November wedding to Freegard had been postponed because Freegard's 'sources' said the security situation post-9/11 made it too dangerous to fly, John had experienced a growing sense of unease. Over the Christmas period his wife Dianne and several friends had encouraged him to find out what was going on. His mind made up, he told his daughter that he was coming over and, brushing away Freegard's objections, had booked a ticket for the next available flight to London.

As he exited customs, he scanned the crowds, looking for his daughter's familiar face.

Freegard bounded up to him. 'You must be John.'

'Where's Kim?' he asked, disappointed that she wasn't there to greet him.

'She's not well,' said Freegard. 'We'll catch up with her shortly.'

Freegard led the way towards the car park. 'Anyway, I want to show you something of London first.'

The two men climbed into Freegard's car. It was about as

comfortable as a mousetrap, reckoned John as the car nipped his knees and elbows. He shifted his large frame, slouching forward to avoid grazing his head on the roof. Why couldn't these goddamn Europeans build cars like they did in America?

'That's the Tower of London,' Freegard shouted, pointing out the landmark as they sped past.

'When I am going to see my daughter?' John asked, beginning to feel short of air in the confined space.

'Soon. This is Big Ben, and over there is Westminster Abbey,' waved Freegard as they sailed round Parliament Square, leaving a trail of exhaust fumes behind them.

'We're heading north now,' announced Freegard some two hours later.

Already disorientated by his lightning tour of London's sights, John learned that they were making their way to a place called Worksop. It would take them three or four hours, depending on the traffic. Soon the arid landscape of the motorway was flashing past. 'Slow down, will you!' cried John, unused to such speed in a small vehicle. But the more John complained, the faster Freegard drove.

They made frequent stops at motorway service stations to buy cans of Red Bull. 'I've been awake all night,' explained Freegard. 'The snow meant I had to get up in the middle of the night to get to Gatwick on time.'

John looked at the peppering of snow flakes on the motorway embankment. Call this snow! You should see the snow where I come from, he thought. You could refrigerate a whole month's produce in the snowfalls we get over there. But he kept his thoughts to himself, saying instead, 'Where I come from we call this a snow flurry. Sometimes it snows sideways for days on end and you have snow up to fifteen feet high. Between my place and the Canadian border there's nothing to stop it except for three fence posts. No, Robert, this isn't snow, this is a flurry.'

Finally they drew up at a motorway service station near Worksop and Freegard announced that they had arrived. John noticed a middle-aged woman coming towards them. Only when she was within a few feet of him did he recognise, with a jolt, who she was.

'Hello, Dad,' said Kim. John recalled the startlingly attractive, petite young woman his daughter had been when she'd left America. Now he reckoned her weight had doubled and her delicate features were lost in fat.

Scotland

The trio headed towards Loch Ness in the highlands of Scotland. They had spent the previous day in Wales, checking out the church where Kim and Freegard would eventually get married, then stayed overnight in Liverpool.

The Scottish countryside unfolded, displaying its charms to the sun; its mountains claimed the skyline and small crofts nestled in their shadows. Yet John was restless. He cast a backwards glance at his daughter. It wasn't just the physical change in her that was marked, her whole demeanour was different. Once so confident and self-assured, she now looked to Freegard for confirmation of everything she said. John found that he could never get her alone to talk to her; her fiancé seemed intent on keeping them apart, and this troubled him even more.

At Loch Ness they checked into the White Horse pub and found a café of solid yellow stone nearby. Crisp white paper cloths covered square wood tables, and a waitress in a lacy apron and sailboat hat took their order for tea.

'That'll be iced tea for me,' said John, enjoying the look of consternation on the waitress's face.

Freegard straightened himself in his chair. 'Kim and I are going to live in a lighthouse on an island off the west coast of Scotland. We're going to be lighthouse keepers for the next twenty-five years.'

John choked on his cake.

'You're not serious, right? Lighthouse keepers! Twenty-five years! You're crazy if you think my daughter's going to sit in a lighthouse for the rest of her life. Gee, twenty-five years! I've got no idea what I'm gonna be doing in two and a half weeks,' he snorted, trying to take stock. 'And you're mad if you think we still have lighthouse keepers. They went out with the ark.'

Freegard glanced slowly about the room. 'We'll be lighthouse keepers in name only,' he said in hushed tones. 'What we'll really be doing is monitoring Russian submarine activity in the North Sea. We'll be observing them from a communication centre in the lighthouse.'

John scrambled to process what he'd just heard. He knew the United States and British governments monitored Soviet activities, so the idea that the British might use a lighthouse to disguise their covert operations had some plausibility.

'The lighthouse is just a cover, Dad. They'll have sonar under the water buoys in the North Sea,' added Kim.

'And the important thing is we'll make lots of money,' Freegard chimed in. 'I'll be earning about a hundred and fifty thousand pounds a year, and Kim will get about seventy-five. If we have children the government will take care of their schooling and all that.'

'I can't believe you would want to live on an island for twenty-five years.' John was still trying to square what sounded like endless periods of inactivity with what he knew of his daughter's fertile mind.

'I think I need to slow down, Dad,' she said.

'Kim will have to go through school and pass an exam,' continued Freegard. 'But there are other formalities to take care of first. The British government, via the CIA and FBI, will change her name. They'll obliterate her birth certificate, her college degree and things like that. She will no longer exist. But she does have to pass that exam before they'll post her with me in the lighthouse.' Freegard gave a raffish shrug of his shoulders.

'There's no doubt in my mind about Kim passing the exam,' said John emphatically. 'This is a girl who never got a B in her life. She's a straight A student. No sir, you don't ever want to play Trivial Pursuit with her, she knows the answers to everything.'

'The cost of the exam is thirty-five thousand US dollars,' said Freegard. 'We need you to pay it.'

John sat back in his chair, absorbing this latest twist. 'I've got the money, but not right now. I can get it in a month, maybe six weeks.'

'Too late, we have to have it by this Friday,' says Freegard.

'You're nuts if you think I can get you that kind of money *that* quickly!'

'What about Kim's mother? I know her husband has just won the state lottery,' Freegard suggested, unblinking.

'Dad, we've got to have that thirty-five thousand dollars,' Kim said in a dull voice.

John took a mouthful of his iced tea, glancing at the other customers, who were all minding their own business. 'Tell you what, I'll make a call for you.'

The following day he phoned Dennis Hodgins, the husband of his former wife Ann. He recounted the story about monitoring Russian submarines, saying that he thought it was all legit. 'I'll pay you back Denny, just as soon as I can.'

'OK. Sign a promissory note for me and I'll send the money,' agreed Denny.

'Thanks a million. Do me a favour, though, will you? Don't send it till next Monday or Tuesday, OK?'

'So, thirty-five thousand dollars will be in Kimberly's account by Friday, then?' queried Freegard.

'It'll be early next week.'

'I said it had to be Friday.'

'Hey, Bob. Chill out. You can do things in my time, not yours.'

'Don't call me Bob.'

'Sorry, no offence intended.' John strolled along, hands stuffed in his trouser pockets, enjoying the irritation he knew he was causing Freegard.

'You'd better treat Kim good, Bob. If you mess with her I'll come back with her three brothers, sit you on a fence, nail your testicles to the post and push you off backwards.'

'Have no fear, I'll take care of her,' Freegard retorted witheringly.

It was the eve of John's departure. 'One last thing,' said Freegard. 'Everything we've told you is secret. It's possible that at some point the agency may test you, without your being aware of it, to make sure you don't give away sensitive information. They'll probably ask you if you have a daughter. I'm sure you know the answer to that.'

John nodded; he was supposed to say she didn't exist. All the same, before leaving Scotland he rang his wife Dianne in the middle of the night and told her to go down to the courthouse. 'Get Kim's birth certificate, her diploma, her medical records and her graduation certificates from high school. Put her identity in a safety deposit box. They might tell me my daughter's going away, but they're not going to take away the proof she's mine!'

Chapter 32

A Confirmed
Sighting at Last

Teddington, 19 February 2003

Back at work once more, DC Mark Simpson was on his way to Fulwell Road in Teddington. His accident had left him out of action for two and a half months, but now he had returned to the case of Robert Hendy-Freegard with renewed determination.

Information had come to him that a car parked outside Freegard's mother's home in Blyth near Worksop was registered to the Teddington address he was now approaching. He was hoping to arrest Robert Hendy-Freegard.

DC Simpson pulled up, snow flakes falling gently on his windscreen. The door was opened by Simon Proctor. The officer said who he was looking for, and Simon invited him inside.

Simpson learned that Freegard was Kimberly Adams's boyfriend, and that she had been using Simon's house in Teddington while he was travelling abroad. Simon, however, was convinced that she was missing, and was possibly at risk. There was something else as well, he said. When he returned from his travels just over two weeks ago he found another girl in the house. She had given her name as Juliet Butler, but curiously, as soon as he started pressing her about what she was doing there, she took off.

A sudden thought crossed Mark Simpson's mind. Pulling two photographs out of his pocket, he showed them to Simon. One was of a woman with dark hair by the sea, the other the same woman, only with blonde hair and smartly dressed. They were both pictures of Sarah Smith. Was this the woman Simon knew as Juliet Butler?

Simon Proctor considered the two images carefully, trying to picture the stranger who had met him at his door. The woman he remembered had longer, darker hair and was slimmer than the one in the first picture but, he told Simpson, he was fairly certain that the woman in both photographs was indeed Juliet Butler.

Nether Hale, 20 February 2003

'Mrs Smith? DC Simpson from the Metropolitan Police.'

Jill clamped the phone firmly to her ear and pressed a biro between her fingers and thumb, not wanting to miss anything the officer might have to say.

'I've been giving a lot of thought to this, and we'd like you to list Sarah as a missing person,' said the detective.

Anxiety bore down on the eagerness of Jill's raised hopes.

'Right. If you think that will help. What do we have to do?' asked Jill.

'We need anything that might help identify her: doctor's details, records from her dentist, anything of that nature.'

'It's been such a long time, our local GP might not have any records,' Jill said with a heavy sigh. 'Wait a minute, though, Sarah broke her wrist when she was ten and had to have it set under anaesthetic. Perhaps the hospital in Margate will have kept the records. I can check with the Medical Records Department.'

There was an expectant pause before DC Simpson replied, 'It's possible, although I may have better luck accessing those kinds of details formally. Usually they're confidential. What did you say the hospital was called?'

'The Queen Elizabeth, the Queen Mother Hospital.'

'Leave that one with me,' said the officer. 'Now, what about dental records?'

A faint memory floated across Jill's mind. 'I'll check with the local chap here in Birchington and see if he's got anything. Sarah did have an X-ray there once. I remember that. Let me give him a call and I'll get back to you.'

Sarah, 21 February 2003

I need to remain constantly on my toes if I'm to avoid being noticed by the police. There's heightened security because of tension in the Middle East and the threat of terrorist action. People are being moved on at Gatwick Airport – I see it happening and have to stay one step ahead. I daren't let them clock me. I need to be invisible.

I've been living here for the past three weeks, evading detection, getting my routine down to a fine art: one day at the North Terminal, the next at the South, snatching just a couple of hours' sleep a night. The airport has seats without arms so I can stretch out flat. I try to blend into the background, stay mobile and avoid being moved on.

During the day I sometimes walk up to the nearby town and sit in the public library reading books. I browse round the supermarket, imagining what I might buy if I had more money, but reality is a diet of stale rolls, sold at knock-down prices at the end of each day. One guy obviously thought I was starving, because he bought me a burger from a McDonald's inside one of the terminals with a free token he had. That was such a treat.

Whenever I can, I pick up the newspapers and magazines that people leave around, read them and fill in all the crosswords. But the days still stretch out like a desert. This monotony brings on a strange mixture of lethargy and stress. Nothing good can come out of this cocktail and I can only cope by shutting down mentally again.

Finally, Rob reappears. After picking me up at Gatwick he's brought me to a hotel where I can shower, eat and hopefully get some sleep.

'You need to get your hair changed,' he announces, 'and it's time you started earning some money again. I've arranged for you to stay with someone in London and work as a cleaner.'

'It's not that Polish woman I stayed with before, is it?'

'It's only for a few days, Sarah.'

'No, no, no. There's no way I'm going back there.'

'This is for you, Sarah. You've got to earn some cash. In a week's time you'll be travelling to Europe on an Eastern bloc passport. And here's the good news: once we're there, you'll get your life back.'

West London

Renata inspected the woman standing on her doorstep; she was slim with violet-red streaks in her short-cropped hair. She didn't recognise her as the woman who had stayed with her once before, the abused wife on the run from her husband, yet Renata knew it was her.

When Freegard called and begged a favour, she'd firmly resisted. 'It isn't the woman you brought before, is it?'

'Come on, Ronnie, help me out here.'

'Absolutely no way,' she told him. 'She didn't speak a word last time. She's a freak.'

'That's because she was terrified. She rang and told you so herself.' This was true, Renata had got an apology the same evening the woman had fled from the flat. 'It'll only be for a week,' he had cajoled, 'and she can help out with your cleaning business.' Renata caved in. He just kept finding her weak spot, she thought, telling her what she wanted to hear and taking advantage of her good nature.

Half-heartedly, she beckoned the woman inside. The woman introduced herself as Carrie Rogers. Renata couldn't help noticing that she was wearing Freegard's clothes, his black leather jacket, even his trainers and belt. She wondered why this Carrie person had no clothes of her own.

'You'll have to sleep on the floor,' Renata told her.

'No problem,' said the woman.

Renata didn't understand how such a well-spoken person could turn up on her doorstep with no possessions and with such low expectations. The whole situation was very odd indeed.

Freegard must have sensed the net was closing in on him. He knew the police were on his tail and from this point on started spending much of his time in other parts of Europe, where he may have been putting in place a getaway plan. On the pretext of taking Kimberly on holiday he travelled vast distances across Europe – through Belgium, France, Switzerland, Monaco, Italy, Austria, Germany, the Czech Republic and the Netherlands. He rarely spent more than one night anywhere; only after crashing the car in the mountains of southern France did he and Kimberly stay in one place for a while.

What was he doing in all these countries? He told Kimberly's father, John Adams, that he was going to Berlin and St Petersburg to carry out some 'financial transactions'. Was he opening up bank accounts in which to lodge all the money he had conned from people? If so, was he operating under his own name or one of his aliases?

And what about Sarah? She had now been under Freegard's control for ten years; he had taken all her money, and the circumstances which he'd forced upon her meant her earning power was insignificant. Yet it seemed he had no intention of leaving her behind; on the contrary, it appeared he was planning to take her with him to Europe on a stolen Eastern European passport. But why run such a risk? Especially since keeping Sarah with him meant he would have to continue to organise and pay for her accommodation and food, even in a foreign country. This plan of action would seem to offer him no obvious practical benefit. Surely she was now simply a yoke around his neck?

Or was she?

Sarah herself says there were times when she felt he treated her like his 'confidante'. However, to Freegard in his self-serving, manipulative and sociopathic world, Sarah was the ultimate slave, the one constant, and the living embodiment of his power – proof of his ability to control and dominate. Freegard revelled in being the master of Sarah's daily life: after sleeping rough, she was grateful just for warmth and a roof over her head in Sunninghill; his response was to lock her in a bathroom for three weeks and to control (as he had done many times before) what she ate, when she ate, and when she was allowed out. She existed entirely at his whim.

Yet, after ten years of isolation, there was no one in Sarah's world but Freegard. During these years, his sadistic treatment of her alternated with occasional expressions of approval and the odd gift – such as a camera, which he later removed. Not surprisingly, these 'acts of kindness' reinforced in Sarah's mind Freegard's claim that he was working for the government, and looking after her. When Freegard had sex with her, Sarah's primal instincts kicked in. Giving herself up to him represented a last desperate stab at survival, the vestige of a hope that he might treat her better.

The sheer duration of their 'relationship' appears to have taken it beyond Stockholm syndrome (where the kidnapped victim identifies with her/his kidnapper), and into a far more complex scenario. The abused and the abuser had become locked in a cycle – of hopelessness in Sarah's case, and power and control in Freegard's. Whatever else he might have done or be planning to do, it did not include letting Sarah go.

part seven

Race Against Time

March–June 2003

Chapter 33

Trains and Buses and Planes

Sarah, March 2003

I've just finished cleaning an office at Plantation Wharf, a riverside complex at Wandsworth in south-west London. Rob has phoned and told me to meet him in Wandsworth town centre, which is about a ten-minute walk away. We're going to Oxford Street. He needs me to do something for him.

'Listen,' he says as soon as we're on the train. 'I'm on a special assignment. That means you're going to have to stay with Renata a bit longer and you'll have to carry on cleaning. Save your receipts so I can check how much you've earned – I want to know that Renata is telling me the truth.'

I hand him the cash I've earned since I started working for Renata, but I have some questions of my own. 'When am I going to Europe? And when will I get my new life?'

'You haven't earned enough yet, Sarah. Can't you get more work? As soon as you're on target, then it's Europe, your money and your life back.'

As we get off the underground at Oxford Street, he turns to me, his face a concentrated frown, his voice brusque. 'I want you to find the best exchange rate for Euros. Check out big stores like Selfridges and all the money exchanges along here. Meet me back here in two hours.'

I nod and stride off up the street.

'Oh, and one last thing,' he calls back. 'At some point in the future I'm going to ring you and you'll have to go to a railway station. I want you to pick up a suitcase with a load of cash in it.'

Could this be my money? I hope to God it's not, because it's supposed to be in the police account. If it *is* my money then something's gone seriously wrong. He walks away and I'm alone with the crowd of Saturday shoppers, on a mission to find the best Euro exchange rate in town.

Two hours later we descend into an underground car park. We have another trip to make now, he tells me, to the Midlands.

On the drive north the silence is as heavy as an ocean. I see signs for Leicester and Dunton Bassett. Finally we turn off onto a small side road with an old-fashioned bus shelter at the end of it, and head towards the village. He pulls up at the side of the road and instructs me to stand in the bus shelter and keep an eye on his black Audi, to make sure it doesn't get damaged by anyone and that nobody is following him. I watch him go down the street and into a house.

Sarah, next day

'This is a first. Why are you giving me these?' I ask, holding the keys to Kimberly Adams's silver Polo in the palm of my hand. Rob has never left me with the keys to any car before now.

We've just arrived back in London from the Midlands, dropped the Audi, picked up the Polo and driven it into the Masterpark underground car park in Audley Square, Mayfair.

'If you ever need to make a fast getaway, you know how to do it,' Rob says. 'In the meantime, the car is away from any prying eyes.'

'And how am I supposed to pay for the parking? Where's the ticket?' I ask.

For a moment he doesn't answer. Instead he gives me a look of mild irritation, before seeming to relent. 'When you go to the railway station to get the cash I told you about, you'll find enough money inside the suitcase for it. As for the ticket, you can work that one out for yourself.'

United States, April 2003

John Adams was belted into his seat on a plane bound from Iowa to Washington DC. In his spare time he sat on an Iowa juvenile drug court, and every year he travelled to the US capital to meet congressmen and senators as part of a group lobbying for legislative improvements for the community. He looked out of the small circular window into the vast blue expanse, pinning his gaze on the horizon. The flight was giving him time to think. By now he and his family had paid out close to US$150,000 to his daughter Kimberly. A couple of weeks after he had returned from Scotland, Freegard had phoned to say that Kim had failed the exam for the job at the lighthouse monitoring centre and needed more money to re-sit it.

'Another ten thousand dollars.'

'I don't believe she didn't pass,' exclaimed John.

'She missed it by one point.'

'What kind of questions were on it?'

Freegard put Kimberly on the phone.

'I can't tell you.' Kim sounded vague.

'Where did you take the test? Who were the instructors?'

Freegard cut in again: 'We can't discuss those things.'

John took a sip of water, thoughtfully rattling the ice cubes around the bottom of the glass, then he reached into his top pocket for his wallet and took out a small photograph of Kim. He stared at the picture. Failing exams was not like his daughter at all, and he had said so to Freegard: she had never failed an exam in her life. Something didn't sit right, and he wasn't the sort of man to ignore a niggling instinct, especially when it concerned his daughter.

Dressed in formal evening attire, John made his way through the huge hall in Washington's Capitol Building. 'The Great Sioux Land Steak Fry' was the annual dinner for all those eager to debate Iowan legislation, but that night something else was on John's mind. He took his seat at the table, noting that his neighbour was the Sioux City Chief of Police, Joe Frizby, a man he'd got to know well over the years. Suddenly his mind was made up.

'Joe, I've got a story to tell ya,' he said slowly, looking the police chief in the eye.

'Go ahead, I'm listening,' said Frizby.

'You know my daughter Kim, don't you? Well, she's gotten tied up with someone who says he wants to marry her. But here's the thing; this guy says he works for the British secret service, like a James Bond figure, and that they're gonna live in a lighthouse off Scotland for twenty-five years so they can monitor Russian submarines. D'you think that sounds genuine?'

'Are you crazy?' said his companion.

'Yeah, I have been wondering.'

'I've got land to sell you in Florida if you believe that story. Ah shucks, John, I hate these low-life con guys.'

John turned away from Joe's stare and back to his dinner. He'd been hoping his friend would calm his fears, but in reality he'd just confirmed them. At least he was sure now of what he needed to do.

A few days later, the head of Senator Chuck Grassley's office in Sioux City listened as John recounted his story.

'Kim's just not responsive to me. She's not her normal self,' John said, shrugging his shoulders. There was a languid stillness in the heavy air and the traffic droned monotonously in the distance.

A swift phone call to Senator Grassley's Washington DC office and thirty minutes later Steve Harker and Bob Burney arrived from the Sioux City headquarters of the Federal Bureau of Investigation, the FBI.

The eyes of the two FBI agents narrowed and they looked sideways at each other as they took down details of the case. Kimberly, they concluded, was probably being held captive; she might even have been brainwashed. John couldn't identify her whereabouts because she seemed to be constantly on the move.

Nevertheless, the agents were confident they would get his daughter back.

With John and his ex-wife Ann's authority to mount wire taps on their phones, they would be able to monitor telephone calls between him, Kimberly's mother in Arizona, and Freegard.

Meanwhile, in London, DC Mark Simpson had been given John's number by the FBI. Within hours, the phone at the Adams's home was ringing. 'Mr Adams? Good morning to you. This is Detective Constable Mark Simpson from Scotland Yard.' It was four o'clock in the morning. As he struggled to wake up, John couldn't believe anyone would ring him at this hour, least of all Scotland Yard. He thought it must be one of Freegard's 'tests', so he put the phone down and went back to sleep.

Chapter 34

The Photograph

April 2003

Detective Constable Mark Simpson and Detective Sergeant Bob Brandon were on their way out of the courtroom at Middlesex Guildhall Crown Court in Parliament Square, London. Grey-wigged barristers bustled along the hallways of the gothic gargoyled building, the weight of centuries of law bearing down on them.

Out of the corner of his eye DS Brandon spotted a couple of familiar faces; senior Crown Prosecution lawyer Andrew West and his colleague Michael Hick, a barrister and specialist in serious fraud.

Hailing the two men, DS Brandon scanned their faces closely. 'I have a rather unusual case,' he said slowly. 'It involves a man who we think has been kidnapping people over what seems to be a very long period of time.'

Andrew West nodded for Brandon to continue. 'Bizarrely, he appears to have been raising money from the victims' families to equip a lighthouse in Scotland to monitor Russian submarines,' concluded DS Brandon.

The prosecutor's face wrinkled into a bemused smile, 'You can't be serious! This isn't a real case, surely?' said Andrew West.

'It is a real case,' insisted Brandon. 'We're still investigating, but when we've got a bit further down the line, can we set up a conference in chambers to discuss it?'

There was a concentrated stillness in the air, then West took out his diary. They would meet on 20 May. The men parted company and the lawyers headed back to the courtroom.

'I can't believe people can be so stupid,' muttered the prosecutor to his legal colleague.

Nether Hale, end April 2003

The taxi shot down the farm track, sending up clouds of orange dust. After taking a right turn through a gap in a row of conifers, DC Mark Simpson and DS Bob Brandon arrived at the main farmhouse of Nether Hale. The customary introductions completed, Jill Smith led the two detectives into the dining room where the officers seated themselves around the table.

'We should never have let her have any money,' Peter said ruefully.

'Every phone call was always about money,' added Jill, setting down a tea tray. 'The stories all seemed so plausible.'

'It was a mistake, and I should never have let her go after we met her at the Pomona. I should have marched you both off. I've kicked myself ever since that day,' said Peter.

DC Simpson looked out over the garden. 'We'd like to take a statement from you, Mr Smith,' he said, turning back to the room and nodding in the direction of a large and rather ancient-looking tape recorder the officers had brought with them. 'If you don't mind, Mrs Smith, we'll take a statement from you afterwards as well. It's important we keep your accounts independent of each other.'

'Have you spoken with John and Maria?' asked Jill, handing DC Simpson the photograph of the 'gang of four', which she'd taken so many years ago.

'Yes, we have. And let me reassure you that we'll do everything we can to locate Sarah and bring her home, Mrs Smith,' he said, taking a good long look at the picture.

May 2003

Renata Kister's suspicions about her house guest were deepening. She wasn't sure whether 'Carrie' was being duped by Freegard or was in league with him. She couldn't understand why the woman never opened up or confided in her. What was she hiding?

When Carrie had first arrived, Renata asked her over breakfast why she was wearing Robert's clothes. 'Rob lent them to me,' Carrie replied, munching on a piece of toast.

Renata had leapt to her feet and crossed the room. 'Well, since you're wearing his clothes you might as well add this to your collection.' She opened a drawer, extracted a rugby shirt and brandished it in front of the other woman. Carrie looked perplexed.

Later that day Renata put the same question to Freegard. His answer didn't tally. Renata knew instinctively that something was wrong. Something was going on between Freegard and this Carrie woman, and she was going to find out what.

Renata, her daughter, and the woman she knew as Carrie strolled through the west London park. Ostensibly, on this warm and sunny day, they had come to feed the ducks, and little Ola scuttled about, clapping her hands excitedly.

'Ciocia, ciocia!' she yelped.

Carrie laughed at the child's exuberance. 'What does she mean?' she asked Renata.

'It's Polish for auntie. She thinks of you as family now.'

The mallards waddled up from the pond in a regimented line, squawking urgently. Ola threw out a handful of breadcrumbs, spraying them over a wide circle, and then jumped up and down, gurgling with laughter.

Renata fingered the camera in her pocket nervously, waiting for the right moment to take a snap. She bit her bottom lip.

'Ola, run towards me!' she shouted to her daughter. The little girl turned around brightly and did as she was asked. This is it, thought

Renata. She whipped the camera from her pocket and squatted lower as if to snap her daughter.

'Smile!' she shouted, and a wide smile like a sunbeam lit up her daughter's tiny face.

In the background Renata saw Carrie flinch and turn, as if trying to hide her head in the folds of her black leather jacket, but Renata knew it was too late: she had got the picture she wanted – she had photographic proof that the woman existed, should she need it.

Chapter 35

French Holiday

France, 10 May 2003

Chambéry lies in the heart of Alpine France, between Annecy and Grenoble. The narrow cobbled alleyways and courtyards of the old town lend the place a sense of history. This was once the capital of Savoie, and an important frontier town on the way to Italy.

Robert Hendy-Freegard was effusive as he checked into the two-star Hotel Buffalo. 'Actually, I'm a doctor. I've got a practice in the States,' he said silkily to the admiring smiles of the receptionists. 'I have a place in London as well.' He ran a hand over his hair, as if stroking a pet. 'Haven't had a holiday in five years, though, so we're spending three months travelling round Europe, aren't we, darling?' Freegard turned towards Kimberly, who stood sullenly at his side.

'Well anyway, here we are!' He signed his name with a dramatic flourish – not 'Sinclair' or 'Adams', aliases he had used before, but this time 'Robert Hendy-Freegard'.

'Stop acting so miserable,' Freegard snapped at Kimberly as they took possession of their narrow room. 'Haven't I told you I'll marry you in Italy?'

The following day, perched on the edge of the bed, Kim slowly dialled Arizona. It was Mother's Day, a good enough reason to be ringing home, although wishing her mother a happy day wasn't the only purpose of this call. She had other orders: to squeeze more money out of Ann Hodgins.

Freegard hovered in the background, a dark, tormenting shadow. Neither he nor Kim was aware that the conversation was being recorded by the FBI.

KIM: 'Happy Mother's Day!'
ANN: 'Thank you!'
KIM: 'How are you?'
ANN: 'I'm good. How are you?'
KIM: 'Oh, we've had a shitty week.'
ANN: 'How come?'
KIM (*sniffling and crying*): 'Coz I failed that exam again.'
ANN: 'You gotta be kidding me.'
KIM: 'Can you ring me on my phone?'
ANN: 'Give me the number real quick.'

Ann phoned her daughter back and, following her instructions from the FBI, casually introduced the idea of a visit to London.

ANN: 'There is this deal online, but it's only through Memorial weekend, where I could fly into London for, I think it's two nights, at a central London hotel and it's, that's included in it, it's one hundred and forty-nine dollars each way.'
KIM: 'What!'
ANN: 'Yeah.'
KIM: 'And can you stay longer than just two nights?'
ANN: 'I think it's just two nights. I think if ya' pay extra, I could stay longer than two. But the thing is I'm still in school then, so it'd have to be that Memorial weekend.'
KIM: 'Which weekend is that?'
ANN: 'That's the second to last weekend in May, like the twenty-third, twenty-fourth of May.'
KIM: 'That's very interesting. I don't know if I'll be around or not, but I'll look at the diary and see because [*sigh*] it's been one of the worst weeks of my life. Tuesday night we sat these exams again . . . and I had a message to call my insurance company.

And they said they won't cover the cost of the repairs to my car. And then Wednesday I found out that I didn't pass the exam again, so we've spent the last however many days begging and pleading with them to let us take the exam again. They've finally agreed to do it, but only if we pay the cost of the exam, which is another two thousand pounds.'

Kimberly agreed to meet her mother in two weeks' time at Heathrow airport, where she would be given another $10,000 for repairs to her car and to re-sit the exam.

If she had hoped the call home would put her in Freegard's good books she was wrong. Without warning, almost as soon as she put the phone down, his mood turned ugly.

'What was in those text messages between you and Paul?' he raged at her.

'That was a year ago – I can't remember what I said to him in a text message a year ago.'

'You do remember,' he screamed. 'You're lying to me. You're lying.'

Kimberly tried to placate him. 'Rob, please. I don't know what was in them.'

'What do you *think* might have been in them?'

'I don't know. I don't know.' She began to cry.

Freegard showed no sympathy. He brought his face up close to hers as she sat on the bed, and looked her right in the eyes. 'If you say I don't know again, I'm gonna punch you in the face, and then you won't see your mother again.'

Like a dog that had been thrashed in a frenzy of unprovoked cruelty, Kimberly sat quietly saying nothing.

Chapter 36

The Sting

Inner Temple, 20 May 2003

London's Inner Temple has been home to lawyers since the fourteenth century. The air is heavy with tradition and the buildings suffer from an absence of light as though smothered in velvet curtains.

Inside 5 Paper Buildings, four men sat in chambers: the Crown Prosecution Service's lawyer, Andrew West; Michael Hick from Chambers; and the two Metropolitan police detectives, DS Bob Brandon and DC Mark Simpson.

'I was sceptical at first myself,' conceded DC Simpson, 'but we've now got statements from John Atkinson, his father Russell and his uncle William; from Maria Hendy – she's the mother of Freegard's two children – and Caroline Cowper. The evidence against this man is mounting.'

'John Atkinson and Maria Hendy both allege that Hendy-Freegard claimed he was a government spy and persuaded them to leave college,' kicked off DS Brandon. 'Atkinson claims that Freegard obtained money from him and his family to keep him safe from terrorists, and Cowper claims he obtained money from her for a car-leasing business that never materialised. He also transferred money out of her account without her consent.'

'We've got one person missing,' added DC Simpson. 'Sarah Smith. Her parents haven't heard from her for over a year.' He glanced at his colleague. 'They don't know if she's alive or dead.' Privately, both officers thought it would be a miracle if Sarah were found alive. 'We also understand a young American woman, Kimberly Adams, is with him at the moment.'

'We want to arrest him,' said DC Simpson. 'We just have to be sure that when we do, Kimberly Adams is there with him, otherwise we may never find her.'

Andrew West listened attentively, slowly running his hand over the bristles on his chin. He had been working nights lately, but inevitably found himself working days as well so that officers could keep in touch with him.

'What's your plan, then?' he asked the detectives.

The idea was to set Freegard up and stage a sting operation. Kimberly's mother had agreed to fly to London and hand over $10,000, as long as she could give it directly to her daughter.

'So with any luck, we'll pick him up at Heathrow airport.'

Andrew West considered the plan. 'I think you're doing the right thing.'

'What we need to know is which way to take the investigation after that,' said Bob Brandon. 'There are a number of layers of complexity here, and I'm sure we've only scraped the surface. But already we can see several possible lines of inquiry. The thing is, which can we pursue? And what charges can we sustain?'

'Well, we're certainly looking at theft, and obtaining money by deception,' assured Andrew West. 'Where the people are concerned, we won't be able to go for a charge of false imprisonment. I am right, aren't I, in understanding that both John and Maria could go for a drink or go to the shops?'

'Absolutely,' confirmed DC Simpson.

'Right. False imprisonment consists of the unlawful and intentional or reckless restraint of a victim's freedom of movement from a particular place. We could charge him with this on the basis that he kept them away from college, but as I understand it they could have gone back to college for a visit. In my view, therefore, we couldn't sustain such a charge. However, we can look at kidnapping.'

Mark Simpson raised his eyebrows. 'Don't we have exactly the same problem? These people were not physically restrained. They could have walked away at any time.'

'True, but there is a charge of "kidnapping by fraud or deception", where the victim is induced to go with the offender as a result of a deception practised on him or her by the offender.'

'How easy is that to prove?' asked DS Brandon.

'Has a case like this ever come to court?' The prosecutor turned to his colleague.

Michael Hick confirmed that one had. 'About thirty years ago a man was sentenced for kidnapping after claiming he was a policeman looking for drugs. He persuaded a woman to walk a hundred yards with him to his car and get in. Even though the man drove off when the woman's boyfriend showed up and pulled her out, all that was required was to prove the offence was deprivation of liberty and the carrying away of the victim to a place that person would not otherwise wish to be.'

'That's useful,' mused West. 'However, I'm worried on two counts. Firstly, it's such a fantastic, unbelievable story that we need as much corroboration as possible – phone bills, bank statements, bank books showing money going out, and the movement of cash into accounts controlled by Freegard. But perhaps more important at this moment is to get the people away from him, and to find out whether there are other victims. The more witnesses we have the better.

'Clearly we need to be very concerned about the whereabouts of Sarah Smith. Let's just hope it all goes according to plan and we can find her. And pray that when we do, she's still breathing.'

Heathrow, 23 May 2003

Behind the scenes, events were moving quickly. Officers from Scotland Yard escorted Ann Hodgins to a corner of Heathrow airport, where it would appear as if she had just stepped off a flight. In fact, she had arrived from Arizona the day before and spent much of the intervening time being briefed on the operation and her part in it.

As Ann was being moved into position, Freegard was driving up the ramp of the airport terminal. He parked the car in the adjacent multi storey, telling Kimberly to wait while he fetched her mother. He walked over to the airport terminal, wearing a smart new pair of Church's shoes he'd just bought from Lester Bowden in Epsom. He had paid over £375 in cash for them, along with a pair of riding gloves.

Checking the flight arrivals board, Freegard saw the plane had landed and waited by the barrier. Meanwhile the police were surreptitiously monitoring the man in the dark leather jacket, blue jeans and red shirt, standing to one side among a small group of cab and limo drivers. They had noted that he was on his own.

The arrivals board refreshed itself like a giant pack of shuffled cards. The crowd by the barrier scanned the faces of emerging passengers. Freegard glanced at his watch. A few minutes later Ann Hodgins swung through the exit doors.

'Ann!' he exclaimed. 'Great to see you.'

'Where's Kim?' Ann tried to keep her voice light.

'She's in the car park. Third floor.'

Ann looked around again anxiously. Why hadn't the police wired her, then they'd know what Freegard had just let slip.

'Give me a second, will you,' she excused herself. 'I need to go to the bathroom. Long flight and all that.' As soon as she was out of sight, she pulled out the mobile phone the police had given her, dialled Bob Brandon and reported what Freegard had just told her.

'Just stay with him,' urged the officer. 'Everything's under control. Go, go, go.'

Her heart fluttered and her stomach churned, but Ann knew she must stay calm so as not to arouse Freegard's suspicion. If anything went wrong she might not get her daughter back.

She rejoined Freegard and followed him through the teeming arrivals hall with its crowds of zigzagging travellers trailing small black suitcases. As they rode up the escalator towards the car park, she wondered when the police would move in and arrest Freegard.

'Here she is.' Freegard pointed to Kimberly, who was sitting in the passenger seat of the car.

'Kim!' exclaimed Ann as her daughter got out to greet her. 'Let me take a look at you.' She was relieved beyond measure to set eyes on her daughter again, but Freegard was in a hurry to get going. 'We've got to get into the car,' he cut in, opening the boot and piling Ann's cases inside, 'Hurry, we have to get going.'

Ann's mind was racing. Where were the police? She needed to stall him somehow. 'Just a minute.' She put up a halting hand. 'I'm cold. I need my jacket from my suitcase.' Ann began to rummage in the boot, fumbling with one suitcase zip after another.

Freegard was getting impatient. 'We don't have a lot of time, Ann. We must get going.'

Where were the police? Where *were* they? Ann thought, trying not to panic.

Just then, in a squeal of tyres, cars converged on them from all corners. DC Mark Simpson jumped out of one of them, holding up his warrant card. 'I'm DC Simpson from the Fraud Squad.' His jaw moved animatedly with the rapid volley of words. After cautioning Freegard, he continued: 'I need to question you about the kidnap of Sarah Smith, John Atkinson, Maria Hendy, and Kimberly Adams, and the theft by deception of their parents' money over the last ten years.'

Freegard looked baffled. 'What? Me?'

'Yes you. You are therefore under arrest for kidnap and false imprisonment of four persons and for deceptions,' continued DC Simpson.

Plain-clothes police officers snapped handcuffs on him.

'I don't believe this,' protested Freegard with an air of innocence and bewilderment.

The chaos at the arrest scene was punctuated by the insistent horn of a frustrated driver, blocked by the unmarked police vehicles and unaware of the drama unfolding.

As Freegard was placed into the rear of a police car he shouted back to Kimberly, 'Kim, baby, just remember I love you!'

Dazed and confused, Kimberly climbed into another police car with her mother.

Slowly, in a whirl of revolving blue lights, the cavalcade set off towards central London and Charing Cross police station.

Nether Hale, the same day

Peter Smith answered the phone. 'Some good news for you,' said DS Brandon. 'We've arrested him at the airport.'

Peter absorbed the information quickly. 'Congratulations. Any news of Sarah?' he asked crisply.

'Well, we found some spare passports on him that aren't his. With any luck it won't be long before we find out where Sarah is. We'll keep you informed.'

'Excellent! That's great news.'

It was well over a year since Sarah had last been in touch, and Peter and Jill didn't know if their daughter was alive or dead. They often talked about what could have happened, but assumed, and desperately hoped, that Freegard wouldn't kill her because he would think her more valuable alive than dead. They didn't believe she was the sort to commit suicide, but where could she be? Was she even in Britain, or could he have taken her abroad? In the absence of any communication, the possibilities were endless.

At least Freegard's arrest had brought them a step closer to the moment of truth.

Chapter 37

Seeking Sarah

Charing Cross, 24 May 2003

The tape recorder whirred quietly in the interview room at Charing Cross police station. A bare light bleached the room as detectives Simpson and Brandon prepared to interview Robert Hendy-Freegard.

A female solicitor reminded the officers of her client's right to remain silent.

DS Brandon set Jill Smith's 'gang of four' photograph in front of Freegard and asked him to name the people in it. Freegard obliged. 'This is John Atkinson, this is Sarah Smith, Maria Hendy, and this chap at the far end is me.' Freegard paused and looked ingratiatingly at DS Brandon. 'May I just ask your Christian name?' he said with exaggerated politeness.

'No,' replied DS Brandon dryly.

'I was only trying to do away with some of the formalities.' Freegard looked wounded.

'My name is Detective Sergeant Brandon, and that's what you can call me,' the officer said coldly.

DC Simpson cut in. 'We're told you're still in contact with Sarah Smith. Is that correct?'

'I still keep in touch with Sarah,' Freegard replied playfully.

'Where is she?'

'I don't know.'

'How do you keep in contact with her then?'

'I'm not saying I don't keep in contact. I'm saying I don't exactly know where she is right now.'

'What about the Polish girl?' DS Brandon interjected.

'That's anyone's guess,' said Freegard coolly. 'DC Simpson, with the greatest respect in the world to you, I believe you have decided what you think. You are wrong, and when it comes to court it will be proven that you are wrong. It is very difficult when you say things to me which I have never heard of before and which I know nothing about, but I am not the liar you think I am.'

Freegard scrutinised the backs of his hands, then lifted his eyes to the officer's face. They were sharp and focused now as he added, 'As things stand at the moment I will make a "no comment" interview.'

There was enough prima facie evidence to charge Freegard with kidnapping, theft and fraud, and to hold him on remand, but as DC Simpson left the interview room he felt frustrated that they were no closer to finding Sarah. At least he had a number of new leads. On searching Freegard yesterday he had found a hotel key ring with the name 'Buffalo' on it. Stuffed in a pocket, he also found a Polish passport in the name of Renata Kister and a scrap of paper with a mobile phone number scribbled on it under the name 'Ronnie'.

Kimberly Adams had already told the police that Freegard had left a briefcase behind in the Hotel Buffalo in Chambéry. DC Simpson believed it might hold crucial information. He grabbed a phone, worried that unless he moved quickly the hotel would dispose of anything left in the room – the staff must by now have realised that its occupants had disappeared without paying and weren't coming back. There was no time to lose.

Across the capital, senior Crown Prosecution lawyer Andrew West picked up the phone.

'We need a formal letter of request from our Home Office to the French Interior Ministry asking for their assistance,' said the government lawyer. 'Any evidence from a foreign source is otherwise inadmissible.'

'Understood,' said DC Simpson.

'Leave it with me,' said Andrew West. 'I'll get onto it right away.'

Chambéry, 4 June 2003

Accompanied by the French Regional Crime Squad, DC Simpson and DS Brandon entered room 229 of the Hotel Buffalo in Chambéry. The room was full of personal items, and as they sifted through them it was clear that most belonged to Freegard. Among the items were two car number plates and three domestic telephones.

Finally, DC Simpson spotted the briefcase. He snapped open the two locks and threw back the lid. The case was full of documents. Letters from Sarah's family to Sarah, Guy Smith's birth certificate, a new driving licence for Sarah and her passport. Simpson frowned and handed them over to DS Brandon. He continued to rifle through the remaining contents of the case and found applications for car loans in the names of Leslie Gardner and Elizabeth Richardson.

DC Simpson cast an anxious look at his colleague. Freegard's web of victims seemed to be getting bigger and bigger.

Finally, Simpson discovered papers in the name of Renata Kister. It was the second time her name had shown up recently and she was certainly someone DC Simpson wanted to talk to.

Hammersmith, 6 June 2003

'When did you last see Robert Hendy-Freegard?' DC Simpson asked Renata Kister.

'About two years ago,' came a guarded reply from a mobile phone.

'So how do you explain the fact that I have your passport then?' said DC Simpson.

Renata remembered that her passport had disappeared on a recent trip with Freegard to Berlin. However, Freegard had warned her that she might be asked about him, and if that happened, he said, she must not, under any circumstances, give anything away.

'I have no idea,' she said flatly.

'We have some documents here in your name. They show you've lived at various addresses in west London.' The officer reeled off the street names. 'There's also a letter in the name of one Darius Mazurek. Ring any bells?'

Renata was silent. How come they had her passport? And what about the other papers? How did they know all her previous addresses? They must have got these details from somewhere.

'OK,' she said slowly. 'I'll be happy to meet you at the police station, to verify the documents are mine.'

Renata sat opposite DC Simpson at Hammersmith and Fulham police station. The office buzzed with activity, broken by the spasmodic, disembodied voices straining through walkie-talkies. It reminded Renata of those conversations with astronauts in space.

'When did you first encounter Robert Freegard?' asked DC Simpson.

Her arms folded across her chest, Renata was in no mood to divulge information about Robert. Not until she was convinced he had done something wrong.

She flicked a strand of loose blonde hair behind her ear. 'Could I see my passport?' Just then her attention was drawn to an officer walking purposefully towards them. His fresh face and solid build were familiar. She knew this man. She had seen him a few years before in a Fulham bar where she'd been doing some casual work. He always sat alone, kept himself to himself and was unfailingly polite. She thought him a kind sort, but hadn't asked his name or occupation.

'Morning, Bob,' said DC Simpson to his colleague.

'Ms Kister, I'd like to introduce you to Detective Sergeant Bob Brandon. He's working with me on the case.'

The two exchanged looks. Renata knew the officer recognised her too. Suddenly her doubts about DC Simpson's claims against

Freegard began to evaporate. She had observed DS Brandon and had a feel for the sort of person he was; she sensed he was someone she could trust. If *he* was on the case then it must be genuine. Her defences started to tumble, and with it her silence about Robert Freegard. 'I'll help you all I can,' she said.

The interview over, Renata looked awkwardly at the two officers. There was one matter that had been bothering her for the past half-hour or so. She wanted to mention it, but felt torn with concern over where it might lead. Despite her initial reservations, she had grown fond of Carrie, and her daughter absolutely adored her. She was good company and seemed so straight and honest. But then Renata remembered the clothes, Carrie's refusal to disclose anything about her private life, her obvious shortage of money and the bizarre Venezuelan episode. What if she was Robert's accomplice? Wouldn't that mean her daughter was at risk?

'I have somebody staying with me,' she said hesitatingly. The two officers looked up, suddenly alert. 'I'd like to find out who she is,' Renata's voice trailed off uncertainly. DC Simpson and DS Brandon glanced at each other. 'I'm very unclear about the whole situation. I have a photograph of her.'

'Can you bring it in?' asked DC Simpson.

Back at the police station, Renata handed over the photograph she'd taken of Carrie in the park. DC Simpson and DS Brandon, standing shoulder to shoulder, shot a sideways glance at each other.

DC Simpson opened a drawer and extracted another photograph. 'Is this the same person?' he asked, unable to hide a shiver of excitement.

Renata examined the woman in the photograph, the spiky blonde hair and the short skirt. She recognised her instantly as Carrie, and shifted uncomfortably in her seat, still unsure about blowing the woman's cover.

'She is registered as "missing" by her parents,' prompted DS Brandon.

Renata pondered this last piece of information. If her parents had registered Carrie missing, then maybe she was on Freegard's side after all. Renata felt she had no option but to tell them.

'It is her, yes,' she whispered.

Both DC Simpson and DS Brandon took a deep breath. They knew they had found their missing person.

'Do you know where she is right now?' asked DC Simpson.

Renata hesitated, then nodded. The officers realised they had to tread carefully. 'It's important that you say absolutely nothing of this to her. It might scare her, and she might take off again.' Renata nodded; she wouldn't say anything.

That night Renata and Carrie sat in Renata's new flat, sharing a drink and a takeaway pizza to celebrate moving in.

'You know, I feel so at home,' said Carrie munching on a slice of tomato-covered dough. 'I really haven't felt so much at home for a long time.'

Renata's heart sank; she felt like a traitor.

Chapter 38

The Pick-Up

Battersea, 11 June 2003

DS Brandon and two other officers were on their way to a house in Battersea where Sarah was currently doing a cleaning job. 'You say the house is near the river?' asked DS Brandon.

'Yes. Just over Wandsworth Bridge and to the left a bit,' confirmed Renata.

Sarah

It's almost twelve o'clock. I have a heavy schedule today and there's no time to spare between jobs. I'm going to leave on the dot so as not to be late for my next appointment. I hate being late.

The police drew up in a cobbled street on the opposite side of the road from the Battersea house. DS Brandon marshalled everyone together. 'OK. Let's pick her up.'

Sarah

I leave the house by the garden door, pulling the blue metal gate behind me with a clang, pausing only to make sure the owners' cat hasn't sneaked out while the gate was open.

Bob Brandon rang the bell. There was no reply. He stepped back from the door and looked up at the windows of the three-storey building.

'Try ringing the bell again,' he told his colleague.

Still no answer.

'She's not here,' he said with exasperation.

Sarah

Cutting across the Homebase car park, I can see the Fulham bus about to pull up at the stop, so I dash across York Road and jump on board just in time.

'I don't understand,' said Renata. 'Let me ring her mobile.'

'You'll have to explain why you want to come and see her,' warned DS Brandon.

Renata tapped in the numbers and a voice answered.

'Where are you?' asked Renata.

'On the bus heading towards Fulham.'

'Listen, I've locked myself out. Can I come and pick up your keys from you at your next appointment?'

It was the excuse the police needed for Sarah to open the door.

Sarah

I've arrived at Chiswick Quay, a small estate of town houses surrounding a marina on the River Thames. It's a lovely afternoon and I'm looking forward to getting back to Renata's new place tonight. I start to hum as I grab the cleaning things.

I leave Renata's keys on the dining-room table and take off my sweatshirt. It'll be too hot for anything more than a T-shirt today.

I've just got upstairs when my phone rings. It's Renata, waiting down below for the keys.

I open the door, and...

'Hello, Sarah.'

The soundtrack to the everyday world disappears. There are two men and a woman on the doorstep – people I've never seen before. How do they know my name? No one, except Rob, calls me Sarah any more. I want to slam the door, to run, but the sight of Renata holds me back. What is she doing here with these strangers?

'Robert Hendy-Freegard doesn't work for the government. He has never worked for the government,' says the man. I hear the words, but they make absolutely no sense. I look at Renata; isn't she on the same side as Rob?

'We need to talk to you,' says the man. He leads me back inside. He says he's Detective Sergeant Bob Brandon.

'Robert Hendy-Freegard is not a secret agent,' he repeats. 'I'm very sorry, Sarah, but the last ten years have basically been one huge lie.'

I feel giddy. My pulse is racing. Sheer panic. The words I'm hearing are not registering. I look towards Renata, beseeching her to tell me that what I'm hearing isn't true.

'He's conned me, too.' Renata shuffles awkwardly. 'I'm sorry. I feel a complete shit giving you up to the police, but I wasn't sure if you were in some kind of trouble.'

I blink at her in a trance. My world is a complete blank.

'We need to take you down to the police station, Sarah. There are some questions we want to ask you,' says the detective. 'We've already spoken to John Atkinson and Maria Hendy.'

My emotions are all over the place. I cry silently one moment, and the next I'm telling myself to get a grip. Nothing seems real. In the car I consider the possibility that this *isn't* real, it's a trick. My mind is all confusion and turmoil.

We draw up outside the grey, faceless exterior of a police station. As we walk inside, I am overwhelmed by the noise and bustle – there are police uniforms everywhere, phones ringing, members of the public milling around.

'Just in here if you will, Miss Smith.' The officers usher me into a room that is bare apart from a table and four chairs. They sit with me.

What if they *are* telling me the truth? What if Rob *has* been dealing me a pack of lies all this time? Oh, God. That's too awful to contemplate. It means I've thrown away my life for nothing.

Bob Brandon suggests we move to the Rape Crisis Centre in Tooting because I am so distressed. The atmosphere will be more relaxed there and they say they can video my interview.

'I know this will sound crazy,' I say once we're in Tooting police station, 'but I need to know this is real. I'd like to speak to Maria Hendy, please.' I need to verify they are who they say they are and that I really am at a police station. I want to hear from Maria herself that she has been interviewed by them. Right now, Maria's is the only voice I feel I can trust.

The phone is brought to me.

'Maria?'

'Yes, Sarah, it's me. Speak to them. Give them a statement. Just be honest. I can't talk to you further. I've given them a statement, but I'm also a witness.'

'Take your time, Miss Smith,' says the officer. 'There's no rush. Tell me in your own words what has happened to you over the last ten years.'

The words come slowly at first, like a stream struggling over rocks. When you've lived for so long without giving away any details to anyone, the impulse to keep back information is powerful. Now I have to lay bare the last decade, expose all the people I've been, all the things I've done, all the money I've lost, all the people I've hurt. I'm reluctant to tell the police everything – I still don't completely believe what has happened. So at this first interview I keep a few things to myself.

Later the same day

Peter and Jill were walking along a beach in Kent with their son Guy and their eldest grandchild. The previous day Bob Brandon had phoned to say the police thought they knew where Sarah was.

Now, at last, the call they had been waiting for came through to

Guy's mobile. 'They've found Sarah,' Guy told his parents. 'They've told me I should go up to London to collect her right now.'

It took a while for the news to sink in. After ten years of uncertainty, false leads and dashed hopes, it seemed impossible to believe that their daughter would soon be back home.

'Thank you, Guy,' said Peter.

He put a protective arm around his wife and they walked on in silence, each absorbed in their own thoughts. What state would Sarah be in? Would she be scared to meet them? How did they make contact? There had been so many cross words, would she accept them now? 'No doubt it will all sort itself out,' said Peter stoically.

Despite these concerns, they could not suppress a feeling of pure delight and utter joy at the news.

Chapter 39

Opening Up

Sarah, Tooting, the same day

The wheels of the video recorder spin to a halt and the machine clicks off. We've done enough for today, they tell me. Detective Sergeant Brandon says it's not possible to stay with Renata tonight, as she's also a witness in the case.

'We'd like you to phone your parents, though.'

A slideshow of images flashes through my mind, none of them pleasant. All the lies I've told... Nether Hale: that's one place I'm not ready for, one place I can't go. There's too much guilt.

'No. No, I can't,' I say adamantly, flapping my hands as if beating away the idea.

The detective looks at me kindly. 'Well, in the meantime, your brother's on his way up from Kent to collect you.'

I am terrified. What will Guy's reaction be? Having banished my friends and family from my thoughts, it's going to take time to adjust. I've not allowed myself to feel anything for so long. All is emptiness.

When Guy walks through the door, it's his hair I notice first. It's gone grey and there's much less of it. Right now it helps to focus on this small detail.

'My God, what's happened to you?'

He stands there, smiling nervously. '*You* don't look any different.'

I manage a tentative smile, but I'm trembling all over.

We climb into his car, and the urban landscape whizzes past as he drives me to his home in south-west London. I tell him I'm dying for a shower. Over and over again, I tell him I must have a shower. It's all I can think of to say to him. My lost ten years are an abyss that is impossible to bridge right now.

Shock – I'm in shock. This must be how survivors of a bomb attack or a natural disaster feel. The implications of what has happened are too immense, so it's the small things that dominate my thoughts at this moment: the colour of hair, the button on a shirt, the need to stand under a shower.

Guy is his usual phlegmatic self, but I detect a wary hesitancy.

On the way he drops into a supermarket to buy me some clothes. All I've got to show for ten years will fit into two plastic bags; my few clothes are still at Renata's. The one thing I've managed to keep throughout the ordeal is the necklace my parents bought me for my twenty-first birthday, its black opal shines like a little beacon, and has held me together through all the bad times.

When we reach his house, Guy pours me a stiff brandy which spreads warmly through my body like sun melting ice.

Slowly at first, cautiously, I offer up tiny scraps of my life. Gradually, though, the Sarah Smith that has been caged up inside me starts to emerge. I figure that if I've told the police so much, I can tell Guy a little bit more, and I do.

As my ordeal unravels, I drink more brandy. By the end of the evening the bottle is empty, and I know I'm sinking into the blessed oblivion of intoxication. At the same time, one thing is now very clear in my mind: I will annihilate the darkness and let in the light.

Fragments of my experiences spring to mind unbidden. I awake with a gasp. Another nightmare. I tell myself that he is under lock and key, that he's behind bars, but he's only on remand. What if he finds me and tries to take me away again? What then?

Panicking, I get out of bed, gulp down a glass of water and try to stop shaking.

It's not over yet. What if he fools them into believing he did nothing wrong?

part eight

Legal History

June 2003–June 2005

Chapter 40

Building a Case

Central London, June 2003

Andrew West slipped the cassette into the VCR and pressed the remote's play button. An image of Sarah Smith appeared on the television screen in front of him.

The government lawyer had prosecuted some twenty high-profile murder cases at the Old Bailey and even taken on a complex nine-month prosecution involving a Microsoft software counterfeiting ring, but he had never dealt with anything quite like this before.

Truth be told, he remained somewhat ambivalent about the case. Did it really amount to anything more than a few gullible people falling prey to a two-bit conman?

He knew that if they were to achieve the successful conviction of Freegard, then Sarah's evidence was vital. The case rested largely on what she had to say.

The interview with Sarah had been conducted over two days, and there were more than three hours of video tape to wade through. He would make notes during the tape of where he felt offences had been committed, and the nature of those offences; notes that he would later cross reference with John Atkinson and Maria Hendy's interviews.

He sat back and listened as Sarah's long story unfolded.

He said he worked for MI5. I believed. . . he was working as a spy.

He convinced me that if anybody wanted to get at me, then they'd do damage to my parents, or if I went home that damage would be done to my parents.

He told me I had to tell my parents that the situation was looking a bit rough and things weren't finished, so I needed some money, but it was always at that instant, it had to be in cash, it had to be wired directly to such and such a bank, or somewhere he had decided on. He said my parents had spent thousands and thousands of pounds hiring private detectives, and that they hadn't been doing stuff in my interests. He kept on at me to get more money from them. I didn't want to contact them because I'd hurt them so much and borrowed so much off them. He said. . . they obviously hadn't got my best interests at heart, and of course he had.

He always said to me: 'If anybody contacts you, just get out of there. Just go, don't talk to them, especially if it's the police, just go, otherwise you'll lose everything.' He made me believe that I was going to get back what had been taken from me, and that if I did actually speak to anyone then I would lose everything.

I had doubts about a lot of things over a period of time, but I was so far along the line I couldn't see where to go, or how to change it, and the hope that it was real was the only thing that made it halfway bearable. To actually think that I had been so stupid, that it really was all a lie, and that I'd wasted all that time, that money and hurt so many people and everyone I care about, just didn't seem possible, or I just didn't want it to be, so I carried on.

He convinced me that he was what he said he was, and as such he had to be trusted because there was no other option. To leave would be to go nowhere, to have nothing, to be like I was when I was in Birmingham, which was just horrible. Did I consider going home? Yes, I considered going home so many times you wouldn't believe, but I didn't believe that I deserved to be accepted back, and I had nothing. I had less than nothing. I had less than when I was sixteen, except that I was no longer sixteen.

*

The interview ended and white noise burst onto the screen.

A father of two himself, Andrew West was clearly moved by what he had just seen and heard. 'It's so obviously true, so heartfelt and so tragic,' he told his colleague Michael Hick. 'Not only did all these things happen, but she's been manipulated and tricked, *and* consented to having all this done to her into the bargain.'

He walked over to the window and glanced down onto Ludgate Hill below. 'The interview is so anguished, I actually feel awful. It's made me realise that it's *so* important to move a very serious offence against Freegard in relation to what he has done to these people.'

Andrew West and his Crown Prosecution team had six weeks in which to serve papers on the defence. The papers had to include an indictment, witness list statements and exhibits. Freegard had been charged with the kidnap of Sarah Smith, John Atkinson and Maria Hendy. Elizabeth Richardson had not yet been traced, and Andrew West asked the defence team to procure Freegard's help in finding her. Freegard refused.

In the meantime, another witness had surfaced: Leslie Gardner, a civil servant from Chelmsford in Essex. Over three and a half years Leslie had handed Freegard close to £30,000 to 'buy himself out of the police' and start a new life as a taxi driver in Middlesex. On one occasion, he told her he needed blackmail money to buy off some killers; 'IRA bombers,' he said, released under the Good Friday agreement.

The CPS lawyer began to collate the paperwork. One of his concerns was how to differentiate between what had happened in this instance and something more benign; a surprise birthday party for example. After all, even if the intent was honourable, wasn't the birthday boy or girl also being taken from one place to another by fraud? Nobody would argue for kidnap in such circumstances, so how could they argue for kidnap in the case of the students? The key lay in proving malice in what Freegard had done.

Even so, Andrew West feared that they might lose on counts of kidnapping, either because the jury didn't understand the concept, or because they might think Freegard was 'just a bit of a lad'.

Furthermore, the relevant bank records were not proof that the money the victims said they had lost went to Freegard. The prosecution could prove a certain lifestyle, certainly, but it could not demonstrate that money had gone out of one account and into another. There was no direct link. All they had to rely on, therefore, were the witness statements.

West was also bracing himself for a tough defence. What if, for example, Freegard claimed that he thought he had been working for somebody else, who in turn claimed *they* worked for the government, that Freegard himself had had absolutely no idea of what happened to the money; he just took it and passed it on. What then?

When the prosecution team received the defence's case statement, Andrew West breathed a small sigh of relief. In it, Freegard asserted that the witnesses were making up the story; it was all a conspiracy by Peter Smith and that the women were all bitter ex-lovers. He, Freegard, had not told them he was a spy and he hadn't taken money from Sarah Smith and John Atkinson.

It could have been so much worse, West thought. On reflection, the government prosecutor realised that Freegard was too vain to allege he had been duped by somebody else. Image counted for everything, and there was no way Freegard would ever admit to being a fool. Even so, Andrew West knew that proving Freegard had kidnapped Sarah, John and Maria by deception was going to be no easy matter. It would be a tricky case to win.

September 2003

Almost four months after Freegard's arrest, DC Mark Simpson received the call he had been hoping for. It was Elizabeth Richardson.

In an effort to trace her, the detective had written to an old friend of hers, and earlier in the day the friend had rung to say that he'd passed on DC Simpson's number to Elizabeth.

Together with DS Brandon, Simpson travelled to a house in

Dunton Bassett, a village in Leicestershire, where almost six months earlier Freegard had left Sarah watching over his car. There they had found Liz.

She told the officers that as she hadn't been informed by MI5 that Freegard had been killed, she could only assume he was away on a lengthy assignment, so she was just waiting for him to call her with instructions about what to do next. She had been waiting for five and a half months.

Following the discovery of Elizabeth Richardson, Freegard was charged with her kidnap, and the case was joined to those of Sarah, John and Maria. The eventual twenty-four count indictment was made up of four counts of kidnap, eleven counts of theft, eight of deception, and one of making a threat to kill. Hendy-Freegard denied all the charges.

The stage was now set for the trial.

Chapter 41

The Verdict

Sarah, 22 November 2004

I wake up in a state of acute anxiety. I'm due to start giving evidence today. It's taken about a year and a half to reach this point, because the trial has been anything but straightforward.

It got under way at the beginning of the year, but collapsed after only two weeks when Freegard's second set of lawyers said they were 'professionally embarrassed'.

The trial was reset for April, but the new defence team said they thought there might be 'a problem'. Judge Deva Pillay discharged the jury when the defence came back and confirmed there was indeed a problem, and that they were 'professionally embarrassed' too. The case was put on hold until June. In June, a fourth set of solicitors and counsel for the defence presented themselves in court saying they couldn't be ready in time. The judge had no choice but to adjourn the trial yet again, until October.

Now at last it's my turn to go to court. Most of the victims are to give evidence from behind a specially erected partition, so we don't have to see Freegard, and the power of our testimony will be directed towards the jury. Despite this, I am panic stricken, terrified that somehow he'll manipulate our testimony and twist it to suit his own ends. It's bad enough just knowing that he'll be there. I can feel all my hard-won sense of purpose collapsing.

I join my brother downstairs in the kitchen, where he is performing the breakfast rituals. He is his usual calm, composed self, betraying no sense of anything out of the ordinary. Aware of my agitation, he puts the kettle on for a quick cup of coffee before we go.

'Don't worry, I'll be waiting for you when you come out,' he says soothingly. 'I'm here if you need anything or you're upset. It'll all be over soon.'

What would I do without Guy? He calms me when I'm fretful and stops my fragile world from spinning out of control. He picks up the scattered pieces of my confidence and helps me put them back together. He gives me renewed strength and makes me feel that I can cope.

Finally it's time.

'Come on, Sarah. Let's go.'

Guy and I board the train for Waterloo Station. From there it's a short walk to Blackfriars Crown Court. There's a clinical atmosphere inside the modern courthouse, rather like an operating theatre. In here the bad is cauterised, lives are restored and made whole again. At least that's the idea.

The waiting before they call me seems endless, and no amount of pacing, sitting and thinking makes time pass by any quicker. I'm frightened and under stress, but I really want to be in there now, to face the defence, deal with their questions and get it over with. I hope, more than anything, that we will get justice.

The court usher collects me and leads me into the courtroom. I take a deep breath. . .

Sarah, 23 June 2005

The jury has been deliberating for several days now. It is just over two years since Freegard was arrested. Bob Brandon just called me to say the verdict is expected in about ten minutes.

Strangely, I feel very calm, as though I'm standing in a deserted street after a dust storm has settled. There's nothing I can do; it's out of my hands now; the jury will decide.

My mobile phone rings. I know the voice instantly. I brace myself.

'Guilty of eighteen counts of theft and deception, and two counts of kidnap. Guilty of kidnapping you and John.'

My knees go weak. I am ecstatic that the jury came to the right decision. Such relief, such joy. 'That's brilliant,' I say. 'Absolutely brilliant.'

I relay the news to Guy, then I phone Mum and Dad. Shortly afterwards I receive calls from my friends. They've seen the outcome on the news and want to pass on their congratulations. Finally, I can begin to let go of the past and rebuild my life.

Yet one piece of the jigsaw is still missing. Freegard may be awaiting sentencing after the verdict, but I still don't know what made all this happen, and why it happened to me. What was going through Freegard's head at The Swan? Was I just in the wrong place at the wrong time?

part nine

Picking Up the Pieces

Present Day

Chapter 42

New Horizons

Sarah Smith, present day

'Put your bags on the scales, please.' I lift my bags onto the rubber belt, worried in case I'm over the weight allowance.

'That's fine. Window seat or aisle, Miss Smith?'

'Window, please.'

After my ten year ordeal, liberty is still a daily surprise for me. To know that I can go to the shops when I want, see whom I want, go home when I feel like it, sit down to a nice meal, or travel where I fancy – all these simple freedoms still have the power to startle me.

When I was at Heathrow during that harsh winter day in 2003, my fingers and toes numb after a long walk through the snow, and later at Gatwick, surviving off meagre rations and trying to avoid detection by the police, I used to sit and watch the travellers. I would wonder where they were going and why, wishing I could be them. My thoughts would fill with imaginings of far-off places, where *I* would go if I had the choice. They were just dreams then.

It's impossible to describe just how strong Freegard's hold over me was, except to say that he had the power of life and death. I could so easily have died from starvation or hypothermia as a result of his treatment in the last couple of years. He could have made me take my own life at any point, if he'd been so inclined. That's a power no individual should have over another.

Just below the tranquil surface I am still in huge turmoil. People I meet now probably think I'm quite ordinary, reasonably confident even, but it's very hard for me to trust anyone after the experience with Freegard. The damage wrought by mental cruelty is not visible from the outside. For ten years I was indoctrinated and institutionalised, made to believe appalling lies and to hurt all those I care about. I've had to face up to the fact that my life was a charade and, at the age of thirty-seven, try to pull my life back together into some kind of order. Thankfully I have the love and support of my family in this, but learning to trust other people again will take time.

Taking decisions is a struggle, and making choices can leave me floundering and in tears. Most people make such everyday decisions and choices all the time, as easily as driving a car – it's something one does subconsciously – they don't even notice when they change gear or turn a corner. For me, though, there's been a whole new restructuring and reordering to get to grips with in my mind. For a long time I didn't trust myself to make the right decisions about big and small things, about anything. So Guy's challenge to me was to do something that scared me every day and to face up to the things I was frightened of, like contacting old friends who I didn't think would want anything to do with me, and people I owed money to so I could repay them.

And that's what I've done. It's like learning to cross the road all over again. At times things still get on top of me, and my emotional reactions take me by surprise. Some days I feel lost, frustrated or depressed. These days, Freegard rarely pops unbidden into my thoughts; when he does it's usually prompted by some familiar sight or sound, but these flashbacks are receding as time passes. I am getting stronger and my life has improved beyond measure. I am proof that even after a dreadful experience life can still be worth living. I should also add that good things can come from bad times. During my ordeal, the unexpected kindness shown to me by strangers often took me by surprise; they made some of the very worst situations tolerable.

At times I feel as if I've never been away. I've mostly slipped back into the groove of my previous life. And everyone's still here, just a little older, perhaps married, sometimes with children. I am very fortunate to have been blessed with a forgiving and loving family and, despite my fears, all my friends, old and new, have stood by me and given me the support I needed.

My life 'undercover' now has an unreal quality to it, a fuzzy outline. Like a ship on the horizon, it might be there or it might be an illusion. However, the outward reminders of what I've lost are constants. I threw away my degree, so I have no qualifications. I don't own a house or a car. I don't have any money. I've missed the best part of my twenties and half of my thirties, that precious time of life when one builds the framework for the future.

Also, reconstructing one's life after not existing on official records is far more difficult than people might think. A child can open a bank account with a pound coin, for example; not so an adult. Without any ID, you can't get a passport or a bank account. Anything I had that identified me as Sarah Smith – my birth certificate, my passport, driving licence and National Insurance card – was found in Freegard's hotel room in France. As these documents were evidence in the case, I needed to request my driving licence in order to apply for a new passport. Without a passport or a bank account it's difficult to get a job or accommodation. Even if I could get a job, all my references would be in the name of Maria Hendy. Without a utility bill with my address on it, ID and income from a job, I cannot get a bank account.

This vicious circle is almost impossible to break, so in my mid-thirties, having applied for a new passport, I had to be added to a joint account with my mother. That was the only option available to me – and even that took a great deal of time and explanation.

One salvation has been talking to the other survivors, making new friends and knowing I am not alone; that there are others who understand. Renata and I have spent hours comparing our experiences and piecing together the parts, reinterpreting our understanding of events, armed with the knowledge of what was really going on. By seeing how our lives were interwoven, we can make sense of our stories. I have also spent time with Kim. I think it was beneficial to both of us to be able to speak freely about what had happened to us. We are all connected by our shared experience. It's a case of unravelling what Freegard did, how he did it and why – some of which we will never know. This last point brings me to John Atkinson.

I finally met up with John shortly after the verdict. It was the first time I had seen him in over eleven years. I needed to clarify in my own mind what was fact and what was fiction in our time together. He was nervous and wanted to meet on the Millennium Bridge in the centre of London – afraid of the upset he had caused my family, afraid that perhaps Guy might be waiting round a corner. Of course nothing like that would ever happen. None of us blames him. He was being controlled as much as I was, and was only acting as instructed. Our meeting gave me the answers I needed from him and a certain peace of mind, and John now knows I don't hold him responsible for anything.

John has his own views about how all this started, and why it happened, drawn from having sat through Freegard's cross-examination. He believes that in the end Freegard's need for power and status, and indeed the entire underlying reason behind what happened to us, boiled down to one thing: jealousy. John believes that Freegard took against him in a very personal way shortly after they met in Newport. Why? Simply because John was living in the same house as his girlfriend Maria Hendy. Freegard couldn't stand the thought of that, so John, and everything he represented, became the focus of Rob's malice: John's middle-class education, his upbringing and his family's relative wealth. Freegard's jealousy was further fuelled by resentment over his own upbringing and his conviction that he was special and deserved better. He determined to humiliate John in front of his friends. To start with, the lies were concocted only to make John a laughing stock, but when Freegard discovered his talent for subterfuge, he built on it and pushed the boundaries as far as he could.

From what I've learned from John since, it appears that Freegard initially had no endgame in mind; he simply wanted to humiliate and control people, while at the same time stoking his own ego. When I was sucked in, he projected all his hatred of John's privileged upbringing on to me and my family circumstances. Through some twisted logic, he felt entitled to everything that was mine. The huge web of criminal deceit and fraud grew out of simple jealousy and the subsequent discovery that he had an aptitude for conning people. This ability developed to terrifying proportions and has left us all scarred for life.

His pattern of behaviour continued for ten years. Whenever Freegard became insanely jealous, as he was of Kim's former relationships, he would go to almost any lengths to frighten, humiliate, demean or destroy. He revelled in the power that enabled him to do this and felt absolutely no guilt. Jealousy and rage, it seems, were the catalysts that triggered the chain reaction whose slipstream engulfed not only me, John and Maria, but Liz, Leslie, Renata, Caroline and Kim. Who knows where his jealousy and power would have led him had he not been stopped?

I felt it really important to tell my story in the hope that it might serve as a warning to others. Fundamentally I am no different from anyone else. I was just in the wrong place at the wrong time. What happened to me could happen to anyone.

John's life has now moved on, of course. He's a teacher in the Czech Republic and has just bought himself a house. We are close only because our shared past defines and unites us, but neither of us wants to linger in that place. We both want to move on, to keep looking forward, and inevitably our lives have gone in different directions. That's how it should be. We parted company that day knowing that we will keep in touch at Christmas.

As far as my money is concerned, I know it's gone for ever. Yet I still wonder sometimes whether Freegard really did spend it all, or whether he banked it somewhere on the continent. I have thought back to when he told me he would be sending me to a railway station to pick up a suitcase full of cash. Who knows what would have happened to me had he swept me away to mainland Europe? I came within a hair's breath of leaving the country. If I had gone, I would probably have been lost for ever.

When I was being interviewed by the police, I gave Bob Brandon the keys for the silver Volkswagen Polo Freegard had parked in Mayfair's South Audley car park. In the boot Bob found a motorcycle crash helmet and a bag containing the few clothes I owned before arriving at Renata's house from Gatwick airport. The outstanding parking ticket ran to almost £7000 – more than the value of the car.

In Kimberly Adams's case, Freegard was found guilty of obtaining money by deception. The jury didn't find him guilty of kidnapping Maria Hendy or Elizabeth Richardson, probably because they couldn't be sure whether or not the girls had gone with Freegard because of their relationships with him. Freegard was also cleared of one count of theft, and of making a threat to kill.

Simon Young had moved away from Sheffield some time ago and no longer had any communication with Freegard, although he still kept an open mind about Freegard being a government spy. It was only when he saw a newspaper report about the trial that he realised it had all been a sham and volunteered himself as a witness.

Not all the pieces of the riddle have been solved. Among Freegard's personal items, the police discovered a reference to another woman, 'Solange' from Brazil, but they have never been able to find any trace of her. How many other victims might be out there?

There's also the matter of bugging the phones. It seems likely that Freegard was telling the truth about this, since he was often in possession of information that he could not possibly have known otherwise. As for the cars, where did he keep them all? And what was he doing that ran up such high mileage on each of them? Finally, what of Roberta? Whatever she told my parents, I never met her. To me she remains a mystery.

In the end, Freegard's need for power became all-consuming and the conspiracy so elaborate that it was impossible for him to control all its components. Experts agree that, for much of the time,

Freegard probably knew he was telling lies, but eventually his fabricated persona became so complete that he could no longer distinguish between the fictional Freegard and the real one. He may well have recognised what was happening to him but was unwilling to break free. It would have meant admitting to his victims that he was nothing but a charlatan and his vanity would not have allowed him to own up to his insignificance. For this reason he will probably never admit to what he's done, nor reveal the whole truth about his crimes.

When passing sentence Judge Deva Pillay told Hendy-Freegard, 'You are an opinionated confidence trickster who has shown not a shred of remorse or compassion for the degradation and suffering to which your victims were subjected. There are substantial grounds for believing you will remain a substantial danger to the public, and to other women in particular.' The judge said there was a 'heinous pattern of offending' against his victims, all of whom fell prey to his 'devious charm'. 'In my judgement the verdicts of the jury in this case represent a vindication of your victims. It is a telling testament to their courage, tenacity and spirit to survive and overcome adversity, despite the depths of despair to which they were driven by you.'

Will Freegard ever change? To date, his exposure as a fraudster appears to have made no impact on him. While on remand, he was apparently the only prisoner who managed to persuade his guards to order takeaway meals for him from the outside. And when he finally began his prison sentence in Wandsworth, it wasn't long before he was getting fellow inmates to do things for him on the promise that they'd be paid once he was free. He told them he had money stashed away in Belgium. The police quickly stepped in, and he has since been moved to Long Lartin maximum security prison in Worcestershire.

I don't have a boyfriend yet; the opportunity hasn't arisen and I don't know how I'll react if and when I do meet someone. It's all about building trust, and that's going to be a slow and difficult process for me. One day, maybe, but I can't see that far ahead just yet. Instead I am pursuing photography – a passion of mine since childhood. With every penny I've earned since paying my debts, I've saved for a digital camera, a telephoto lens and special filters. I use every opportunity to photograph wildlife, landscapes and people, and have recently had my first photograph published in a magazine. It's a small start, but it is a start, and I hope to get commissions soon and sell my work.

Finally, I must describe what happened when I met my parents again for the first time. In the end, I put off seeing them for a week after the police found me. I felt deeply ashamed and full of remorse for the untold number of times I had demanded money, for the myriad lies I had told and for all the distress I had caused them. I considered all this to be entirely my fault and, naturally, was extremely worried about how they would react to me. But when Mum and Dad walked through Guy's front door, after a few awkward moments it was as if the years apart had melted away, and with them my concerns. I realised I needn't have worried. 'That's it,' Dad said. 'Everything's going to be just fine.' He was just happy to see his family unit whole again. There are no other words at such times.

If this experience has taught me one thing, it is that nothing stands in the way of true family love. All differences and all hurt are simply absolved in its endlessly forgiving embrace.

'Here's your boarding pass, Miss Smith. The gate opens at six fifty,' says the stewardess.

I hug my pass to my chest, a big smile on my face, and walk with Guy towards the departure gate. I am off to explore a bit of America and Canada.

'You look after yourself,' he says. 'Try not to take too many photos of the Statue of Liberty.'

'Don't worry, you know I will.' I give him a hug and wave goodbye. I filter through the security checks and mingle with my fellow travellers. Now I'm one of them, today it's me who's flying. Being free is a miracle. I count my blessings every day.

Robert Hendy-Freegard was originally convicted of two counts of kidnapping by fraud of Sarah Smith and John Atkinson, ten counts of theft, and eight counts of obtaining money by deception. Before sentencing, a psychiatric report on Hendy-Freegard was requested, but the defence chose not to disclose its contents. Freegard was given two life sentences to run concurrently in respect of the kidnapping charges, and a further nine years for the theft and fraud offences.

In April 2007, Freegard's appeal against the two kidnapping convictions was upheld, meaning the life sentences were quashed. The three appeal judges – the Lord Chief Justice, Lord Phillips, Mr Justice Burton, and Mr Justice Stanley Burnton – ruled that when Sarah and John were taken away from Harper Adams College they had not been falsely imprisoned – not totally deprived of their liberty – and therefore the strict legal definitions of kidnap did not apply. At the time of writing, this judgement may yet be tested again in the House of Lords. At the same appeal hearing, Freegard's attempt to have his sentence reduced on the other convictions was dismissed. Sarah's dismay at the quashing of the kidnapping convictions is matched only by her determination that nobody else should face an ordeal similar to hers.